Selena Fragassi
Foreword by Local H's Scott Lucas

PEARL JAM LIVE!

35 YEARS OF LEGENDARY MUSIC AND REVOLUTIONARY SHOWS

EPIC INK

CONTENTS

Foreword 4
"Once" (An Introduction) .. 6

Opening Act (1984-1991)

"Given To Fly" 18
"Do The Evolution" 28
"Better Man" 34
"Off He Goes" 44
"Gonna See My Friend" 52
"Alive" 58
"Why Go" 68

Headliner (1992-2000)

"Oceans" 82
"Immortality" 90
"Lightning Bolt" 94
"Dissident" 106
"Not For You" 118

"Force Of Nature" 126
"Quick Escape" 136
"Push Me, Pull Me" 148
"I Am Mine" 160
"State Of Love And Trust" . 168

Encore (2001-Present)

"Bu$hleaguer" 184
"Who You Are" 194
"Rearviewmirror" 206
"Glorified G" 214
"Nothing As It Seems" 222
"Future Days" 232

Discography 240
Awards 244
Sources 246
Index 248
Image Credits . . . 252
Acknowledgments . . . 254
About the Author 255

FOREWORD

If you wanted to get on the radio in the '90s, your best bet was to get a lead singer that sounded like Eddie Vedder. It didn't matter what particular strain of alternative music you were peddling; as long as your band featured vocals that were within spitting distance of Vedder's soul-stirring baritone, you could churn out warmed-over, golf-shirt rock, and you'd still rule the airwaves. (I think we all know whom I'm referring to.) Not since Robert Plant had there been a rock voice so shamelessly imitated.

But I didn't sound like him, so I did the next best (or worst) thing: I went ahead and wrote a song called "Eddie Vedder." Sure, it wasn't without its ironies. Ostensibly, it was about a girl who preferred Vedder over me (get used to it, Lucas), but the song also doubled as a shot at all the Eddie clones clogging commercial radio. At the same time, the name drop didn't hurt our chances of getting a little airplay for ourselves. It wasn't *purely* mercenary, but the whiff of calculation wasn't something we could 100 percent plausibly deny.

Eventually, it got back to me that the man himself was onto us. Apparently, Vedder had no real problem with the song, but he didn't understand why it had to be so blatantly named after him. At the time, I might have defensively mumbled something about Mookie Blaylock, but deep down I realized that he had a point. At best, Vedder had every right to feel embarrassed over the song. At worst, I was just another asshole exploiting him. And I felt bad about that.

So years later (nearly twenty of them), I got my chance to square it right with him.

Vedder was scheduled to headline a benefit show at the Metro in Chicago. It was for a Boston-based baseball and rock charity called Hot Stove Cool Music. Being proudly sports ignorant, I had no idea what the name meant, but I loved Boston bands, so I was usually (and happily) involved in the musical lineup most years. Unfortunately, that year I had to miss it because we were playing a festival gig outside of the city that had us opening for a band so shitty I can't even bring myself to name them here. I was pissed.

But I had a plan: We'd play our set, get the hell out of there, and race back to Chicago where I would find Eddie and apologize about the song—after which, he would see what a cool guy I was and then we would become long lost alterna-buddies. It was foolproof.

By the time we got back to Chicago, the show had already ended and I got word that I should meet everybody at The Lodge, a downtown Rush Street staple known for a laissez-faire policy concerning customers throwing peanut shells on the floor. Wearing a Cubs hat that I'd "inherited" from Tom Morello, I walked through the doors and there was Vedder, surrounded by musicians, hangers-on, and a very large security guy. My friend Ed Valauskas (the Eddie V of Boston) saw me and brought me over to Vedder.

"Hey, Eddie. This is Scott. He's a good dude."

Immediately taking a shine to my Cubs hat, Vedder replied, "Well, you look like a good dude. You're a Cubs fan."

He was playing right into my trap.

"Eh. Not really. It's Tom Morello's hat. I stole it off him because he's an asshole."*

Vedder laughed and nodded his head. "Yeah, I was just about to say: Of course, Tom Morello is a Cubs fan, too."

Bingo! With the ice properly broken, I leaned in and said, "Hey, listen, I wrote this song named after you. And somebody told me that it kind of embarrassed you, and I wanted to apologize."

He grinned that grin of his and replied, "I don't think I was embarrassed."

I pushed on.

"Yeah. No, I heard that you said it's a good song, but why did they have to name it after me."

Vedder cocked his head. "Yeah, I don't think I said that." As if to say, *Easy, fella. I'm Eddie Vedder. Your puny songs can't hurt me.*

And then he turned away and started talking to someone else.

Just like that, all my machinations had blown up in my face and I was thwarted. Where did I go wrong? Was I given bad intel all those years ago? Was Vedder just fucking with me?

Okay. Plan B.

Undeterred, I walked over to the jukebox, fired up "Baba O'Riley" by the Who, and started a sing-along with my group of mighty Bostonians by the bar. Out of the corner of my eye, I could see Vedder suddenly perk up and look over at us. Hey, that's MY song! Like a cobra drawn to a snake charmer's tune, he was powerless to resist—and by the time the song had reached its chorus, there was Eddie Vedder standing right next to me. Singing with that voice that so many had tried to imitate. Singing with that voice that so many had *failed* to imitate. And in that moment, with us laughing like idiots and shouting the words "teenage wasteland" at each other, it was all too easy to see why.

Yeah, that was a pretty great night.

You are correct in your suspicion that the story behind the pilfered Tom Morello Cubs hat is a good one—but that's a story for another foreword to a different book.

Scott Lucas is sometimes recognized as the singer and guitarist for the two-man Chicago rock band Local H, whose latest release is their critically acclaimed ninth album entitled LIFERS. He also co-hosts a podcast called LIFERS and just released his directorial debut, an immersive concert movie called (you guessed it) LIFERS. He also does other stuff that ISN'T called LIFERS.

"ONCE"
(An Introduction)

Once upon a time it was October 1990. Around the world, it was a period that brought people together in significant historic and cultural moments. This was the month East and West Germany reunited, ending forty-five years of political division. It was when radio stations banded together across the world to honor John Lennon on what would have been his fiftieth birthday. And it just so happened to be when Pearl Jam came *alive* with their first-ever show and began a career that has brought people together in a way that few other bands have been able to replicate over the past thirty-five years, especially at concerts.

"When you see Pearl Jam, you never know what kind of show you're going to get," said *Rolling Stone* in a reader poll that ranked the band number 8 on a list of the Top 10 Live Acts of All Time. "Pearl Jam approaches every show with . . . passion and respect for their fans," the magazine added. "It's one reason why they continue to pack giant venues without radio hits or much mainstream media attention."

Through it all, Pearl Jam fans have become a fervent community that travels the world and caravans to countless shows (though they *are* keeping count) because they know each night will provide a unique experience. The band curates every concert with distinctive set lists that are finalized minutes before taking the stage. Band-sanctioned bootlegs, collectors' edition posters, and limited merch add to the one-time-only vibe of each night and result in epic lines of fans trying to secure mementos.

Many have also become part of the massive Ten Club fan community that Pearl Jam has fought fiercely to protect over the decades, such as by continuing to give the diehards first access to tickets, even as the fan club model has largely perished. And remember Taylor Swift's late 2022 kerfuffle with Ticketmaster? That, too, came almost thirty years after Pearl Jam did it first in 1994, when the band members brought antitrust allegations against the monolithic ticketing company to keep concerts fairly priced and accessible, even to the detriment of their own careers.

The band has also rallied for women's rights, voting rights, environmental causes, and the homeless, particularly through their Vitalogy Foundation, which has raised over $50 million since 2006, largely via ticket sales. Pearl Jam has always been a band of and for the people, one keenly aware that it takes a village to push art and ideals forward. "Over the past three decades, the band has a long history of standing up for what it believes in and putting its resources behind those beliefs," a recent press release declared.

And it all started, in typical Pearl Jam form, with a live show. Specifically, the night of October 22, 1990, with the band's debut at Seattle's Off Ramp Café—a date we know so much about all these years later thanks to Pearl

Jeff Ament and Eddie Vedder at an early gig, when the band is still known as Mookie Blaylock, February 1991.

Jam members' and fans' meticulous recordkeeping. From the beginning, the official band website, along with fan sites like Pearl Jam Concert Chronology and Five Horizons and the podcast *Live on 4 Legs*, have logged every single show date over the past thirty-five years—more than 1,100 along the way—and provided set lists, show posters, and extra details to help drive home the nostalgia.

The Pearl Jam Concert Chronology website first went online in 2020, though earlier iterations appeared in 1996 with Five Horizons and in 2005 with Two Feet Thick, before the reins were handed over. "So many people have helped out with sending stuff like ticket stubs, info about set lists, and photos of the band," the site's current curator Richard Jeansson shared in an interview, adding that his own research has come into play. "I've checked out libraries, social media, and contacted many Pearl Jam fans and photographers, and even people who work with the band. It's been an interesting process." The site is a work in progress, updated through 2002 at the time of writing, and with additional years on the very near horizon. "The plan is to add more years and things continuously," Richard shared.

With the help of these resources, plus interviews with industry figures and archival band member interviews, Pearl Jam's full history and key tour moments have been retold throughout this book. The complete tour log from 1990 to 2025 has also been compiled with official info from PearlJam.com to further celebrate the band's latest milestone and show the breadth of their work. (All tour dates

Eddie Vedder, Mike McCready, Dave Abbruzzese, Jeff Ament, and Stone Gossard, February 1992.

presented at the beginning of each section are for regular ticketed events, excluding record store appearances, TV show appearances, and band members' individual shows. Special benefits, anniversary concerts, and major festival dates are noted in bold. When the band appeared multiple times at one venue, all performances are noted together.)

By the end, what comes to the surface is just how much these two facets—the band's chronology and their touring legacy—became intrinsically intertwined as one fed off the other and nourished the monolithic act.

Designed to bring that live feel to the page, this book features twenty-four chapters—about the number of songs Pearl Jam currently plays on a given night—titled after specific songs in emulation of a set list. The book also highlights specific show memories throughout, submitted by a range of fans and journalists who have followed Pearl Jam's journey—from a Dutch fan who took in the tragic events of the Roskilde Festival in 2000 but chooses to remember a happier time hitchhiking his way through Australia to see the band, to a woman who considers herself the "world's oldest Pearl Jam fan" and caught a memorable show in Seattle, to this book's author recounting the nostalgic PJ20 weekend at Alpine Valley in Wisconsin.

But back in 1990, on that late October night, no one had any clue that any of this would happen or that Pearl Jam would become cultural demigods and the mainstream faces of the Seattle rock scene just a few years later. If you happened to live in Seattle and be of age (or had a good fake ID) to get into the notorious Off Ramp Café and had also gotten the memo about a last-minute add-on to the bill that night and decided to check them out, you would've been part of the lucky crowd, unaware you were witnessing music history.

There had been whispers of the new band—at the time called Mookie Blaylock after the New Jersey Nets basketball star—but it was one that came with some heavy baggage. Just seven months earlier, a central figure in the Seattle enclave, singer Andy Wood, had succumbed to the effects of a drug overdose, leaving his grieving bandmates in the once buoyant Mother Love Bone without their anchor. MLB guitarist Stone Gossard and bassist Jeff Ament decided to carry on with a new project—Mookie Blaylock—assembling Stone's grade school friend, guitarist Mike McCready, plus early drummer Dave Krusen (who they knew through mutual friends in the band Son of Man) and a relative unknown from San Diego named Eddie Vedder on vocals.

October 22, 1990 was their trial by fire. Mookie Blaylock was only days old at this point. Eddie had just arrived in Seattle on October 8, fourteen days prior to that first gig. "We were still learning the songs. It was nerve-racking," Dave Krusen told *The Seattle Times,* noting that the band members "just wanted to set up and play, get on stage and see how it felt."

"My first instinct was to say, 'This is insane, we can't play a show after a week,'" Stone shared with *Uncut*. But Jeff knew it was the right move. In the same interview, he said, "I think Stone and I both knew the potential that he and I had together—but we needed to get out and play, and get better."

On a Facebook tribute page to the Off Ramp Café, the infamous hole-in-the-wall club named for its physical location tucked in a corner near the off-ramp for the southbound Interstate 5, it's described as "a little dirty, a little nasty, a whole lotta fun and hella historic." (It still exists, though in 2005, it was renamed El Corazon.)

The club has long been considered the "CBGB of Seattle," with its small stage as influential to Seattle's burgeoning grunge/alt-rock community as CBGB was to New York's punk/new wave heyday. Soundgarden, Alice In Chains, and Mudhoney all broke through at the Off Ramp.

> **The Off Ramp Café was a spot where many acts would try out new material before taking it into the studio or on the road.**

Nirvana even debuted an early iteration of their hit song "Aneurysm" there in November 1990, before releasing the track in 1991. It's the spot where Cameron Crowe hosted the afterparty for *Singles*.

Shelly Underwood, a writer and expert on the '90s Seattle scene, shared an excerpt of her book *Dive* on Medium that unearths the legacy of the historic hall: "Hole's first show in Seattle was there [and] almost any band you could think of played the Off Ramp. Mark Lanegan said how much he hated the place, but nonetheless was there hanging out from time to time. Kurt Cobain passed out in the green room while his very drunk wife, Courtney, was on stage.... Chris Cornell sat up in a corner booth and watched his brother and sister in Inflatable Soul play to packed rooms. Crash Worship almost burned the place down with their pyrotechnics every time they played. That fairly small, not-so-special room was everything."

Eddie Vedder greets fans on tour in Sweden, June 28, 2014.

Eddie Vedder and Jeff Ament onstage together in 1991.

Especially on the night of October 22, 1990, as Mookie Blaylock was getting ready to take the stage. The night brought in a modest number of onlookers who wanted to see what the new post–Mother Love Bone project was all about, as the Seattle community typically came out to support their own. The 299-capacity room was about a quarter full at the start, Dave Krusen estimated. "By the time we were done, it had filled up a little," he told *The Seattle Times*. Chris Cornell was in the crowd. So was his Soundgarden bandmate Kim Thayil. Heart's Nancy Wilson also had a front row seat, as did the Seattle scene's de facto manager, Susan Silver.

What they and everyone else in the room saw was a raw forty-plus-minute set, one in which the band sound-checked a slower tempo version of "Even Flow" in front of the audience. That warm-up showed all kinds of promise even before the set officially began. Someone thankfully had a camcorder that night, and in well-documented footage, you can feel the passion in Eddie Vedder's voice as he belts out each note. You can see Mike McCready dialed in as ever, with one of his soon-to-be-notorious guitar solos. And there were Jeff Ament and Stone Gossard bouncing around, already becoming the backbone of the incredibly important rhythm section. Dave Krusen is not totally in view (this is VHS from 1990, remember), but that's kind of fitting, as he remains a kind of shadow figure in the pantheon of drummers that would fill the seat before Matt Cameron got the permanent spot.

Unsurprisingly, the applause picks up after each subsequent song, as the band gets more comfortable. But what's most interesting is seeing Eddie uncharacteristically shy and demure at the start, with a ball cap pulled over his head, hands in pockets or arms crossed over his chest, teetering from foot to foot. He eventually loses the cap and his jacket and moves around the

A handwritten set list adorns the sound board for a performance at the Hollywood Palladium in Los Angeles on May 13, 1992.

stage some. But where is the rafter-jumping, Tarzan-swinging, dead-staring banshee that nearly risked his life on the early tour runs? He wasn't totally done incubating yet. In the beginning, Eddie's confidence level was a far cry from the incredible frontman he would become. "It was a bit hard for me in the beginning to come out," he told Cameron Crowe in the *Pearl Jam Twenty* documentary. "It wasn't a neutral zone, it was their zone," he said of joining forces with Stone, Jeff, Mike, and Dave.

Even so, all the hallmarks of Eddie's power were there at that Off Ramp Café debut. Even the person recording that precious VHS footage zooms in and focuses on the singer several times, especially as the band started with the incredibly emotional deluge of "Release." It was actually Eddie's idea to open with the song that night, hoping to start slow and reel people in, according to Mike McCready. It's a strategy the band has stuck with over time, as "Release" remains one of their favorite ways to open a show.

> **Of the 184 times the band has played "Release" live, according to data from Setlist.fm, it's typically featured at the top of the set.**

During their first performance, Pearl Jam also played "Alive," "Black," "Even Flow," and "Once," all songs that, along with "Release," wound up on their groundbreaking debut album, *Ten*, less than a year later. To think that the band was just days old and had already formulated such iconic songs is remarkable and hints at their early chemistry. Chris Cornell has been quoted as saying, "It definitely to this day was absolutely the best inaugural show I've ever seen in my life. Hands down, no comparison."

It truly was the catalyst that set Pearl Jam alight and begat one of the most successful careers in modern rock history. Since then, the band has sold more than eighty-five million copies of their twelve studio albums globally and was inducted into the Rock & Roll Hall of Fame in 2017. In the last year alone, Pearl Jam was handsomely nominated for three Grammy awards for their latest album *Dark Matter,* including Best Rock Performance, Best Rock Album, and

Best Rock Song, and their tour to support the record debuted on *Pollstar*'s Live75 charts in September 2024, with the first few tour dates bringing in close to $20 million.

Even when tragedy struck, like Kurt Cobain's death by suicide in 1994 and the horrific events of the Roskilde festival in 2000, after which the Pearl Jam members considered disbanding, they've soldiered on and remained as relevant as ever. Even as all their Seattle comrades went by the wayside, either through untimely deaths or unfortunate breakups, Pearl Jam still reigned supreme. Quite ironic for a band that was once considered commercialized "synthetic grunge," as noted by *SPIN*. In their thirtieth anniversary oral history of the band, the magazine pondered, "Why were Pearl Jam, virtually alone among their peers, the ones who kept the flame alive?" Yet, there is a tangible hunger that continues to be stoked, not only for the band but the community Pearl Jam continues to bring together.

At a show in Colorado in 2015, remarking upon the twenty-fifth anniversary of that fateful first night, Eddie Vedder shared with the crowd, "We're proud to still be together. We're proud to be in a long relationship." And in good times and bad, they've stayed faithful to that sentiment.

SET LIST SPOTLIGHT

The First Show Ever
(October 22, 1990, The Off Ramp Café, Seattle, WA)

1. Release
2. Alone
3. Alive
4. Once
5. Even Flow
6. Black
7. Breath

— ENCORE —

8. Just A Girl

HIDDEN PEARL

"Just A Girl" has only been played twice in Pearl Jam's entire history. The last live performance was in 1991.

OPENING ACT
(1984-1991)

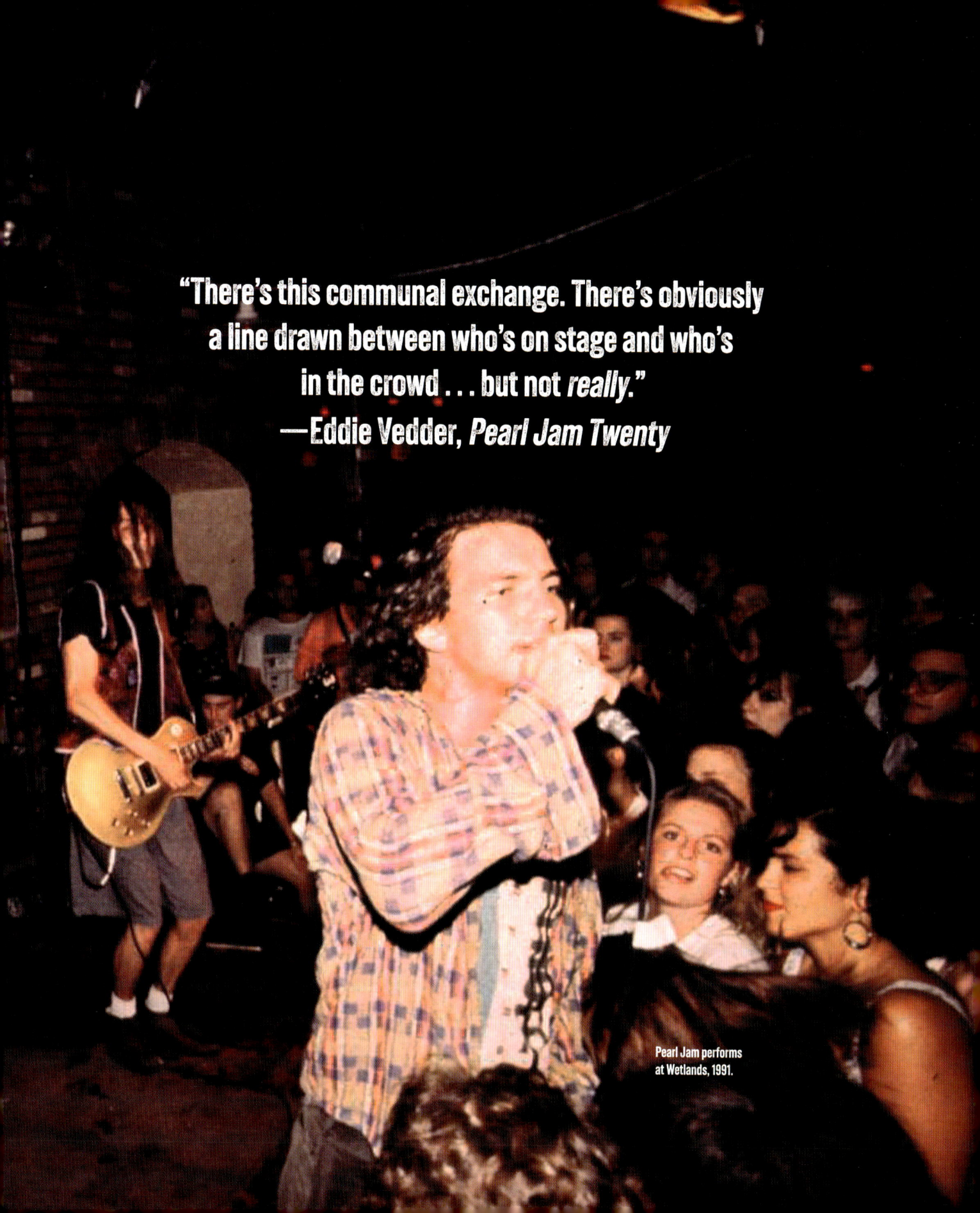

"There's this communal exchange. There's obviously a line drawn between who's on stage and who's in the crowd... but not *really*."
—Eddie Vedder, *Pearl Jam Twenty*

Pearl Jam performs at Wetlands, 1991.

TOUR DATES: 1990–1991

1990
Performing as Mookie Blaylock
October 22: Seattle, WA @ Off Ramp Café
December 19: Seattle, WA @ Vogue
December 22: Seattle, WA @ Moore Theatre

1991
Performing as Mookie Blaylock
January 10: Victoria, BC, Canada @ Harpo's
January 11: Vancouver, BC, Canada @ Town Pump
February 1, February 25, March 1: Seattle, WA @ Off Ramp Café
February 7: Los Angeles, CA @ Florentine Gardens
February 9: Long Beach, CA @ God Saves The Queen
February 10: San Diego, CA @ The Bacchanal
February 11: Los Angeles, CA @ Club With No Name
February 12: Los Angeles, CA @ Riki Rachtman's World Famous Cathouse
February 13: San Diego, CA @ Winter's
February 14: Oakland, CA @ Real Rock Club
February 15: San Francisco, CA @ I-Beam
February 16: Sacramento, CA @ Cattle Club
February 17: Eugene, OR @ Union Trade Hall Woodmen of The World
February 20: Portland, OR @ Melody Ballroom
February 26: Seattle, WA @ Vogue
March 2: Seattle, WA @ O.K. Hotel

Officially performing as Pearl Jam
May 17: Seattle, WA @ Off Ramp Café
May 25, July 4, August 3, August 19, August 29, and September 3: Seattle, WA @ RKCNDY
July 10: Boston, MA @ Avalon
July 12: Philadelphia, PA @ JC Dobbs
July 13: New York, NY @ The Marquee
July 15: Providence, RI @ Club Babyhead
July 17: New York, NY @ Wetlands Preserve
July 21: Chicago, IL @ Cabaret Metro
July 22: Minneapolis, MN @ First Avenue
August 23: Seattle, WA @ Mural Amphitheater
September 25: Victoria, BC, Canada @ Harpo's
September 26: Vancouver, BC, Canada @ Town Pump
September 28: Portland, OR @ Satyricon
September 30: San Francisco, CA @ I-Beam
October 1: Los Angeles, CA @ Riki Rachtman's World Famous Cathouse
October 2: Los Angeles, CA @ Troubadour
October 3: Los Angeles, CA @ Foundations Forum
October 5: San Diego, CA @ Winter's
October 6: Los Angeles, CA @ Palladium
October 7: Phoenix, AZ @ Mason Jar
October 9: Austin, TX @ The Back Room
October 10 and December 11: Cedar Hill, TX @ Trees
October 11: Houston, TX @ The Vatican
October 13: Atlanta, GA @ The Point
October 14: Chapel Hill, NC @ Cat's Cradle

October 16: Madison, WI @ Oscar Mayer Theatre
October 17: Dekalb, IL @ Duke Ellington Ballroom at NIU
October 19: Ames, IA @ CY Stevens Auditorium, Iowa State University
October 20: Omaha, NE @ Peony Park Ballroom
October 22: Milwaukee, WI @ Eagle's Ballroom
October 23: East Lansing, MI @ MSU Auditorium
October 25: Pittsburgh, PA @ A.J. Palumbo Center
October 26: Cleveland, OH @ Cleveland Music Hall
October 27: Rochester, NY @ Rochester Auditorium Center
October 29 and October 30: Toronto, ON, Canada @ Concert Hall
November 1: Boston, MA @ Walter Brown Arena, Boston University
November 2: Burlington, VT @ Memorial Auditorium, University of Vermont
November 3: Springfield, MA @ Civic Center Springfield
November 4: Amherst, MA @ Student Union Ballroom at UMass
November 5: Troy, NY @ Houston Field House at Rensselaer Polytechnic Institute
November 6: Ithaca, NY @ The Haunt
November 7: Syracuse, NY @ The Landmark Theatre
November 8: New York, NY @ CBGB's
November 9: Washington, DC @ Bender Arena, American University
November 11, November 12, November 15, and November 16: New York, NY @ Roseland Ballroom
November 13: Warwick, RI @ Rocky Point Palladium
November 17: State College, PA @ Rec. Hall, Pennsylvania State University
November 19: Columbus, OH @ Veterans Coliseum
November 20: Kalamazoo, MI @ The State Downtown Theater
November 21: Ann Arbor, MI @ Blind Pig
November 22 and November 23: Detroit, MI @ State Theatre
November 24: Indianapolis, IN @ Convention Center
November 26: Normal, IL @ Braden Auditorium, Illinois State University
November 27: Cincinnati, OH @ Cincinnati Gardens
November 29: Chicago, IL @ Aragon Ballroom
November 30: St. Paul, MN @ Roy Wilkins Auditorium
December 2 and December 3: St. Louis, MO @ The American Theater
December 4: Lenexa, KS @ Memorial Hall
December 6: New Orleans, LA @ State Palace Theater
December 7: Houston, TX @ Unicorn
December 8: Austin, TX @ City Coliseum
December 10: Houston, TX @ The Vatican
December 11: Dallas, TX @ Bronco Bowl
December 12: Norman, OK @ Hollywood Theater
December 14: Denver, CO @ Denver Coliseum
December 15: Salt Lake City, UT @ Club DV8
December 27: Los Angeles, CA @ Los Angeles Memorial Sports Arena
December 28: San Diego, CA @ Del Mar Pavilion
December 29: Tempe, AZ @ Arizona State University Center
December 31: Daly City, CA @ Cow Palace

TOUR DATES: 1990–1991   17

"Given To FLY"

Like any good story, there is so much that happened *before* that is key to understanding the evolution of Pearl Jam, starting with its birthplace of Seattle. With roots in the mid-'80s and picking up steam with 1991's "Smells Like Teen Spirit," the Seattle sound came from unexpected music capital far away from the geography and infrastructure of a Los Angeles, New York, or Nashville. Yet the region still became a once-in-a-lifetime sonic breeding ground for a litter of amplified greats, among them Pearl Jam, Soundgarden, Nirvana, Alice In Chains, Mother Love Bone, Green River, Mad Season, Screaming Trees, Mudhoney, Temple of the Dog, and so many more.

The movement also influenced scores of post-grunge bands well into the '90s and beyond, inspired clothing designers and brands with their aesthetic, and has long been called the voice of a generation looking to find enlightenment in their disenchantment. "It's all too apparent that grunge remains an essential element of rock's ever-evolving DNA," said UDiscover Music.

Some call it the last great rock scene. Some wonder if the Seattle magic could ever happen again, especially as artists splinter off into the ether of the digital age rather than finding a physical creative community. And still others wonder if that storied nebula was somehow cursed, especially after all the unfortunate losses of luminaries like Andy Wood, Kurt Cobain, Layne Staley, Chris Cornell, Mark Lanegan, Mia Zapata, and Kristen Pfaff.

Though the scene has been mired in more tragedy than would seem possible for one collective group of artists, it has persevered and the legacy has lived on. As you read this, a teenager somewhere is picking

TOP: Influential grunge band Alice In Chains in Chicago on October 1, 1990.

BOTTOM: Grunge band and close friends of Pearl Jam, Soundgarden, in Chicago on November 8, 1991.

OPPOSITE: Pearl Jam performs on February 26, 1991.

GIVEN TO FLY 19

Grunge band Nirvana in Germany on November 12, 1991.

up their first copy of *Ten* or *Nevermind* and will soon fall down the rabbit hole.

Like Detroit's Motown, Chicago's Chess Record blues, New Orleans jazz, the San Francisco hippie sound, and New York punk, the Pacific Northwest music scene that spawned Pearl Jam was the perfect alchemy of the right place (an isolated, rainy metropolis with little to do), the right time (appealing to music fans who were over the facade of hair metal and pop), and the right people (a hugely supportive network) that turned a devoted local scene into a national and international treasure.

Before "grunge," Seattle was notable for other non-music developments too, like being ahead of the dot-com boom, as Microsoft set up its headquarters there in the '80s (Amazon would soon follow in 1994). Seattle also became the unofficial café capital of the United States with the advent of Starbucks in the '70s that continued the legacy of the first roasting business in town from nearly a century prior.

There was a dark side, too, the gloom and doom of which seeped into the grunge scene, which expressed the vibe through heavy lyrics and aggressive guitars. As *Far Out Magazine* explained, a series of events in '80s Seattle brought more dark clouds than usual. There was the 1983 Wah Mee Club massacre that claimed the lives of thirteen people (then referred to as the "deadliest mass murder" in the history of Washington State); there was a serial murderer, the Green River Killer, on the loose; and the region was still picking up the pieces from the so-called "Boeing Bust" in the early '70s, after the Supersonic Transport Program (an effort to build an American version of the Concorde) tanked. This led to one of the worst unemployment rates of any city since the Great Depression, standing at almost 12 percent.

As has become apparent across music history, from bad times often comes great music, and the youth wave in Seattle in the 1980s had a lot to make noise about. To do so, they soon started taking cues from the punk bands that came through town. Major label acts of the time weren't stopping in remote and out-of-the-way Seattle. Instead, it was the get-in-the-van-and-drive punk bands traversing the country on their own dime who made frequent appearances on their ad hoc West Coast tours—and thereby made their mark with the young musicians in town who craved live music and could be seen out and about on a near nightly basis.

As *Rolling Stone* explained in a sweeping 1992 feature, "In the early Eighties, any band that made it to Seattle stood to make a big impression," with the article citing acts like Hüsker Dü, the Minutemen, and Black Flag as cultural and musical beacons that young, disenfranchised Seattle-ites took cues from to create their own sound, as grunge ultimately mixed in influences of anti-establishment punk, metal, garage rock, and noise rock. In a vintage interview from the early '90s, archived on YouTube by *The Grunge Scene*, Pearl Jam's Jeff Ament even shared that "from a playing standpoint, we could relate more to the Ramones." Even the "grunge aesthetic" of long, unkempt hair could be called imitation. As *Rolling Stone* opined, Seattle's "trademark hirsuter-than-thou look was inspired by the longhairs in Black Flag."

But it was more than just punk *music* that influenced the vibe of the Seattle scene in the '80s and '90s—it was also their unflinching aesthetic, a commitment to DIY ideals, devotion to the community, and uncensored creativity that led to that grassroots uprising. "We created everything ourselves . . . it was us basically making records, paying for them ourselves, paying for our own tours, we had nothing to do with the actual music industry," Jeff has said.

Pearl Jam performs at Wetlands on July 17, 1991.

"The Seattle phenomenon wouldn't have been possible without the network of college radio, fan zines, and indie distributors that sprang up in the wake of punk rock," *Rolling Stone* added in their article, citing radio stations like KCMU and KJET and publications such as *Backlash* and the *Rocket* for being unflinching in their support of local bands.

In fact, it was indie rags and fan zines that led to the development of one of the most important enablers of the Seattle scene: Sub Pop Records. The independent label was founded in 1988 by Jonathan Poneman and business partner Bruce Pavitt, and grew out of Bruce's involvement with a radio show and zine called *Subterranean Pop*—which inspired the name of the forthcoming label. Shortly before establishing Sub Pop, he was also writing a music discovery column for *Rocket*. Once there was enough money in the bank, Jonathan and Bruce then started turning their attention to investing in the burgeoning bands in their city, providing modest seed money to artists to put their ideas on tape.

Sub Pop became the first home for a growing roster of acts like Nirvana, Mudhoney, and Soundgarden. The label had their hands on Nirvana's 1988 debut cover single "Love Buzz," which became an early part of a subscription service called the Sub Pop Singles Club. It helped rally an early community behind music emerging from the city. Sub Pop also had the debut Soundgarden single, "Hunted Down"/"Nothing to Say," which was issued in June 1987 (before the label was even a true business), and on its heels came the band's first EP, *Screaming Life*, that October, which helped everything explode.

"The label is often associated with something called 'the grunge movement,' [and] exploitation of this association has frequently proven financially fruitful," the founders sarcastically share on the label's official website. They should give themselves more credit, though. Without Sub Pop, who knows if we would've ever gotten to the '90s takeover of the Seattle sound, and through it, the dawn of bands like Pearl Jam.

Before the grunge era, Seattle was perhaps best known as the birthplace of the one and only Jimi Hendrix, in 1942. His mastery of the electric guitar, at least in an evolutionary sense, could be seen as a small stepping stone toward the impending rock scene that would come five decades later. There were also iconic regional bands, like Tacoma's '60s-era instrumental rock group the Ventures and garage rockers the Sonics, that made their mark. A slew of early '80s acts followed, like the glam punkers Malfunkshun (from Bainbridge Island, Washington, and featuring the inimitable Andy Wood—more on him soon), Seattle's own post-punkers U-Men, and noise provocateurs Melvins (from Montesano, Washington), who were particularly influential on the emerging '90s rock scene. Because, yes, grunge and all that came with it was more than just from Seattle—it extended across a large swath of Washington State. Even

Nirvana truly wasn't from Seattle but from Aberdeen, over one hundred miles away.

Another faction that needs to be mentioned in this history is the riot grrrl scene that grew out of Olympia, Washington, and would soon have its moment to shine via acts like Bikini Kill and Bratmobile and the ever-relevant record label Kill Rock Stars. It was their trailblazing and other rock stars like Courtney Love that invited more women to come out and play.

In Seattle, '70s-born classic rockers Heart also had a multi-pronged influence on the grunge scene, which doesn't always get the credit it's due. In 1990, band members and sisters Nancy and Ann Wilson invested in a local analog studio in their hometown called Lawson Productions, which was eventually renamed Bad Animals Studio (in homage to Heart's 1987 album of the same name). By 1991, Bad Animals Studio was ground zero for many of Seattle's

Ann Wilson and Nancy Wilson of the band Heart perform at the Palladium in New York City on October 22, 1978.

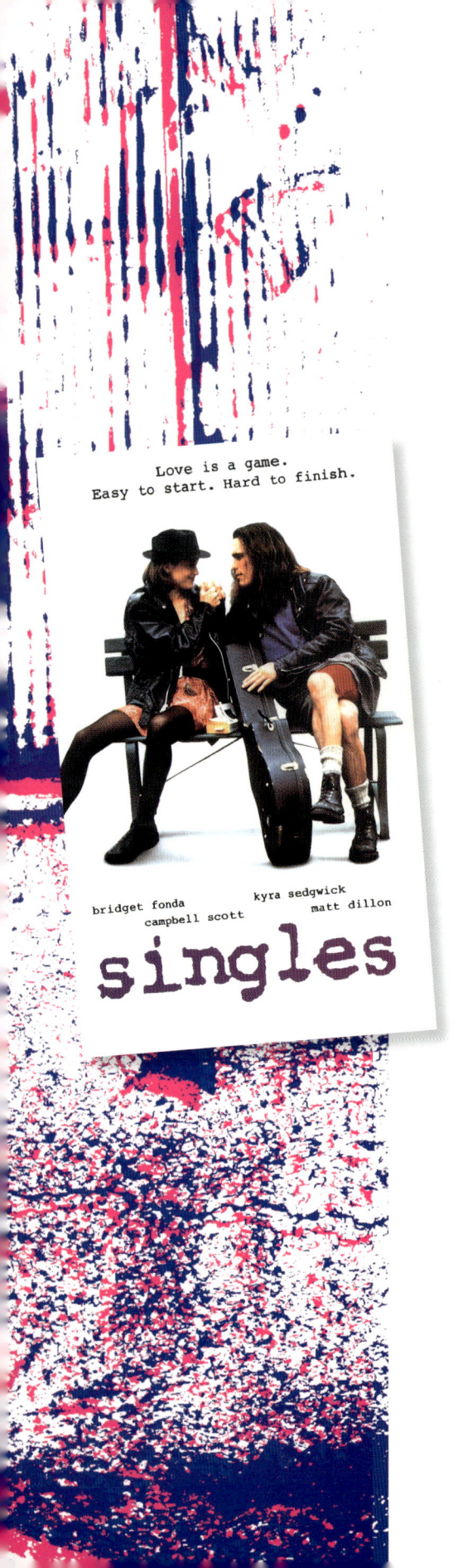

burgeoning acts to record albums before the majors got involved—among the Wilsons' friends and clients were the so-called "Big Four" of grunge: Pearl Jam, Alice In Chains, Soundgarden, and Nirvana.

The earliest connection linking the bands and Bad Animals Studio came through Pearl Jam's eventual manager Kelly Curtis, who had been friends with the Wilson sisters since they were all teens. He was also one of Heart's early publicists. "Through him I guess we went to a lot of events where a lot of the Seattle music bands were playing," Ann recalled to *Ultimate Classic Rock* in 2021.

Another tentacle of the scene came when Nancy Wilson married *Almost Famous* screenwriter, filmmaker, and journalist Cameron Crowe in 1986. His 1992 movie *Singles* was set in this music mecca and has been described as his "love letter" to the Seattle music community. It, of course, featured members of Pearl Jam, Soundgarden, and Alice In Chains in various cameos.

In 2011, Cameron famously spearheaded the *Pearl Jam Twenty* documentary and accompanying book, a heartfelt two-decade visual retrospective of the band. In the first few minutes of the film, he discusses his awareness of what was happening around him in the '80s and '90s, which made him pay attention to acts like Pearl Jam and their contemporaries: "I became aware of a whole scene of musicians that really worked together to create their own world of influences and bands and community."

That point can't be overstated enough. If it seems like everything was somehow connected in the Seattle music scene, it truly was. The interwoven network of collaborative talents and the allies who supported them was a huge part of the charm and, ultimately, led to the scene's success. Everyone had their own bands and worked on numerous side projects, easily shuffling members from one to the other, multiplying the number of acts and helping the community to grow.

The population of Seattle in 1990 was just over half a million people, and the big "small town" meant that everyone knew each other and

US poster art for the 1992 film *Singles*.

became quite chummy. In terms of music, it was a lot of friends looking to impress one another with their latest works. This sense of community has permeated the career of a band like Pearl Jam, which has since expanded the invitation to fans the world over.

As Ann Wilson shared with *Ultimate Classic Rock*, it was hard to escape the scene if you lived in Seattle at that time. "I lived right in town, [so] whenever I went to see music, [the bands] usually would come back to my house. That's really how I met a lot of people—just by going to see them and then hanging out later. Eventually, we all became friends, and we began to trust each other."

In fact, Eddie Vedder shared in *Pearl Jam Twenty* that the "comradery and healthy competition part" was something he only found out after the fact was "unusual." It was Johnny Ramone who pointed out to him that the friendships he saw in bands like Soundgarden and Pearl Jam weren't common. "He told me, 'I've never seen that before, in New York we hated each other.'"

In Seattle, the competition in cutthroat music capitals like NYC and LA was replaced with comradery, where friends became collaborators, bandmates, and lifelong muses—even, and especially, when tragedy befell the scene. "You learn from each other, you get inspired by each other," Eddie revealed in the *Pearl Jam Twenty* documentary. Everything felt real, not artificially dictated by record label heads or other influencers—from the thrift store clothes they wore to the modest clubs (like the Off Ramp Café, the Showbox, Moore Theatre, and Central Saloon) where the scene converged when one of their own had a show, to the unpolished demos that were dirty and, well, "grungy."

The bands weren't exactly fond of that term—especially in the beginning—as it became as much of a cliché as the flannel and combat boots it rode in on. As Soundgarden's Kim Thayil told *Loudwire* in 2021, "'Grunge,' as a term, nobody liked that. Everyone thought, 'Oh this is a marketing thing. This

US poster art for the 2011 *Pearl Jam Twenty* documentary.

GIVEN TO FLY 25

is a way to file Seattle on a retail display in a record store.' We thought that was it. Initially, people just rejected the term." Though, he conceded, "Eventually, we all just came to embrace it." Eddie Vedder also shared in a 2009 interview, "It feels like a word with a lot of baggage . . . but there's some good stuff in there if you take it out and spend the time to open it. . . . It was really good for us, I suppose, because we ended up being lumped together with a bunch of other great bands as well. But we were all really different. There were similarities but we're crazily different."

None of the bands really sounded like each other. If you take the Big Four acts alone, you get a platter of sludge and prog-leaning alt metal with Soundgarden, the unpolished and raw punk-influenced rock of Nirvana, a more harmony-infused melodic rock with Alice In Chains, and a '70s-loving classic rock act with Pearl Jam.

As Jeff Ament explained in *The Love Bone Earth Affair* home video, released by PolyGram in 1992 as a posthumous tribute to Mother Love Bone, "Everybody was just kind of making music and doing what was natural . . . stylistically if there is some Seattle sound, some Seattle visual thing, it's just from being cooped up in the city."

But there was a unifying ideology to it: "Grunge was an intersection of social activity, distortion, and a genuine sort of mind-bending wonder. And hormones," Sub Pop's Jonathan Poneman somewhat jokingly told Noble House Hotels in a guide to discovering the places that made the Seattle scene.

There were also so many acts beyond those mainstream stalwarts that were truly the godfathers who kicked open the gates, even if they didn't always reach marquee status. The true harbinger of what would become known as the Seattle sound was Green River, a punk-loving, Stooges-reminiscent band formed in 1984 and allegedly named for the serial killer dominating headlines at the time. The quintet was relatively short-lived and already on the way to its demise in 1988, the first casualty in the scene's continual battle of going commercial vs. remaining independent and underground; the band members differed on the matter, which eventually broke up the band.

What rose from the ashes, though, was foundational and helped kick-start the genesis of the scene's growing family tree. On the one hand, you had Mudhoney (started by Green River's Mark Arm and Steve Turner—the ones who wanted to stay homegrown and indie), and on the other hand, there was Mother Love Bone (started by Green River's Stone Gossard, Jeff Ament, and Bruce Fairweather, who were eyeing a major label breakthrough).

Soundgarden was also getting warmed up in 1984, as was Screaming Trees that same year, and Skin Yard followed shortly thereafter in 1985. The latter band was notable for its

A collection of Pearl Jam posters.

lineup, including Soundgarden/Pearl Jam drummer Matt Cameron and Jack Endino, who would go on to become one of the most frequent recording engineers and producers on Seattle sound albums in the years to come.

Green River was notable within that early crop of rock acts out of Seattle's underground as the first to release a record, the 1985 EP *Come On Down*, released via the small imprint Homestead Records. But a year later, in 1986, came another big turning point, when a half-dozen of the reigning acts in Seattle contributed tracks to the *Deep Six* compilation issued by local punk label C/Z Records. Among the bands featured were Green River, Melvins, Malfunkshun, Skin Yard, Soundgarden, and the U-Men. Although the compilation wasn't a commercial hit at the time, it's long been regarded as the scene's unparalleled debut, introducing the sound to the rest of the world before Sub Pop took the reins.

One musician who was also intent on making sure the rest of the world knew about the Seattle sound after *Deep Six* was Andy Wood, the lovably flamboyant singer of Malfunkshun and, later, Mother Love Bone. In the *Pearl Jam Twenty* documentary, several of the key figures who were interviewed frequently discussed how Andy had dreams to play coliseums and arenas and acted like it every time he came on stage—even if it was just at one of Seattle's hole-in-the-wall venues. "He was a rock star, he knew it, and something about that made us believe we were too," said late Soundgarden singer Chris Cornell in the film; in addition to being a close friend and contemporary, he was also Andy's one-time roommate.

Andy was the heart and soul of the scene, and his premature passing in March 1990 left a hole that some believed would never be filled.

GIVEN TO FLY 27

"Do The EVOLUTION"

Thirty-five years ago, many first uttered the question that the Seattle scene would come to grapple with over and over in the years to come: Who could possibly replace a beloved frontman? Especially when it came to Andy Wood.

"I walked out," Mother Love Bone's photographer Lance Mercer told *The Seattle Times* about being in the crowd for Mookie Blaylock's live debut. "Seeing Jeff and Stone onstage was really difficult, because I felt Andy was the one who deserved to be there, not Eddie." Eventually, Lance would come around on the band; he shot the photos for *Ten* and toured with the band early on.

If it sounds harsh, Lance's statement has to be taken in the context of just how much of a behemoth Andy Wood was to the Seattle scene or to anyone who had ever seen him command a show. There was no replacing Andy, and Stone Gossard and Jeff Ament knew that when they chose to put Mother Love Bone to rest, while never forgetting Andy's legacy. The supergroup tribute Temple of the Dog grew out of that adoration. Seattle's Museum of Pop Culture even crafted a bronze statue of the singer as part of its Pearl Jam exhibit, which was on view from 2018 to 2023.

> Over the years, Pearl Jam has paid homage to their fallen comrade in concert, performing Mother Love Bone songs like "Chloe Dancer/Crown Of Thorns" and "Stardog Champion" at many formative shows.

(l-r) Mike McCready, Eddie Vedder, Dave Abbruzzese, Stone Gossard, and Jeff Ament of Pearl Jam.

Notable instances include the 2005 and 2006 shows at the Gorge Amphitheatre in George, Washington, as well as Madison Square Garden in 2003, and the PJ20 mini-festival at Wisconsin's Alpine Valley in 2011.

Andy was born in Mississippi in 1966, and he kept a bit of that accent and lots of Southern charm throughout his adult life, even though the Wood family eventually settled in the Seattle

OPPOSITE: Eddie sings during a Pearl Jam performance at Wetlands on July 17, 1991.

DO THE EVOLUTION 29

BELOW: The band Mother Love Bone.

OPPOSITE: Mother Love Bone onstage.

area when its patriarch got a job as an Air Force recruiter. Andy began his music career at just fourteen years old, tapped as the bass player and singer of the band Malfunkshun, a groovy, noisy glam rock trio that took cues from T. Rex and KISS. Malfunkshun also featured Andy's older brother Kevin Wood and drummer Regan Hagar. (Early short-lived members included bassist Dave Rees and original drummer David Hunt.)

Mom Toni Wood recalled in an interview with *Grungery* that older brother Kevin once took young Andy to a rock concert when they were kids and the lightbulb went off. "I can't remember who was playing but they were watching the concert and then Andy poked Kevin with his elbow and said, 'Hey, I want to be a rock star,' and Kevin said, 'Me too.' And they went home and started the band," Toni shared, noting that during a family Easter gathering in 1980, the brothers stayed home and made their first demo.

Andy always dreamed big when it came to his music, which he liked to refer to as "love rock"—coalescing all his feelings about being a frontman and what he wanted to give to his crowds. In the few interviews that exist of Andy, you can hear him constantly name-dropping, in the most innocent way. He shared in the *Love Bone Earth Affair* home video that, "in my mind, I was as big as Peter Frampton in the '70s." Later, he recalled coming up with the Mother

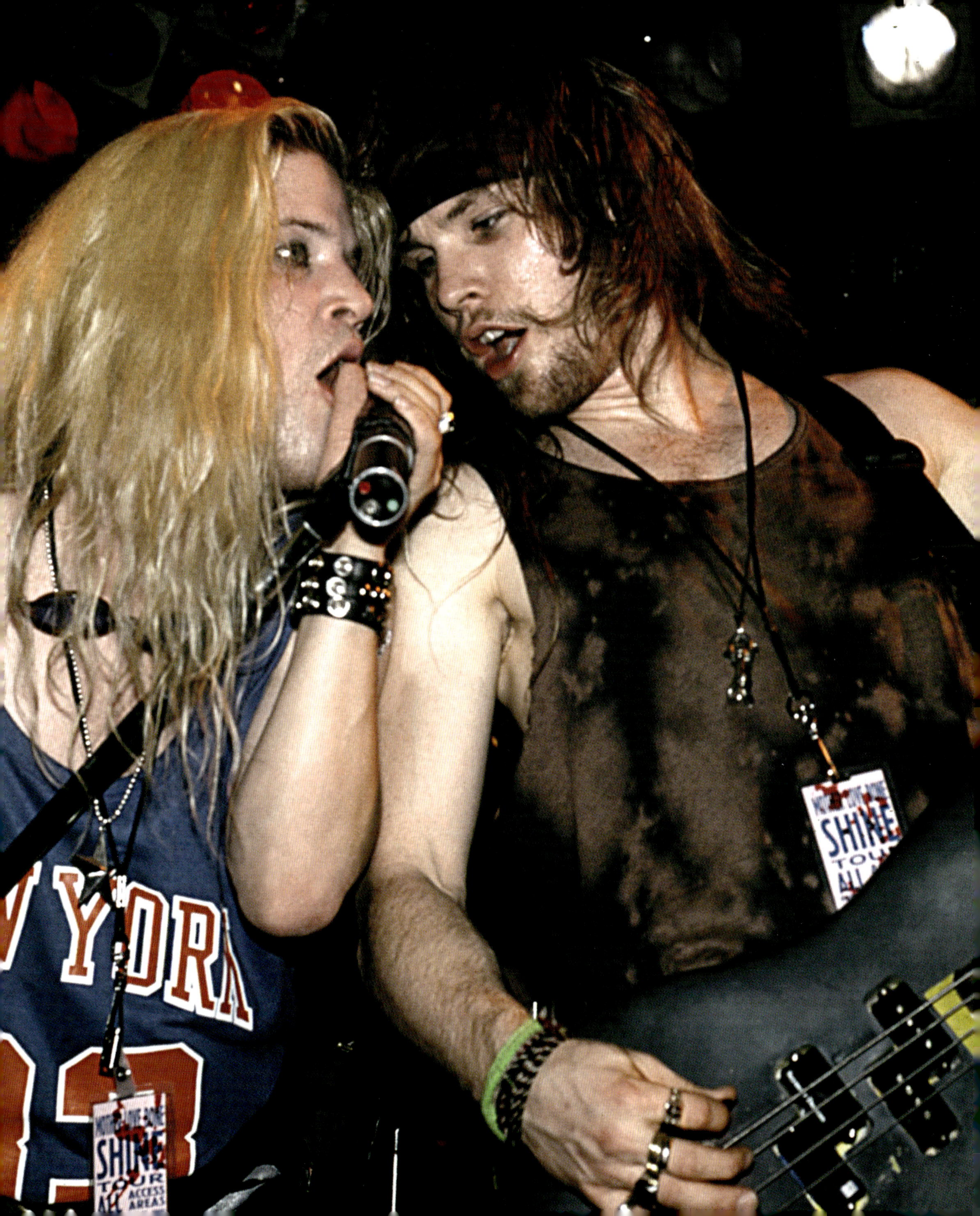
SHINE
TOUR
ACCESS
AREAS

Love Bone name after toying with short-syllable monikers like Led Zeppelin because he believed "that might be the secret to huge success."

Andy also bargained with the universe to get him to an arena stage. "I want to get on an arena tour with some band—Warrant, for that matter; what the hell, let's go on tour with Warrant just so we can play arenas," he joked of teaming up with the glam metal band. "I want the world to know that Mother Love Bone is coming to take over the world, a plethora of delights, a fruit salad compote of delights," he famously said in archived footage included in the *Pearl Jam Twenty* documentary.

And everyone believed he could get there, if only time had been on his side. Malfunkshun gave him his first shot to rile people up. Performing under the ostentatious alter ego L'Andrew the Love Child, Andy wore satin outfits and makeup that made him look "outrageous" (his own words) and was well-known for antics like eating cereal during sets, throwing gummy bears into the crowd, and tossing around sheep doll props. "The first time I saw Malfunkshun, there was this girl in a furry coat. She was walking up to the front of the stage, and people were trying to pick her up. I was looking at her, and she was pretty huge. Then she got on stage and started playing bass," Melvins' Dale Crover has recalled seeing Andy onstage. He gained a lot of attention for this onstage persona, which was described by the magazine *Kerrang!* as a mix of "equal parts Marc Bolan, Freddie Mercury, Prince and Gene Simmons." But underneath it all was a person grappling with his own modest reality.

Mom Toni admitted that addiction runs in the Wood family and it was a demon Andy fought as well, with several attempts at rehab (the first in 1985). It especially reared its head as Andy turned to substances to cope with matters of the heart. "He was so emotional about girls. If he had lived, he may have become a stronger person," Toni shared in the *Grungery* interview.

Jeff Ament believed that flaw was part of Andy's greatness, even if it sadly came at a price. "Not to glamorize what he did, but I think a lot of his lyrics were drawn out of that confusion and not understanding his feelings," Jeff shared in the *Love Bone Earth Affair* video.

Malfunkshun's only true release while Andy was alive was on that *Deep Six* compilation for C/Z Records, before Andy decided to leave the band to embark on Mother Love Bone. "He felt awful about leaving them," mom Toni shared. "He had to. He said to me, 'This is all going to happen before I'm twenty-five. I'm going to be big before I'm twenty-five. And then, after I make it big and ride that wave for a while I'm going to kind of pull back and write music for movies and do quiet things.' That was his plan."

So, when Jeff and Stone's previous band Green River broke up in 1988, it came at "the right time" said Andy in the home movie. Malfunkshun and Green River shared a practice space and a public address system, so Jeff, Stone, and Andy became close and started jamming together and saw fresh opportunity. "They were the guys I needed to be in the band I wanted to form," Andy added. Soon, label heads were zeroing in on Andy's It factor and the great musicianship behind Mother Love Bone, which, in addition to Stone, Jeff, Andy, and Bruce Fairweather, also included drummer Greg Gilmore of 10 Minute Warning (another Seattle band, which notably included Guns N' Roses' Duff McKagan).

MLB was courted by Geffen Records but ultimately wound up with PolyGram subsidiary Mercury Records, who released the EP *Shine* in March 1989. Mercury also released the band's one and only full-length album, *Apple*, the following year—though Andy sadly never got to see that day. He died from the effects of a drug overdose on March 19, 1990, at the young age of twenty-four, and the album was released four months later to the day, on July 19, 1990.

"In our minds, there was never a doubt we wanted the record to come out," Stone shared in an early '90s interview alongside Jeff, which has been archived on YouTube via *The Grunge Scene*. Though PolyGram/Mercury gave the members space to figure out what they wanted to do with *Apple*, the band decided to release it and dedicate it to Andy's memory. Mother Love Bone members did what they could to help promote the album and make sure fans heard it—Stone helped piece together live footage for a video for track "Stardog Champion" and Jeff designed T-shirts. "Hopefully people will hear it," Jeff said in the interview, "because there's no opportunity for us to go out and tour like we wanted to."

Andy's death, rightfully, put a pause on everything. "We're not really looking at this point just to find a singer to replace Andy and go on with Mother Love Bone," Stone shared in the vintage interview. "Andy's personality was such an integral part of the band and the whole image of the band and his lyrics and all the colorful kind of Andyisms, all tied into the whole trip that we decided it just wouldn't be right just to go on and find some other long-haired rock guy to be the singer," Stone continued. "And so at this point I think everyone really wants to kind of take a break . . . and just kind of let things happen naturally to a certain extent and see where we want to go with it. We're not in any huge rush to be rock stars at this point. Something will happen, regardless of what it is, we don't know."

That door would open again a few months later with Eddie Vedder. Although it meant working with someone from outside the Seattle scene for the first time, what Stone and Jeff found was an incredible connection as Eddie, too, was grappling with his own sense of loss. Together, they grieved . . . through music.

"Better MAN"

Finding a singer they not only liked but truly loved, was nothing Jeff nor Stone expected to happen so soon. By mid-1990, Stone and Jeff weren't even jamming together. There wasn't bad blood, of course; they were just two people trying to find their own ways forward while tangled in a complicated grieving process.

"To be honest I didn't have much of a safety net at that point, so I felt a teeny bit of desperation like how am I going to pay my rent? I'm 27 years old. Do I need to go back to school? Does lightning only strike once? Is it over?," Jeff shared on the *Broken Record Podcast* of his mindset at the time. "I was scrambling, I didn't know if I was going to play music anymore." On the other hand, he added, "Stone hit the ground running and wrote a bunch of beautiful tracks. That was how he responded to Andy passing."

Stone's instrumentals became the bedrock of that folkloric demo tape known as Momma-Son (or Mamasan, as it was also called before 2009's *Ten* box set reissue revealed the correct spelling). But, in its earliest iteration, the tape was simply labeled the *Stone Gossard Demos 91*. It featured not only some of the emerging riffs Stone had started writing for Mother Love Bone and was looking to repurpose (one of them being "Dollar Short," which eventually became Pearl Jam's uber-hit "Alive"), but also new arrangements bringing him to all-new territory.

As Cameron Crowe wrote in his 1993 *Rolling Stone* profile of the band, Stone was "playing constantly, moving away from the trippy atmospherics of Love Bone and toward a hard-edged groove."

And Stone knew exactly who he needed to help fill out that sound: Mike McCready, his once schoolyard friend and a solid guitarist. "I had known Stone . . . before he had even begun playing guitar," Mike told *Guitar Player* in 1994. "We used to trade rock pictures and stuff like that." They both were obsessed with metal and glam rock and bands like KISS. Mike also had a soft spot for guitar gods like Jimi Hendrix and Stevie Ray Vaughan while Stone loved Led Zeppelin. (Funny enough, Mike was not Stone's only classmate-cum-collaborator; when Stone attended the Northwest Boarding School, he did so alongside Steve Turner, his later cohort in Green River.)

OPPOSITE:
Mike McCready performing at the Pinkpop Festival in Landgraaf, the Netherlands on June 8, 1992.

Mike McCready at a Lollapalooza gig in Scranton, Pennsylvania on August 15, 1992.

Mike was born in Pensacola, Florida but moved to Seattle as a young child and also began his rock dreams early. He formed his first band Warrior (later named Shadow), which some compared to Def Leppard, in the eighth grade. A few years in, the act tried to cut a record deal in Los Angeles but had no luck. Returning to Seattle, Mike was despondent. He cut his hair and enrolled in community college while working in a video store to make some money. He was close to giving up all of his ideals, on music, and on the punk attitude behind it. "I was becoming a staunch conservative, because I was so depressed," Mike told Cameron Crowe for the '93 *Rolling Stone* feature.

But anyone who possesses an ounce of the talent Mike McCready does knows that it's not long before music reels you back in, and eventually he started a new project, a psychedelic blues band called Love Chile. Stone happened to be at one of Love Chile's shows, and after seeing Mike's undeniable magic on stage, Stone called on his old friend, attempting to fill the gap he felt. The two started plugging in and playing together in the attic of Stone's parents' house where he had been holing up.

That attic was the breeding ground for so many of Stone's musical projects, starting with the short-lived March of Crimes (featuring Soundgarden's Ben Shepherd), then Green River followed by Mother Love Bone. So, it felt natural to begin charting out the new project in the same spot.

Conversations soon turned to convincing Jeff Ament to join the fold. Mike had been working at Piecora's Pizza across the street from a café where Jeff worked, when he wasn't moonlighting with acts like hard rock/glam rockers War Babies and groovy jammers Luv Company. So, when Stone and Mike showed up at a War Babies gig to talk Jeff into the idea, he agreed to "listen to the songs or play along or whatever."

Jeff grew up in Big Sandy, Montana, where his father was once the mayor. The bass player loved skateboarding and punk music, in particular the Ramones, the Sex Pistols, and the Dead Kennedys. And by the time he was college-aged, he had his first band, Deranged Diction (he was known as Jeff Diction). Although Jeff intended to become a graphic designer and attended the University of Montana to take courses in that field, the school abandoned the program in his second year and Jeff gave up, too. Rather than stick around Montana, he headed to Seattle.

It was a city and a scene he fell in love with in the early '80s, after embarking on a "life-changing trip" to see punk band X one night, then the Clash open

Jeff Ament performing at Lollapalooza in Scranton, Pennsylvania on August 15, 1992.

for the Who on night two. "The next two months, I kept calling my one friend in Seattle, and saying, 'Hey, man, if I came out there, could I sleep on your floor until I get a job?' He said, 'No problem,'" Jeff recalled to *Juice Magazine*. Jeff did get a job, working in a coffee shop called Raison D'être in an artsy part of Seattle called Belltown, where he met many music contemporaries, including Mike McCready.

Soon enough, the newly formed trio was in the groove. Jeff and Stone were back in their element as collaborators, or as Matt Cameron once called them, "full-on partners." And Mike found his niche, too. "Stone and I just clicked together," he told *Guitar Player*. "Our guitars really

Soundgarden (with Matt Cameron, second from left) during a photo shoot in Tokyo, Japan, February 1994.

complemented each other; his sense of melody and rhythm, my lead style." They were just out a drummer and a singer.

Matt Cameron, the drummer of '80s Seattle rock band Skin Yard, was a natural suggestion. By 1986, he was the drummer of Soundgarden and by 1990/91, he was working alongside Jeff, Stone, and Chris Cornell on material they intended to be a tribute to Andy Wood (what would become Temple of the Dog). Though Matt couldn't commit to Stone/Jeff/Mike's budding project, he did offer to lend his hand for the *Stone Gossard Demos 91* tape to help lay the groundwork. The fact that Matt appeared on this original demo has led many fans to hail him as the technical first drummer of Pearl Jam (of course, a role he'd return to for the long haul in later years).

Now, here's where it gets interesting. While Dave Krusen was ultimately hired as Pearl Jam's skinsman, the group first approached a different drummer—Jack Irons— who, in a twist, eventually led them to Eddie Vedder. Jack was known for his early work in Red Hot Chili Peppers and came as a recommendation via record label executive Michael Goldstone, who had originally signed Mother Love Bone to PolyGram and retained Jeff and Stone before they even had coalesced a full band.

Like Matt Cameron, Jack was a busy man. Post-RHCP, he was involved in his own project, Eleven, and had a baby on the way, and so he passed on the opportunity. (Of course, this is not the end of Jack.) But he did know

Jack Irons drumming with the band Eleven in London on July 2, 1992.

BETTER MAN 39

someone that might be interested in the singing role, someone he called "Crazy Eddie." Though Jack cautioned that Eddie wasn't from Seattle, Jeff, Stone, and Mike rather liked that idea.

Jack first met Eddie Vedder in San Diego in November 1989. Eddie, a native of Evanston, Illinois, was by then living in the coastal SoCal town and was fighting to find his way into the music scene. In San Diego, he was involved in a smorgasbord of projects like Surf and Destroy, the Butts, Bad Radio, and the funk rock-leaning band Indian Style (with Rage Against the Machine drummer Brad Wilk).

Eddie was also an avid surfer, often out riding the Pacific Coast waves when he wasn't working. He held a few odd jobs in this era: as a nightwatchman at a hotel, an attendant at a local gas station, and a stagehand at a music venue, the Bacchanal. In November 1989, the Clash's Joe Strummer had a gig at the Bacchanal and superfan Eddie was waiting backstage to meet him. He also met Joe's then-drummer Jack Irons. "I had no idea that that day really was going to affect my life in ways that no one—well, especially me—could not imagine," Vedder shared in his Audible Original offering *I Am Mine* in 2021.

Jack Irons and Eddie Vedder at the *Singles* premiere in Hollywood, California on September 11, 1992.

Jack and Eddie stayed close; the two would meet regularly to play rounds of basketball. And after Jack heard of the new band in Seattle looking for a singer, he handed the *Stone Gossard Demos 91* tape to Eddie. "These guys have been around, they were members of [Mother Love Bone]. It looks like they've got a deal going, it's a serious thing, so see if there's something there for you," Jack told Eddie, as recounted in *Goldmine* magazine. The tape only had instrumentals, five songs in total—with working titles like "Dollar Short," "Troubled Times," "E Ballad," "Richard's E," and "Agyptian Crave"—but Eddie heard something incredibly compelling in them.

As Eddie recounted to *CBS Sunday Morning* in 2024, the day he got the tape from Jack, he was set to work an overnight shift and had been listening and relistening to the tape while at work. The next morning, he still had the music rolling around in his head as he set out on his morning surf and the words for three songs came to him. Long-time Pearl Jam journalist Jessica Letkemann, behind the *Music For Rhinos* mini-book, reported that this was the morning of September 13, 1990. As soon as he got back to shore, Eddie rushed to the nearby apartment of his then-girlfriend, musician Beth Liebling, to write everything down on sticky notes and then recorded his takes on a four-track. "I was still wet when I hit record," Eddie shared.

As Jessica wrote in her book, "Out came three songs, a brief rock opera [with] shades of his beloved Who's *Tommy*." The journalist added that at a show in 1994, Eddie described those three early songs as a "little mini opera . . . about birth . . . incest . . . and death." The lyrics and storylines of each track were "based on things that had happened, and some I imagined," Eddie added in the 1993 *Rolling Stone* interview.

Much of it hinged on the very real experience Eddie went through as a teen learning that the man he grew up believing was his father (Peter Mueller) was actually his stepfather, and his biological dad (Edward Louis Severson Jr.) had already died, leaving no opportunity for Eddie to really connect with him. Eddie did meet him a few times as a kid, but in those instances his real dad was just described as a "family friend." It was an unimaginable loss he was still grappling with much in the same way that Stone and Jeff were still dealing with their own personal tragedy after the death of Andy Wood.

Working to lay down the vocals on the instrumental tracks "brought out emotions I hadn't felt in a while; this natural thing came out," Eddie shared in the *Pearl Jam Twenty* documentary. "In a way, we were strangers but coming from a similar place and all that came out on the first batch of songs."

The song "Alive" (originally "Dollar Short" in the instrumental version) relives the trauma Eddie felt after he was given the news, though the lyrics soon veer into fantasy as the fictional mother attempts to sexually assault her son, unable to deny his resemblance to his father. As dark as it initially was, Eddie has said that Pearl Jam concerts have changed the meaning of the song over time. As throngs of fans wildly sing along to the refrain—"I'm still alive"—the intonation has morphed into a kind of self-empowered creed. "They lifted the curse. The audience changed the meaning for me," Eddie has said.

The three-song demo tape narrative continues with "Once" (originally "Agyptian Crave") in which the son, unable to handle the distress of the situation, turns into a deranged serial killer. It then wraps with "Footsteps" (originally "Troubled Times") in which the killer is caught and looks back on the situation while jailed and awaiting his execution date. Eddie told *Rolling Stone* that also woven into the narrative were the background stories of the Green River Killer in Seattle and a serial killer of sex workers in San Diego.

"Alive" and "Once" would go on to appear on Pearl Jam's debut album *Ten* while "Footsteps" wound up as a B-side for the *Ten* single "Jeremy." In an interview with Jessica Letkemann, Eddie clarified that everything heard on the tape was fictional. "It never happened . . . But that was my right as a writer to be able to do whatever I want with it."

Eddie put the new Momma-Son label on the tape, added some ad hoc artwork, and shipped it off to Seattle.

Jeff Ament can still remember his initial reaction after pressing play for the first time. "I listened to it, and then I remember I left and got a coffee, and then I came back. I listened to it again and I remember calling Stone and I said, 'You need to come over here right now,'" Jeff recalled on *CBS Sunday Morning* in 2024. "As soon as we heard the work that he had done, I was pretty much beside myself," Jeff added with Jessica Letkemann. "[We said] we gotta get this guy up here somehow."

What Jeff—and then Stone and Mike—heard on the tape was that intense passion that Eddie would soon become synonymous with. "Stone and Jeff saw talent in Eddie that no one else did," legendary Seattle journalist Charles R. Cross told *The Seattle Times*. "One part of the story that never, ever gets told, is they could have picked 20 other lead singers. There were other people in Seattle that certainly would have approached them. What those guys saw in [Eddie] . . . was when his voice opened up, he had the ability to sing an anthemic song with scary power."

Or, as PolyGram/Epic A&R rep Michael Goldstone told *Billboard*, "You've got to believe there's some kind of higher force when the first singer that they stumbled onto was some security guard in San Diego named Eddie Vedder."

OPPOSITE:
Eddie Vedder strutting onstage circa 1992.

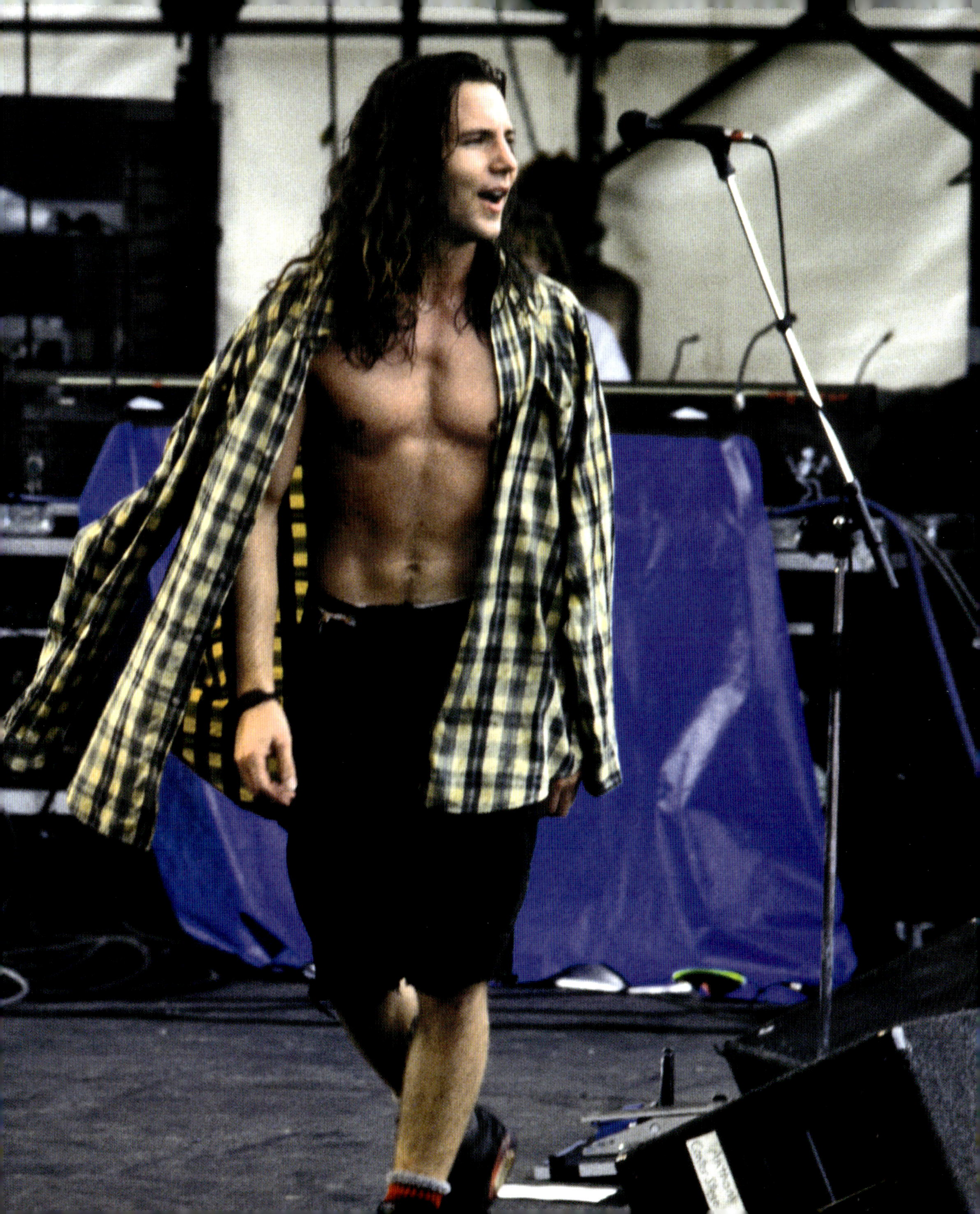

"Off He GOES"

After weeks of schlepping back and forth from San Diego, Eddie was fully living in Seattle by the end of 1990. Jeff Ament remembers there was "a lot of snow on the ground, which is pretty rare for Seattle," as he told *Uncut* magazine. And the weather, and sheer will, enticed the five-piece band—soon to be known as Mookie Blaylock—to keep forging ahead. "We were stuck in the city, stuck in our basement."

OPPOSITE:
Stone Gossard onstage at a Seattle gig in 1991.

That basement was a space in the lower level of a building called Galleria Potatohead, an art gallery that operated from 1989 to 1993 located on Second Avenue between Bell and Battery Streets in the same creative, young Belltown neighborhood where Jeff worked days at the coffee shop. According to a co-owner named Jan Cook, who has posted memories on Facebook, "The gallery space was in the front and we rented out studios in the building to several artists including [blacksmith] Black Dog Forge and Pearl Jam." The idea, Jan said, was to "create a unique space for the artistic community to come together."

Seattle's Museum of Pop Culture (MoPOP) recreated the modest 30 x 30 space for its "Pearl Jam: Home and Away" exhibit that ran from 2018 to 2023, offering more than five hundred artifacts that helped tell the story of one of the city's great bands. On the walls of MoPOP's model replica hung a painting of director John Waters, just one of several images that once decorated the space near "posters of basketball players and guitar god Stevie Ray Vaughan," according to *The Seattle Times*.

In 2017, the paper interviewed the Black Dog Forge blacksmiths who once worked upstairs from Pearl Jam's spot. They noted that rent back in 1990 was about $75 a month—and the band definitely got their money's worth. Not only were they toiling over new material at all hours, but Eddie made a corner one of his first "homes" in Seattle. "Ed was couch surfing between the practice place and my apartment and Kelly [Curtis], our manager's house," Jeff shared with *Uncut*. In fact, one of his roommates at Kelly's house was none other than Alice In Chains's Jerry Cantrell.

It didn't really matter where the band members slept, as they didn't do much of it in these days. From the moment that Eddie flew into Seattle the first time on October 8, the five-piece had been incredibly productive. In the *Pearl Jam Twenty* documentary, Eddie recalled being picked up from the airport by Jeff and telling him, "I don't want to fuck around," insisting Jeff head straight to the rehearsal spot to get to work. And that's what they did, writing a near-full album, then getting signed to a label, logging tour dates, and filming parts of a movie (*Singles*) before most bands can even complete the audition process.

OFF HE GOES 45

It's important to remember that much of the young twenty-somethings' restless energy was driven by an incessant want to succeed. Not only were Jeff and Stone hoping on a wish and a prayer to find the "lightning strikes twice" magic, but Mike was also looking for any sign that he still belonged in music, and Eddie wasn't so confident about his future as his former group Bad Radio had recently broken up. "I gave myself a timeline," he said in 2011, per *Classic Rock Magazine*. "I don't think I ever would've sold my guitar—as Pete Townshend would say, never spend your guitar or your pen—but I [thought I] would be resigned to being the assistant manager of a drug store."

Eddie was hell-bent on avoiding that fate, and to do so, he threw himself into the creative process. "Eddie would stay there in the rehearsal studio, writing all night. We'd show up and there was another song," Mike shared in *SPIN*. "I'd never been in a situation where it clicks [like that]."

The chemistry was truly palpable, Eddie telling *CBS Sunday Morning* that those early days working together was something like "heaven." In their haste, the newly minted group

SET LIST SPOTLIGHT

The Night Eddie Came Alive
January 10, 1991, Harpo's, Victoria, BC, Canada

1. Once
2. Alive
3. I've Got A Feeling (The Beatles cover)

HIDDEN PEARL

This short opening set was Pearl Jam's first gig outside the United States, although Jeff and Stone had previously played Harpo's with Green River.

created masterworks that would soon become the band's signature calling cards. Beyond "Alive," "Once," and "Footsteps" on the Momma-Son demo, there was "Black" (developed from the instrumental dub "E Ballad") and "Alone" (born out of the instrumental "Richard's E"). The sessions also produced "Even Flow," "Release," "Breath," "Just A Girl," and "Oceans."

Eddie wrote the latter as an homage to the surfer's beloved waterways; he got the idea when he got locked out of Galleria Potatohead in the pouring rain and waited in vain for the other band members to hear him pounding on the door. While waiting to be rescued, Eddie tuned into a bass line that Jeff had been playing over and over and wrote "Oceans," using the thumping pulse as his guide.

But it is "Release" that has perhaps the most interesting origin story, an unexpected gem that "was never really even written," Eddie

Pearl Jam's Eddie Vedder and Stone Gossard onstage in Los Angeles, California in 1991.

OFF HE GOES 47

Alice In Chains at the Off Ramp Café in Seattle, where Pearl Jam opened, in February 1991.

shared with *Billboard* in 1991. It's a haunting, spiritual-level song with a gutteral refrain that tapped even further into Eddie's unresolved emotions about the earth-shattering father/stepfather revelation.

"What he was writing about was the space Stone and I were in. We'd just lost one of our friends to a dark and evil addiction, and [Eddie] was putting that feeling to words. I saw him as a brother," Jeff told *SPIN*. "That's what pulled me back in [to making music]. It's like when you read a book and [it's] describing something you've felt all your life."

That first week of the band working together in early October 1990 was, in a word, "intense," Eddie told *Billboard*. "These aren't like rock 'n' roll songs where we kind of like sit and smile afterwards and give each other high-fives and light up another cigarette or pop open a beer. It was more like . . . having to take a huge deep breath, and the silence that followed." The band recorded each of those early Galleria Potatohead sessions by overdubbing several tossed-out Kipper Jones tapes Eddie got from his friend who worked at Virgin Records. Within a week, they knew they had something special, and then they spent another week rehearsing the material ad nauseum. On the fourteenth day, they had their first show. They didn't even have a name yet but took their moniker from a Mookie Blaylock basketball card that was lodged inside their early demo tape, believing it was a sign.

Soon, Mookie Blaylock booked two more shows in Seattle that December alongside local comrades Alice In Chains, where more of the scenesters came out to see the fledgling post–Mother Love Bone act. But focus soon turned to getting *out* of Seattle, and the band did so at the beginning of 1991, with an invitation to again open for Alice In Chains during their promotion of the newly released album *Facelift*, which was making noise with singles like "Man In The Box." In January, the tour headed to Canada and then to Los Angeles (where they played Riki Rachtman's World Famous Cathouse), while February brought more West Coast stops in Sacramento, Oakland, and San Francisco, as well as Eugene and Portland, Oregon. There was also San Diego, where Eddie and Co. got to play the singer's old stomping grounds at the Bacchanal.

The band grappled with some interesting circumstances.

Several of the venues early on in the tour wrongly billed the band as Mother Love Bone, not even realizing Andy Wood had died and that the band was no more.

Soundgarden's Chris Cornell onstage in the Netherlands in June 1992. Chris opened his arms to Eddie to welcome him to the scene.

"Not many people knew about Andy's death, because we had no internet back then," Chay Wilkerson Moore, a crew member at one of the Canadian venues, told Pearl Jam Concert Chronology. "So [fans] were quite blown away to hear this band." Other venues billed the group as "formerly Mother Love Bone," which also did them no favors to strike out on their own.

Jeff told *SPIN*, "It was good for us to get out of town and out where nobody knew anything about us. The first three or four shows were in Seattle and all eyes were on the new guy. [Leaving] was the best thing we could have done."

There was also a perception that Eddie was having to fight being "an outsider," Mike recalled to *Mojo* magazine. The gatekeepers in the scene were "very small, very provincial," added Mike, "and my so-called friends were kind of dicks to him."

One person who had open arms, however, was Chris Cornell. The late Soundgarden frontman took Eddie under his wings and found a close kinship with him. Eddie filled a void Chris was also feeling since Andy Wood's passing. As Mike recalled, Chris really "helped Ed integrate into the scene, took him out for beers, talked to him. He was very engaging when he didn't have to be." And that, in turn, gave Eddie the confidence to step out of his shell more and more.

Because, in the beginning, Eddie had only a mere sliver of his unyielding power as a frontman. "He was genuinely 'quiet and loving Eddie' when we first met him," Jeff told Cameron Crowe for *Rolling Stone*'s 1993 feature. As Cameron added, "In the band's earliest shows, Vedder had been so self-effacing, he barely looked up . . . and at a certain point, he changed."

The curtain came crashing down at one of those January 1991 gigs opening for Alice In Chains in Canada—at Harpo's in Victoria, British Columbia, to be exact. As Cameron astutely described the night, "It was Pearl Jam's maiden tour, their first appearance away from a nurturing audience of Seattle friends. But this Canadian crowd was far more interested in getting drunk. Midset, Vedder decided to challenge the jaded audience, to wake them up."

> **"Unscrewing the 12-pound steel base of the microphone stand, Vedder sent it flying over their heads, like a lethal Frisbee. The steel disk crashed into the wall of the back bar. They woke up. Vedder would never fully be the same."**

Nor would the band.

The buzz around Mookie Blaylock was starting to grow, especially as a prime opportunity came barking with Temple of the Dog.

My Pearl Jam Moment

RIKI RACHTMAN'S WORLD FAMOUS CATHOUSE, LOS ANGELES, CA, 1991

We had Alice In Chains scheduled to play, and I believe it was Jerry Cantrell who took me backstage and said we can't play because so-and-so is dope sick. So, they had to cancel the show. But they said, "We're going to come back and we'll play another show for you, and we're going to bring our friends that are starting this band called Mookie Blaylock, with some of the guys from Mother Love Bone."

I remember when they played, I was watching their singer climbing all over these amps. People didn't do that at the Cathouse. Eddie was climbing all over stuff. And I'm like, who the hell is this guy? You know, they're the opening band. We didn't even know who they were. There are two or three bands that I've seen do that. And I remember when a band does that. It's like, holy shit, this guy can die right now.

The thing about Pearl Jam is I don't think they ever really fit into a mold. And I don't think Pearl Jam ever cared about fitting into a mold. I truly believe with all my heart that Pearl Jam did whatever they wanted to do, and they kept on putting out great songs. To be completely honest, it was the later records I became a fan of, like *Lightning Bolt*. That to me was the best Pearl Jam record. When I heard it, I gained a new appreciation and it made me want to go back through their catalog once again.

—*Submitted by TV/radio host and Cathouse owner Riki Rachtman*

"Gonna See My FRIEND"

As Mookie Blaylock was starting to gel, a concurrent development would help thrust the band members in the spotlight as Jeff, Stone, and Mike became part of the supergroup Temple of the Dog.

The idea for the project—meant to be a musical tribute to Andy Wood—came from Chris Cornell. The day Andy died, Chris had just gotten back from a tour with Soundgarden and was able to say goodbye before Andy was taken off life support. Chris was devasted. And like Stone, he tried to numb his pain with music. "I started writing songs, that was the only thing I could really think of to do," Chris told Seattle rock station KISW in 1991.

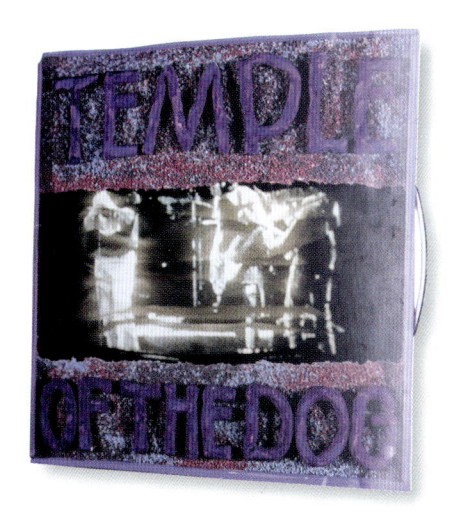

There was just one issue, as Chris explained: The material was a bit too slow and off-the-mark for the Soundgarden catalog, yet he knew Andy would have liked it. "So I didn't really want to just throw it out the window or put it away in a box," Chris told KISW. "I thought it would be good to make a single, and I thought it would be really great to record it with these guys, Stone and Jeff, because they were in his band." In fact, Chris shared that he was just starting to get well acquainted with the two right before Andy died, and he thought recording music together would keep that lifeline going. In many ways, it was like Andy had "reached down" and put it all in motion. He was still the great connector, even in the great beyond, and brought all of his friends together.

In November and December 1990, Stone, Jeff, and Mike started logging time with Chris Cornell and drummer Matt Cameron at London Bridge Studio for the eponymous Temple of the Dog album.

Two of the songs they worked on, "Say Hello 2 Heaven" and "Reach Down," were Chris's obvious obituaries for his dearly departed. But the rest of the album would end up being filled by additional, random songs Chris had written (like "Wooden Jesus" and "All Night Thing") as well as recycled riffs from the *Stone Gossard Demos 91* tape that became fully fleshed out ideas—among them "Times of Trouble" and "Pushin Forward Back."

The most prominent from the bunch, of course, was "Hunger Strike," featuring the recognizable duet between Chris and guest star Eddie that, in later years, would become an anthem of the Seattle scene. The song was actually the first time Eddie ever had a featured vocal on a major label record. And it all was happenstance.

ABOVE:
The cover of Temple of the Dog's eponymous 1991 record.

OPPOSITE:
Chris Cornell performing with Soundgarden in Allentown, Pennsylvania on August 19, 1990.

GONNA SEE MY FRIEND

Per Chris, the lyrics for "Hunger Strike" were written about an unrelated matter, in response to the "existential crisis" Soundgarden were in as they became involved in a major label bidding war and worried about becoming commercialized. (Sound familiar?) It was only included on the *Temple of the Dog* album because, at the time, the group had only finished recording nine songs and, Chris said, "it seemed like 10 songs was a complete album." And he believed the message of "Hunger Strike"—about staying true to yourself and your art—was a fitting way to wrap it up. But it was also incomplete and Chris was struggling with where to take it. During one of the supergroup's rehearsals, Chris was working on the song as Eddie sat in the corner waiting for Mookie Blaylock sessions to begin. When he heard Chris struggling, Eddie had an idea.

Chris recalled, "I was singing the chorus in the rehearsal space and Eddie just kind of shyly walked up to the mic and started singing the low 'going hungry' [part], and I started singing the high one. When I heard him sing, the whole thing came together in my brain. I just felt like, 'Wow, his voice is so great in this low register. He should sing on it.'"

"That was the first time I heard myself on a real record," Eddie shared in the *Pearl Jam Twenty* documentary. "It could be one of my favorite songs that I've ever been on—or the most meaningful."

Temple of the Dog was recorded in just fifteen days at London Bridge Studio. Stone told KISW that the members paid for the project themselves, and that was all the time they could afford. It was released on April 16, 1991 via A&M Records (Soundgarden's label), just four months ahead of the release of Pearl Jam's *Ten*.

Temple of the Dog only sold seventy thousand copies in its infancy; it would take more than a year for the music to fully take off thanks to a renewed marketing push. By the summer of 1992, grunge was a household name and Pearl Jam and Soundgarden were both on their fast ascent as a result of huge returns for their respective 1991 albums *Ten* and *Badmotorfinger*. It had A&M seeing dollar signs.

The label reissued *Temple of the Dog* and hyped "Hunger Strike" with that iconic sitting-around-the-bonfire music video. It was helmed by director Paul Rachman, who had some cachet in the scene for having just worked with Alice In Chains on their breakthrough video for "Man In The Box." The obvious choice for the *Temple of the Dog* video, Paul was quickly hired by Alice In Chains/Soundgarden manager Susan Silver and Pearl Jam manager Kelly Curtis—but there was one caveat: Paul had to get the two sides to agree to a concept.

OPPOSIITE:
Soundgarden onstage at the Whisky-A-Go-Go in Los Angeles, California on December 7, 1989.

GONNA SEE MY FRIEND 55

"Early on, there was a little bit of disagreement between the Soundgarden camp and the Pearl Jam camp. Basically, the Soundgarden guys didn't want to be in the video. They didn't want a video with the band members. They wanted something a little more cinematic, filmic. A little more of a pure tribute to Andrew Wood," Paul recalled to *Stereogum*. "The Pearl Jam guys . . . they really wanted to be in the video. They needed the exposure."

Paul's pitch was to keep it in Seattle and find an iconic location that reflected the guts of the scene. "The idea was to make something very organic. Keep it connected to the city, keep it connected to the place, and in turn, keep it emotionally connected to Andrew Wood in that way," Paul added. With that idea, Chris had a change of heart. In fact, the singer was the one who came up with the perfect spot: Seattle's Discovery Park.

The video became a ubiquitous pick at MTV, and the *Temple of the Dog* album would go on to sell one million copies. It was the only album ever put forth by the supergroup. And although Chris Cornell would sometimes pop up at Pearl Jam shows to create mini-reunions (like the PJ20 weekend), there was only one proper tour logged for it, twenty-five years later and without Eddie.

"Every time we got around Chris, the topic of a reunion would come up. At PJ20, I said something like, 'Man, it would be fun to go and play those Temple songs at some point if you're up for it,'" Jeff told *Rolling Stone*. "I knew he'd been playing some of the songs in his solo show. . . . It felt like there was some unfinished business."

A completely sold-out, five-city Temple of the Dog tour occurred in 2016, featuring Chris, Jeff, Stone, Mike, and Matt. It made stops in Philadelphia, New York, San Francisco, Los Angeles, and of course Seattle. The set list featured eight of the ten songs from the studio album (with the audience filling in Eddie's parts every night) as well as covers of Mother Love Bone songs and tracks from Mad Season, Led Zeppelin, David Bowie, The Cure, and Black Sabbath.

> **It wrapped just six months before Chris's tragic passing in May 2017, bringing devastating new meaning to the songs on the album.**

Talking with *Rolling Stone* about the future of Temple of the Dog in late 2016, Chris left the door open on possibly reforming the band, saying, "There's always a chance [we'll record more songs]. Just from my perspective, it would have to feel great. It's a scary thing. I don't want to say it would have to live up to the [first] album, but I wouldn't want to take away from it. That's the issue with me. I don't want to detract from what happened before."

SET LIST SPOTLIGHT

Temple of the Dog's Only Tour
November 21, 2016, Paramount Theatre, Seattle, WA

1. Say Hello 2 Heaven
2. Wooden Jesus
3. Call Me A Dog
4. Your Saviour
5. Stardog Champion (Mother Love Bone cover)
6. Stargazer (Mother Love Bone cover)
7. Seasons (Chris Cornell song)
8. Jump Into The Fire (Harry Nilsson cover)
9. Four Walled World
10. I'm A Mover (Free cover)
11. Pushin Forward Back
12. Hunger Strike
13. Hey Baby (New Rising Sun) (Jimi Hendrix cover)
14. River Of Deceit (Mad Season cover)
15. Heartshine (Mother Love Bone cover)
16. Holy Roller (Mother Love Bone cover)
17. Reach Down

– ENCORE –

18. Man Of Golden Words (Mother Love Bone cover)
19. Missing (Chris Cornell song)
20. Times Of Trouble
21. Achilles Last Stand (Led Zeppelin cover)
22. Quicksand (David Bowie cover)
23. Fascination Street (The Cure cover)
24. War Pigs (Black Sabbath cover)

– ENCORE 2 –

25. All Night Thing

HIDDEN PEARL

As the show was wrapping up, and before the final song, Chris teased the audience with undue hope for a revitalization of Temple of the Dog: "One more song and then, who knows, maybe we'll play this again. Then we'll go on a massive world tour! But we're not going to. But you never know . . ."

"ALIVE"

On February 22, 1991, Jeff, Stone, Mike, Eddie, and Dave flew to New York to officially sign a contract with Epic Records. Getting a label deal happened pretty quickly thanks to an ongoing relationship with A&R rep Michael Goldstone. As previously mentioned, he was the exec who landed Mother Love Bone on the roster at his previous label, PolyGram. But, when it came time for Stone and Jeff to sign on the dotted line again, they weren't so keen to stay with PolyGram, especially since Michael had jumped ship and Stone and Jeff felt he was the one truly passionate about their work.

It's been reported that Michael had to get Epic to pony up a half-million dollars to release Jeff and Stone from their contractual obligations, and he went to bat for them. "In fairness to PolyGram, the band really wanted a fresh start, and [the label was] really gracious about it," Michael told *Billboard*. "I think they felt like the band had been through so much that they really supported them starting fresh. So we all dusted ourselves off and started over."

Starting over also came with a new band name. The legal team at Epic was concerned with trademark issues over the Mookie Blaylock tag as the basketball star had just inked a deal with Nike, and the suits encouraged the band to figure out another way to brand themselves. The five guys complied, but still found ways to pay homage to their basketball hero, like naming their debut *Ten* (Mookie's jersey number) and, by extension, dubbing their fan club the Ten Club. Pearl Jam's first T-shirt also featured a photo of the sports star.

So, how'd they get the name Pearl Jam? In early interviews, the band claimed it was inspired by Eddie's great-grandmother and the hallucinogenic-laden spreads she used to make. But the singer finally confirmed to *Rolling Stone* in 2006 that that was "total bullshit." Another rumor circulated that the name was innuendo for, well, pearly-colored male fluid, but that seems to be farcical too. The most plausible story is that the band already had the idea for "pearl" (it really is the name of Eddie's grandma) and took inspiration for "jam" after seeing another soon-to-be hero, Neil Young, in concert. The same day band members were in New York to sign with Epic, the band

OPPOSITE:
Eddie Vedder onstage at Melkweg, in Amsterdam on February 12, 1992.

BELOW:
Neil Young and Crazy Horse at Farm Aid in New Orleans, Louisiana on September 18, 1994.

made a trek thirty minutes away to Nassau Coliseum to see a headlining set from Neil Young & Crazy Horse. "He played, like, nine songs over three hours," Jeff told *Rolling Stone*. "Every song was like a fifteen- or twenty-minute jam. So that's how 'jam' got added on to the name. Or at least that's how I remember it."

On March 2, 1991 at Seattle's O.K. Hotel, the band played what would be the final show with the Mookie name on the poster. By March 10, the band appeared on Seattle rock station KISW to share that they'd changed their name.

> **And by May 17, once again at the Off Ramp Café, they'd mark another big first, officially emerging as Pearl Jam.**

Between March and May 1991, Pearl Jam took a two-month sabbatical from shows to make *Ten*, though it wouldn't be long before they hit a stage again. "Essentially *Ten* was just an excuse to tour," Jeff told *Bass Player* magazine in 1994. "We knew we were still a long way from being a real band at that point . . . we told the record company, 'We know we can be a great band, so let's just get the opportunity to get out and play.'"

Pearl Jam booked time at London Bridge Studio, a hallowed hall they had become comfortable with when making the *Temple of the Dog* album. London Bridge truly was a de facto clubhouse for the Seattle scene in the '90s. Started by the late Rick Parashar and his brother Raj, the studio was also where Mother Love Bone put the pieces together for the *Shine* EP and where Soundgarden crafted *Louder Than Love*. So it only made sense to have that good energy hanging around during the sessions for *Ten*.

Pearl Jam already had an incredible wealth of music to bring forward to the sessions—in addition to "Alive" and "Once," from the Momma-Son demo, "Oceans," "Release," "Black," "Jeremy," and "Even Flow" were already formed, and there were blueprints for "Porch," "Why Go," "Deep," and "Garden." Stone and Jeff wrote most of the instrumental material, with the exception of "Oceans," where Eddie gets a credit, and "Release," where all five members are attributed. Additionally, "Porch" is the sole track written by Eddie alone; and all lyrical material is his incredible contribution.

Since the studio recording of "Alive" was already done, it became the album's first single—Pearl Jam first put that song to tape back in January 1991, when they attempted to make a more pro-sounding demo. That early session also netted the outtake "Wash" and a cover of the Beatles' "I've Got A Feeling."

The *Ten* recording sessions also produced "Yellow Ledbetter," which would be placed as a B-side for the "Jeremy" single and gain popularity on its own merit by 1994. There was also

"Alone," "Footsteps" (from the Momma-Son demo), "Hold On," and "Brother" that ended up on the *Lost Dogs* rarity collection released in 2003. Plus, "Just A Girl," "2,000 Mile Blues," "Breath And A Scream," and "Evil Little Goat," all of which appear on the 2009 reissue of *Ten*.

Remarkably, the band racked up all of that material in just two months. They had a shoestring budget to work with and not much time to spare. "I think we spent about $25,000 making [*Ten*] and about three times that mixing it," Jeff once shared with *Classic Rock*. "It was still a third of the money that we'd spent making the Mother Love Bone record. We didn't expect the record to be a huge deal."

As Stone told *RIP* magazine in 1991, there was also a sense of urgency to tap into their raw feelings as Pearl Jam embarked on their maiden album voyage: "It was exactly what we didn't do with Mother Love Bone, and that was to actually get some of the spontaneity and freshness of the songs, to get really close to them when they were written . . . I wanted to get back to making a record that was a little bit more raw, with a little more emphasis on getting the intensity."

That certainly came out in songs like "Black." It's regarded as one of Pearl Jam's best songs ever—a total bullseye for capturing the emotions of a passionate first love and what happens when it ends. In 1991, Eddie was in a happy relationship with long-time girlfriend and future first wife Beth Liebling (of Seattle band Hovercraft), but "Black" has long been rumored to have been written as a soliloquy to his early love Liz Gumble, who Eddie first met in high school theater classes. The couple were, "by all accounts, inseparable," said *Rolling Stone* in a profile of Eddie in 1996. "When Gumble went away for a brief vacation with her family, [Eddie] expressed his grief with typical theatricality. He wore her scarf wrapped around his neck every day till she came back," the article continued, adding, "he was inconsolable after [their] breakup."

Even from the beginning, Eddie has always had an incredibly poetic way of tapping into very real emotions, whether personal (as on "Black" and "Release") or distant ("Jeremy"). Yet while "Jeremy" soon took off as one of *Ten*'s most identifiable songs, thanks to that haunting video by Mark Pellington, it was actually "Black" that elicited the biggest fan reaction—and the most fan letters.

Guitar World shared snippets of how many of those letters often read: "I was recently considering suicide, and then I heard your music."

> **The publication noted that it was Pearl Jam's very visceral performance of "Black" in the band's momentous 1992 *MTV Unplugged* episode that hit fans like a ton of bricks.**

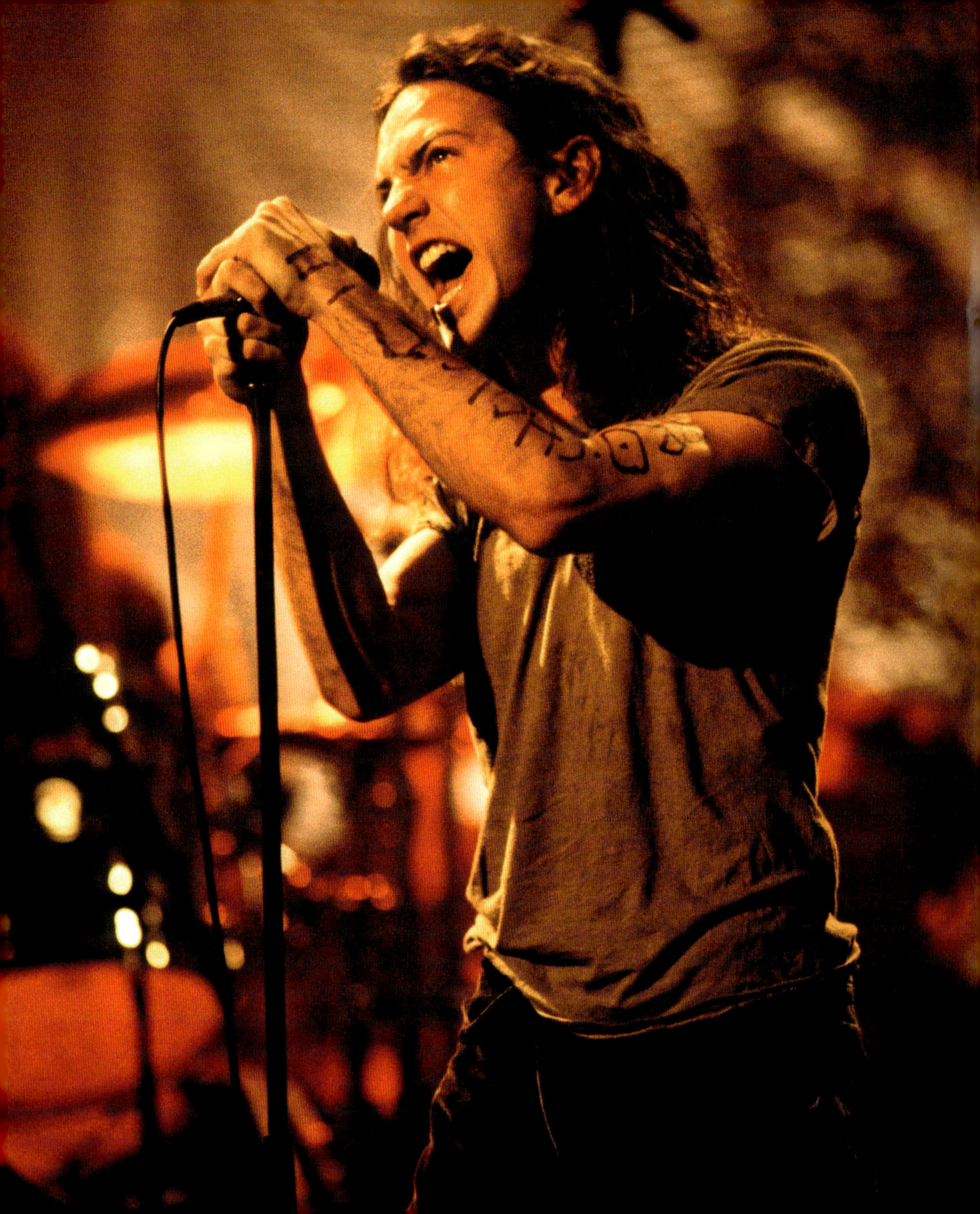

Especially the part where Eddie declares that the subjects of the song "belong together" (an addendum borrowed from the 1981 Rickie Lee Jones song, "We Belong Together").

Other songs on the album also sparked important conversations that were incredibly topical for the time: like the plight of the many living in 'Prozac nation,' a saga which Pearl Jam earnestly tells on "Why Go." The liner notes of *Ten* reveal a dedication to a woman named Heather; in interviews, Eddie shared that she was someone he knew in Chicago who was institutionalized after she was found smoking pot.

"Even Flow" is also notable as the song the band spent the most time on in the studio, around thirty to fifty takes in all, Mike McCready has estimated. He told *The Daily Record*, "I swear to God it was a nightmare. We played that thing over and over until we hated each other. I still don't think Stone is satisfied with how it came out." Lyrically, though, Eddie was. The song puts a spotlight on the homelessness epidemic, a cause Pearl Jam continues to advocate against.

OPPOSITE:
Eddie Vedder performing during Pearl Jam's episode of *MTV Unplugged* in New York City on March 16, 1992.

> **During two "Home Shows" at Seattle's Safeco Field in August 2018, Pearl Jam raised nearly $11 million for causes to fight homelessness.**

The band set up an advisory council that worked with 170 philanthropic organizations, nonprofits, and local businesses in the larger metro area to help disperse funds. "The Home Shows initiative is about bringing the issue of homelessness closer to all of us—increasing our understanding of a complex issue, our empathy for our neighbors experiencing homelessness, and our resolve for working together," Stone shared in a statement at the time, picked up by *Billboard*.

Given this focus, Eddie also chose the Home Shows as the first time he opened up about the inspiration for "Even Flow," twenty-seven years after the song was first released. While he was first getting his bearings in Seattle, the frontman would frequently visit a local sandwich shop for lunch and often ran into another guy, also named Eddie, who was a Vietnam veteran currently living under a viaduct. Vedder tried to keep tabs on his name twin when he could, but after returning from a tour, he discovered the veteran had passed away.

In June 1991, Pearl Jam headed to England to mix *Ten* with the sought-after pro Tim Palmer at his Ridge Farm Studios, housed on a converted farm in a remote part of Sussex. Tim added new sonic flourishes to the album, including some interesting percussion for "Oceans" in the form of a fire extinguisher and pepper mill. "The reason I used those items was purely because

ALIVE 63

Pearl Jam performs during the Home Shows at Safeco Field in Seattle, Washington on August 10, 2018.

we were so far from a music rental shop," Tim told *Guitar World* in 2002. "Necessity became the mother of invention." Tim also worked with Mike to add that delicious guitar solo at the outro of "Alive," which Mike said was inspired by his childhood idols KISS and their song "She."

Ten was released August 27, 1991, neatly packaged with art concepts from Jeff Ament. If you recall from earlier pages, Jeff was in the graphic arts program at the University of Montana before Pearl Jam, and if fate had worked another way, he might've become a bread-and-butter-making designer. Instead, he infused that passion for visuals into the band's iconography over the years. When life got too busy, Jeff still kept it in-house, as his brother Barry and the Seattle design team the Ames Bros took over.

The art is "still some of the most recognizable and well-loved in all rock music," *Consequence of Sound* declared in their *Opus* podcast series. Jeff designed the iconic stick man figure that became an emblem for Pearl Jam over the years and hand-carved the large block letters (over 5 feet, or 1.5 m, tall) that were in the background of all those photos in the album spread. The photos themselves were the work of Lance Mercer, Mother Love Bone's one-time photographer, and they were taken in the band's rehearsal spot at Galleria Potatohead. If you think it looks like a basketball team huddle, you wouldn't be too far off—the sports-loving members had that team idea in mind for the shoot. According to Jeff's words in a press release for the *Ten* reissue in 2009, the concept "was about really being together as a group and entering into the world of music as a true band . . . a sort of all-for-one deal."

Ten has been certified 13x platinum by the Recording Industry Association of America® (RIAA®), for selling thirteen million copies in just the US alone. The album has been hailed as "arguably *the* greatest rock debut record of all time" by *Kerrang*; *Rolling Stone* readers agreed, tying *Ten* and Guns N' Roses' *Appetite for Destruction* as their top pick in a list of the greatest debut albums.

But it didn't get that reputation or that interest overnight; surprisingly, it was a very slow build. A&R rep Michael Goldstone told *SPIN*, "When we were working 'Alive,' the initial feedback was, 'This isn't rock enough for rock radio and it isn't alternative enough for alternative.'" *Ten* didn't get the best reviews in the beginning, either. *NME* only gave it a 5 out of 10 rating. *Entertainment Weekly* and *The Village Voice's* Robert Christgau each graded the album a "B-" finding it derivative of other Seattle bands' efforts.

Grunge hadn't totally exploded yet—it would take Nirvana's *Nevermind* and "Smells Like Teen Spirit" to really open up the floodgates. But, a year later in 1992, *Ten* would find its footing and breakthrough into the Top 10 of the *Billboard 200* charts, entering at No. 8 the week of May 30 and spending 265 weeks (more than five years!) on that chart in varying positions. That included four weeks at No. 2 that August, sitting only behind Billy Ray Cyrus's *Some Gave All*. *Ten* would even outsell *Nevermind* at one point in 1993; by that point, two full years after its original release, the album was the eighth best-seller in the United States, according to Nielsen SoundScan data. Over time, the critical opinion would largely change, too, as more came around to the significance of the album and its role in modern music history. *AllMusic* came to hail it a "flawlessly crafted hard rock masterpiece."

Pearl Jam was also nominated for various awards, including Favorite Pop/Rock New Artist and Favorite New Heavy Metal/Hard Rock Artist at the American Music Awards in early 1993 (they won both); Best Rock Song and Best Hard Rock Performance for "Jeremy" at the 1993 Grammys, which they lost (to date, they've won two Grammys and have had very vocal opinions on it); and a slew of MTV VMAs including Best Alternative Video for "Alive" in 1992 as well as Video Of The Year, Best Group Video, Best Metal/Hard Rock Video, Best Direction, and

Viewer's Choice for "Jeremy" in 1993. They won all except Viewer's Choice for "Jeremy" and the nomination for "Alive." (Fun fact: "Alive" was the first video ever shown on MTV to not be lip-synced.)

Band members have even changed their own opinions about the album over time, though more related to the sound on the first edition. Eddie has said he can't even listen to *Ten* because he isn't a fan of the sound of it. Jeff also told *SPIN*, "I'd love to remix *Ten* . . . just [to] pull some of the reverb off it." They did that in 2009 with the aforementioned reissue, helmed by a go-to producer Brendan O'Brien. He had his qualms at first, telling *SPIN*, "The original *Ten* sound is what people bought, dug and loved, so I was initially hesitant to mess around with that."

That can't be overstated enough. *Ten*'s sound became a juggernaut example of its time, especially as Pearl Jam started a grueling tour in support of the album, and fans were able to see the band's visceral approach to the music. "People didn't know what [*Ten*] was," manager Kelly Curtis told *SPIN* of the initial reaction. But, "once people came and saw them live, this lightbulb would go on."

Michael Goldstone said that was just the way the band wanted it, too—rather than "having it shoved down everyone's throats the first five minutes," he said, "people got to discover Pearl Jam on their own: The kid on the street took all of his friends, and then the next time through everyone came."

Pearl Jam at the 1993 MTV Music Video Awards in Los Angeles, California on September 2, 1993.

My Pearl Jam Moment

LIMELIGHT, NEW YORK, NY, 1992

I won't say that I'm a "day one" Pearl Jam fan. But if it wasn't "day one," it was close. In the late '80s, I became a big Soundgarden fan, and they led me to Temple of the Dog and from there to the Mother Love Bone album *Apple*, which I also loved.

So, I was curious about what these guys would do in their next band. I don't even know if I was aware that the "other" guy singing with Chris Cornell on "Hunger Strike" was the singer of Stone and Jeff's next band. (Before the internet, you couldn't "Google" something.)

I did not pick up Pearl Jam's *Ten* on August 27, 1991, but I definitely got it pretty soon after. Like so many other people, I was stunned when I heard the album. It may have sounded hyperbolic at the time when I told people that every song was a classic, but I think history has proved that I was right about that. I couldn't wait to see them live. I got tickets to see them on an insane tour: They were opening for Red Hot Chili Peppers, and Smashing Pumpkins was on the bill as well. And then I couldn't get off of work, so I gave my ticket away. I know, I know.

But in the spring, Pearl Jam headlined their own tour and they were playing New York City's Limelight, so I got tickets for my friend and I. Ticket price: $12! It was Sunday, April 12, 1992. I remember taking the Long Island Railroad to New York City and seeing Scott Ian from Anthrax in our train car. My friend and I moved closer to where he was sitting and he was cool and chatted with us, asking who we were going to see. "Pearl Jam? I think I've heard of them." Who knew that they soon would be the band that dominated rock music for years?

I'd been looking forward to the show for about two months and it did not disappoint. They opened with a ballad, "Oceans." This seemed so unusual. Most hard rock bands like to blow your head off the minute they hit the stage. I sensed that they had a confidence and range that made them stand apart. They could ease you into their show with a slow song. But the second song was "Even Flow" and the place erupted.

It was as aggressive as any metal show that I'd been to, but there was a warmth to the band that made it feel different. It was definitely a different kind of community. They played almost all of *Ten* (except "Garden") and two new songs: "State Of Love And Trust" and "Leash." They covered the Beatles' "I've Got A Feeling" and Neil Young's then-recent song, "Rockin' In The Free World," which would go on to be one of their encore jams for the next few decades.

I left the show realizing that I just saw something pretty incredible and I knew that the next time I saw them, it probably would be in a venue many times larger. I was right about that: I've seen Pearl Jam many times since then, from floor seats to way in the outfield at Fenway Park. They empty the tank every time. I've never seen a show that wasn't at least great. But I'm really grateful that I experienced April 12, 1992.

—Submitted by journalist Brian Ives

"Why Go"

In July 1991, Pearl Jam's wish to use *Ten* as an excuse to tour was granted. The band's first jaunt through the Midwest and East Coast was booked, with nine showcases in Boston, Philly, New York, Providence, Chicago, and Minneapolis (there were also shows scheduled for Columbus, Cleveland, and New Haven, but those did not go through as planned). It was all an effort to help develop a wider audience before the release of *Ten*. The route began with a typical hometown warm-up show at Seattle's RKCNDY on July 4, but this time Pearl Jam looked a little different, with a new drummer in tow.

Dave Krusen was out of the band at this point due to what were described as personal issues (he does receive credit for his work on *Ten*, however). "They had to let me go," the drummer told *Punk Globe* magazine, admitting that the band's decision likely saved his life. "I couldn't stop drinking, and it was causing problems. They gave me many chances, but I couldn't get it together."

> **Dave's last appearance was an invite-only *Singles* wrap party at RKCNDY on May 25, 1991—the first documented time Pearl Jam played "State Of Love And Trust," the song they contributed to the *Singles* soundtrack.**

Dave Krusen did come back to the fold thirty-one years later in a ceremonious and need-based occasion on May 16, 2022 for a date in Fresno, California, when Matt Cameron was out sick with COVID-19. As Rolling Stone reported from that date, "Eddie Vedder not[ed] the drummer didn't have the chance to play many live shows with Pearl Jam in the early Nineties, but added, 'It looks like this week we're going to get to make up for it.'"

Back in 1991, Dave was replaced in a pinch by Matt Chamberlain. Due to the timing, Matt was the drummer featured in the "Alive" music video, which was filmed at RKCNDY on August 3. Because of the visibility of the video, many fans just assumed he was Pearl Jam's original drummer. (Dave, who?) But Matt's time behind the PJ kit was short-lived too, as he left to join the house band at *Saturday Night Live;* in his wake, he suggested his friend, Texas native Dave Abbruzzese, to take over. New Dave was so psyched about the gig, he even tattooed the infamous stickman logo on his arm. He was in place by August 23.

This would be a good point to discuss that dizzying drummer situation. Or as the band refers to it in the *Pearl Jam Twenty* documentary, their "*Spinal Tap* situation." Pearl Jam has had five drummers in thirty-five years, and all had an important role to fill. As *Seattle Weekly* once stated, "Each

OPPOSITE:
Eddie Vedder onstage at the Pinkpop Festival in Landgraaf, the Netherlands on June 8, 1992.

drummer helped shape the band's trajectory, if not its sound. Had just one of them joined or left at any other time, Pearl Jam might not be headed to eternal acclaim as a still-relevant act." It's likely the reason why Pearl Jam invited all five men to their Rock & Roll Hall of Fame induction in 2017, even though only Dave Krusen and Matt Cameron were officially part of the ceremony.

So, after the short-lived Dave Krusen (1990–1991) and Matt Chamberlain (1991) era came Dave Abbruzzese, who entered at an incredibly exciting time (1991–1994) as the group embarked on their first international tours, Lollapalooza, and the making of *Vs.* and *Vitalogy*. Ultimately, this Dave was dismissed after he publicly aired his grievances about the Ticketmaster fracas, believing Pearl Jam should have been doing more press and videos during the blackout period. Then came Jack Irons (1994–1998), who of course was first approached for the gig ahead of Dave Krusen. Jack always remained close to his friend Eddie and came on board around the time that Pearl Jam worked on *No Code* and *Yield*, stepping aside when a medical issue necessitated some time off from touring.

(l-r) Dave Abbruzzese, Stone Gossard, Eddie Vedder, Mike McCready, and Jeff Ament backstage at the Pinkpop Festival in Landgraaf, the Netherlands on June 8, 1992.

The role was soon filled by long-time friend of the band and Seattle stalwart Matt Cameron, who had time open up after the dissolution of Soundgarden in 1997. Though it was only supposed to be a temporary situation, he's remained Pearl Jam's official drummer ever since, a remarkable feat considering Matt worked double time from 2010–2017, rejoining Soundgarden in their reformation period before the death of Chris Cornell.

With the addition of Matt Cameron, the core Pearl Jam lineup has been complete for more than twenty-five years. On tour, long-time mainstay Boom Gaspar has become part of the family, where he's contributed piano and keys since 2002. And as of 2021, utility man Josh Klinghoffer is also part of the touring ensemble, picking up any instruments where needed.

But back to 1991 and that Midwest/East Coast showcase tour. While no one totally knew who Pearl Jam was yet—it was still a month before the release of *Ten* and just on the heels of the first single "Alive"—those who did see the band had a resounding reaction of, "Who are these guys and where did they come from?"

Bill Keough, the promoter for Club Babyhead in Providence, Rhode Island, where Pearl Jam played on July 15, recalled the vibe in a post on Pearl Jam Concert Chronology: "Pearl Jam's agent at the time was a young and upcoming industry guy named John Branigan (Triad Artists), who had a knack for the next thing and a good ear for cool stuff. He knew I was a big supporter of Sub Pop and knew Mother Love Bone. I was always happy to help him out with his 'baby bands' . . . [and] Pearl Jam was an easy yes. . . . The night of the show, Pearl Jam showed up early and got their soundcheck in earlier than usual. Their tour pass laminates were simply NBA Mookie Blaylock cards with their names written in sharpie on the back. After soundcheck, Eddie, Jeff, and Stone asked if there were some outdoor courts nearby where we could shoot some hoops. I took them to some courts in Fox Point at the top of Wickenden St., where we played a friendly but competitive pickup game along with some of their road crew and a few of my friends from the club. The show itself had 60 people [who] paid at the door ($5) and around 30-40 guests via radio and record company lists. Set was raw but great. . . . Long story short, album was released, the ["Alive"] video hit MTV, and [eventually] they exploded way beyond playing a small club."

Paul Adams, an employee of First Avenue in Minneapolis, also recalled the hypnotic appeal of Pearl Jam when they played the hall on July 21, telling Pearl Jam Concert Chronology: "A few people trickled in during their brief set. It only took a song or two before a lot of the employees who were in various places in the building [made] their way to the floor area. After a couple of songs on the stage, Eddie jumped down to the floor and was singing to each of us who were there. I can remember about twenty or so people on the floor and more than half of them worked at the club. We were all into their energetic set as if they were playing in front of ten thousand people. Stone even jumped down to the floor and finished the set in the crowd with Eddie. By the time their quick thirty-minute set was done, we were all blown away and wanted more."

It was the birth as we know it of Pearl Jam, the venerable tour gods who have gone on to transfix crowds, sell out shows, and become the leaders of a master class in how to perform live. And, back then, it was a reputation that was growing quickly—accelerated by Eddie Vedder's death-defying onstage antics that had people believing they were seeing miracles when he survived. Upon the band's return to Seattle in August, they played their first-ever outdoor show at the Mural Amphitheatre on August 23, in which Eddie climbed a speaker stack during a performance of "Porch"—a mere baby step toward his total abandonment of gravity on upcoming dates. By August 29, at RKCNDY once again, Eddie goaded Mike into playing guitar from on top of the singer's shoulders during "Alive," and then the frontman decided to do his own gymnastics, swinging from the rafters during "Porch" once again.

By September 25, Pearl Jam had kicked off a full-fledged North American *Ten* headline tour—but it didn't last long. About fifteen shows in, the band canceled and/or postponed the remaining dates as an even bigger opportunity came up: the chance to open for Red Hot Chili Peppers on their *Blood Sugar Sex Magik* tour. "It's important for us to establish ourselves as a live band because that's what we are first and foremost," Stone shared in an archival video posted to PearlJamOnline's YouTube page.

The opportunity allegedly came at the request of former Peppers drummer and Eddie's friend Jack Irons, who was hoping to help Pearl Jam get some bigger opportunities to push

TOP:
Red Hot Chili Peppers perform at Lollapalooza in Waterloo, New Jersey in August 1992.

BOTTOM:
Smashing Pumpkins pose during a photo shoot in Chicago, Illinois on May 10, 1991.

Ten as the album struggled to find its footing. Pearl Jam was joined on the bill by the Smashing Pumpkins, making it the epitome of a total '90s rock package—the father, son, and holy ghost of what would become the most worshipped bands of the era. Especially when you add in Nirvana, who joined the bill toward the very end.

As RHCP frontman Anthony Kiedis explained in his book *Scar Tissue*, "The longer we toured, the larger the crowds got. By the time we were scheduled to play the West Coast, we had jumped from theaters to full-fledged arenas, so the promoters felt we needed to add another band that was bigger than Pearl Jam. Nirvana's second album, *Nevermind*, had just exploded, and I was crazy about that record, so I suggested we get Nirvana to take Pearl Jam's place." But when Billy Corgan found out, he yanked the Pumpkins from the bill, none too happy with Kurt Cobain, who was dating his former flame Courtney Love. Out of sheer luck, Pearl Jam was brought back on to fill the vacancy.

The tour was a bit slow to start, but as the bands' profiles grew in real time, so did the audiences. As Billy Corgan recalled to Chicago rock station Q101 in 2018, "When the tour started, the first week or so, first two weeks, there seemed to be some unhappy people . . . They said well the Chili Peppers are upset because the record company is not really supporting their record. And Pearl Jam's upset because the record company is not really supporting their record. . . . And then all of a sudden [RHCP's] 'Under The Bridge' hit and then I think it was 'Jeremy' or 'Alive' hit and then suddenly it was like we had this triple crowd . . . and it was like this legendary tour because this was all hitting at the exact same time. Obviously, it was a great time for rock."

> The RHCP/Pumpkins/Pearl Jam jaunt kicked off October 16, 1991 in Madison, Wisconsin, and as the weeks went by, there were scores of anecdotes about Eddie's Evel Knievel-like stunts.

He climbed to reach balconies in Madison, swung upside down and dived into the crowd in DeKalb, injured himself jumping off speaker stacks in Rochester, and needed a dozen stitches when he pounded cymbals in New York.

During the New York run, Pearl Jam also staged several in-store signings at record stores and had the chance to play the iconic CBGB, with Eddie telling the crowd, "Ever since I was 14, I wanted to come to this place." By the time the tour reached Columbus, Eddie was rebuffing security's warnings and brought a throng of fans on stage to mosh together.

Eddie Vedder onstage at the Pinkpop Festival in Landgraaf, the Netherlands on June 8, 1992.

People in the crew even started taking bets on the spots Eddie might jump from. "I think the first time I got really worried, we were in Texas in early December," Mike McCready told Cameron Crowe for the 1993 *Rolling Stone* cover story. "Eddie climbed up on this girder, about 50 feet [15 m] in the air. Nobody knew where he was. And all of a sudden you look up—some guy had a flashlight on him—and it was like 'Fuck!' He's up there clinging to a girder. I'm thinking, 'This guy is insane, but I'm so totally pumped.'"

As Eddie would share, there was impetus for Pearl Jam to prove itself by any means possible. "'We're going to take this to some level that people aren't going to forget," he famously said, "and if that means risking your life, we're going to do it."

Eddie's bravado had come to a fever pitch by the time Nirvana was added to the tour lineup on December 27. At San Diego's Del Mar Pavilion the next night, even Nirvana's Dave Grohl took notice of the risky maneuvering. "I didn't sit and watch them play until the show in San Diego, where Eddie climbed the fuckin' lighting rig," Dave told *SPIN*. "I swear to God he was like 250 feet [76 m] up in the air. It was one of the scariest things I've ever seen in my entire life. . . . Honestly, I was horrified. I was really scared that he was gonna die."

Eddie, admittedly, was scared shitless too. "I got to the top, and I thought, 'Well, how do I get down?' I either just give it up and look like an idiot, or I go for it. So I decided to try it, and it was really ridiculously high, like 100 feet [30.5 m], something mortal. I was thinking that my mother was there, and I didn't want her to see me die. Somehow I finally got back onstage, finished the song, and went to the side and threw up. I knew that was really stupid, beyond ridiculous." But there was a rationale behind it—namely, a bit of healthy competition. "To be honest, we were playing before Nirvana. You had to do something," he said. "Our first record was good, but their first record was better."

As the tour stretched into New Year's Eve 1991 and wrapped on January 3, 1992, everything started to change. "I remember after the New Year's Eve 1991 show, somebody running onto the bus and saying Nirvana had just hit No. 1," Mike recalled to *SPIN*. "I remember thinking, 'Wow, it's on now.' It changed something. We had something to prove—that our band was as good as I thought it was." His new year resolution would soon come true as 1992 moved everything at warp speed.

SET LIST SPOTLIGHT

The '90s Rock Trifecta Tour
December 31, 1991, Cow Palace, Daly City, CA

1. Once
2. Even Flow
3. Suggestion (Fugazi cover)
4. Why Go
5. Jeremy
6. Alive
7. Leash
8. Smells Like Teen Spirit (Nirvana cover)
9. Porch

HIDDEN PEARL

Red Hot Chili Peppers bassist Flea joined on "Leash" during the New Year's Eve 1991 show. A reporter with *Rolling Stone* was in the crowd that night and said the show even eclipsed that of hometown heroes Grateful Dead, who were playing their long-running annual NYE bash down the road.

HEADLINER
(1992–2000)

"Some nights when it hits, I just look out at the audience and think, 'Oh my god, this is the greatest thing in the world, I don't want this to end.' And then the show's over with, but you're still up in that state for hours afterwards."
—Mike McCready to *Guitar World*

Eddie Vedder crowd-surfing during a Pearl Jam show in 1992.

TOUR DATES: 1992-2000

1992
January 2: Salem, OR @ Salem Armory
January 3: Seattle, WA @ RKCNDY
January 17: Seattle, WA @ Moore Theatre
January 24 **(Rock For Choice Benefit)** and May 13: Los Angeles, CA @ Hollywood Palladium
February 3: Southend-on-Sea, England @ The Esplanade Club
February 4: London, England @ Borderline
February 7: Stockholm, Sweden @ Koolkat Klub
February 8: Oslo, Norway @ Alaska
February 9: Copenhagen, Denmark @ Pumpe Huset
February 11: Paris, France @ Locomotive
February 12: Amsterdam, Netherlands @ Melkweg
February 15: Madrid, Spain @ Revolver
February 18: Milan, Italy @ Sorpasso
February 19: Winterthur, Switzerland @ Albani Bar Of Music
February 21: Manchester, England @ International II
February 22: Ponteland, UK @ Riverside
February 23: Glasgow, Scotland @ Cathouse
February 25: Nottingham, England @ Rock City
February 26: Birmingham, England @ Edwards No. 8
February 27: Bradford, England @ Queenshall
February 28: London, England @ Union of London University
March 1: Groningen, Netherlands @ The Vera
March 2: Maurik, Netherlands @ Paard
March 4: Utrecht, Netherlands @ Tivoli
March 5: Eindhoven, Netherlands @ Effenaar
March 6: Rotterdam, Netherlands @ Nighttown
March 8: Cologne, Germany @ Live Music Hall
March 9: Berlin, Germany @ The Loft
March 10: Hamburg, Germany @ Markthalle
March 12: Frankfurt, Germany @ Batschkaap
March 13: Munich, Germany @ Nachtwerk
March 25: Minneapolis, MN @ First Avenue Club
March 26: Madison, WI @ R and R Station
March 27: Milwaukee, WI @ Marquette University Alumni Hall
March 28: Chicago, IL @ Cabaret Metro
March 30: Cincinnati, OH @ Bogart's
March 31: Columbus, OH @ Newport Music Hall
April 2: Cleveland, OH @ Peabody's Down Under
April 3: Detroit, MI @ St. Andrew's Hall
April 4: Toronto, ON, Canada @ Concert Hall
April 6: Lowell, MA @ Cumnock Hall
April 7: Amherst, MA @ Student Union Ballroom at UMass
April 8: Boston, MA @ Axis Club
April 10: Philadelphia, PA @ Trocadero Club
April 12: New York, NY @ Limelight
April 13: College Park, MD @ Ritchie Coliseum, University of Maryland
April 16: Athens, GA @ Legion Field, University of Georgia
April 19 and September 6 **(Lollapalooza)**: Dallas, TX @ Starplex Amphitheater
April 20: New Orleans, LA @ Tipitinas
April 22: St. Petersburg, FL @ Jannus Landing
April 23: Miami, FL @ Cameo Theater
April 24: Orlando, FL @ The Edge
April 28: Austin, TX @ City Coliseum
April 29: Dallas, TX @ Bronco Bowl
April 30: Houston, TX @ Unicorn
May 2: Lawrence, KS @ University of Kansas
May 3: Omaha, NE @ The Ranch Bowl
May 5: Boulder, CO @ Glenn Miller Ballroom, University of Colorado
May 7: Bozeman, MT @ Gallitan Fairgrounds
May 9: Mesa, AZ @ Mesa Amphitheater
May 10: Tijuana, Mexico @ Iguana's
May 12: Ventura, CA @ Ventura Theater
May 15: San Francisco, CA @ Warfield Theater
May 16: Santa Cruz, CA @ The Catalyst
May 17: Portland, OR @ Roseland Theater
May 18: Vancouver, BC, Canada @ Plaza of Nations
June 5: Nuremberg, Germany @ **Rock Am Ring Festival**
June 6: London, England @ **Finsbury Park Festival**
June 8: Landgraaf, Netherlands @ **Pinkpop Festival**
June 10: Stuttgart, Germany @ Kongresszentrum
June 11: Hamburg, Germany @ Grosse Freiheit 36
June 13: Berlin, Germany @ **Go Bang Festival**
June 14: Bremen, Germany @ **Go Bang Festival**
June 15: Nuremberg, Germany @ Serenadenhof
June 17: Milan, Italy @ City Square
June 18: Zürich, Switzerland @ Volkshaus
June 19: Vienna, Austria @ Rockhaus
June 22: Paris, France @ Elysee-Montmartre
June 25: Stockholm, Sweden @ Moderna Museet, Skeppsholmen
June 26: Copenhagen, Denmark @ **Roskilde Festival**
July 18 and July 19 **(Lollapalooza)**, November 1 **(Bridge School Benefit)**: Mountain View, CA @ Shoreline Amphitheatre
July 21: Vancouver, BC, Canada @ Thunderbird Stadium, UBC **(Lollapalooza)**
July 22: Bremerton, WA @ Kitsap County Fairgrounds **(Lollapalooza)**
July 25: Denver, CO @ Fiddler's Green Amphitheatre **(Lollapalooza)**
July 27: Maryland Heights, MO @ Riverport Amphitheatre **(Lollapalooza)**
July 28: Cincinnati, OH @ Riverbend Music Center **(Lollapalooza)**
July 29: Cuyahoga Falls, OH @ Blossom Music Center **(Lollapalooza)**
July 31 and August 1: Clarkston, MI @ Pine Knob Music Theatre **(Lollapalooza)**
August 2: Tinley Park, IL @ World Music Amphitheatre **(Lollapalooza)**

78 PEARL JAM LIVE!

August 4: Saratoga Springs, NY @ Saratoga Performing Arts Center **(Lollapalooza)**
August 5: Barrie, ON, Canada @ Molson Park **(Lollapalooza)**
August 7 and August 8: Norton, MA @ Great Woods Center **(Lollapalooza)**
August 9: Wantagh, NY @ Jones Beach Music Theatre **(Lollapalooza)**
August 12: Stanhope, NJ @ Waterloo Village **(Lollapalooza)**
August 14: Reston, VA @ Lake Fairfax Park **(Lollapalooza)**
August 15: Scranton, PA @ Montage Mountain Performing Arts Center **(Lollapalooza)**
August 16: Pittsburgh, PA @ Star Lake Amphitheater **(Lollapalooza)**
August 18: Raleigh, NC @ Walnut Creek Amphitheatre **(Lollapalooza)**
August 20 and September 1: Atlanta, GA @ Lakewood Amphitheatre **(Lollapalooza)**
August 22: Miami, FL @ Bicentennial Park Grounds **(Lollapalooza)**
August 23: Orlando, FL @ Central Florida Fairgrounds **(Lollapalooza)**
August 25: Charlotte, NC @ Blockbuster Pavilion **(Lollapalooza)**
August 28: St. Paul, MN @ Harriet Island **(Lollapalooza)**
August 29: East Troy, WI @ Alpine Valley Music Theatre **(Lollapalooza)**
September 4: New Orleans, LA @ UNO Soccer Field **(Lollapalooza)**
September 5: Rosenberg, TX @ Fort Bend County Fairgrounds **(Lollapalooza)**
September 8: Phoenix, AZ @ Desert Sky Pavilion **(Lollapalooza)**
September 11, September 12, and September 13: Irvine, CA @ Irvine Meadows **(Lollapalooza)**
September 20: Seattle, WA @ Warren G. Magnuson Park **(Drop in the Park)**
September 25 and September 26: Honolulu, HI @ Andrew's Amphitheater
September 27: Maui, HI @ War Memorial Gymnasium
December 31: New York, NY @ The Academy

1993
May 13: San Francisco, CA @ Slim's Café
June 16: Missoula, MT @ University Theatre, University of Montana
June 17: Spokane Valley, WA @ The Met
June 26: Oslo, Norway @ Sentrum Scene
June 27: Oslo, Norway @ **Isle of Calf Festival (Kalvoya)**
June 28: Stockholm, Sweden @ Sjohistoriska Museet
June 30: Helsinki, Finland @ Jaahalli
July 2 and July 3: Verona, Italy @ Stadio Bentegodi
July 6 and July 7: Roma, Italy @ Stadio Flaminio
July 10: Meath, Ireland @ Slane Castle
July 11: London, England @ Finsbury Park
July 13 and July 14: London, England @ Brixton Academy
July 16 and July 17: Rotterdam, Netherlands @ Sportspaleis Ahoy
July 18: Amsterdam, Netherlands @ Paradiso
August 11: Calgary, AB, Canada @ Max Bell Arena
August 12: Edmonton, AB, Canada @ Convention Center
August 14: Gimli, MB, Canada @ Gimli Motorsport Park Sunfest '93
August 17: Gatineau, QC, Canada @ Robert Guertin Arena
August 18: Toronto, ON, Canada @ Canadian National Exhibition (CNE) Stadium
August 19: Montreal, QC, Canada @ Verdun Auditorium
September 2: Los Angeles, CA @ Viper Room
September 4: Vancouver, BC, Canada @ C. Place Stadium
September 5: George, WA @ Gorge Amphitheatre
September 6: Portland, OR @ Portland Meadows Race Track
October 25: Seattle, WA @ Off Ramp Café
October 27: Santa Cruz, CA @ The Catalyst
October 28: San Francisco, CA @ Warfield Theater
October 30: San Jose, CA @ SJSU Event Center
October 31: Berkeley, CA @ Greek Theatre
November 2 and November 3: San Diego, CA @ Civic Theatre
November 4: Los Angeles, CA @ Whisky A Go-Go
November 5: Indio, CA @ Empire Polo Fields
November 6 and November 7: Mesa, AZ @ Mesa Amphitheater **(Mount Graham Benefit)**
November 9: Albuquerque, NM @ Convention Exhibition Hall
November 11: Denton, TX @ University of North Texas Coliseum
November 12: Dallas Texas @ Moody Coliseum, SMU
November 16, November 17, and November 19: New Orleans @ UNO Lakefront Arena
November 20: Nacogdoches, TX @ Stephen F. Austin Arena
November 22: Little Rock, AR @ Barton Coliseum
November 23: Oklahoma City, OK @ T and T Center
November 24: Wichita, KS @ Century II
November 26 and November 27: Boulder, CO @ Balch Fieldhouse, University of Colorado
November 30 and December 1: Las Vegas, NV @ Aladdin Theater
December 2: Reno, NV @ Lawlor Athletic Events Center
December 7, December 8, and December 9: Seattle, WA @ Seattle Center Arena

1994
March 6 and March 7: Denver, CO @ Paramount Theater, Denver
March 9: Pensacola, FL @ Civic Center Pensacola **(Rock For Choice Benefit)**
March 10: Chicago, IL @ Chicago Stadium
March 13: Chicago, IL @ New Regal Theater
March 14 and March 15: St. Louis, MO @ Fox Theatre
March 17: West Lafayette, IN @ Elliot Hall, Purdue University
March 19: Detroit, MI @ Masonic Theater
March 20: Ann Arbor, MI @ Crisler Arena
March 22: Cleveland, OH @ Cleveland State University Convocation Center
March 24: Louisville, KY @ Louisville Gardens
March 25: Memphis, TN @ Mid-South Coliseum
March 26: Murfreesboro, TN @ Murphy Athletic Center
March 28: Miami, FL @ Bayfront Amphitheater
March 29: St. Petersburg, FL @ Bayfront Arena
April 2 and April 3: Atlanta, GA @ Fox Theater
April 6: Springfield, MA @ Civic Center Springfield
April 7: Rochester, NY @ War Memorial
April 8: Fairfax, VA @ Patriot Center
April 10 and April 11: Boston, MA @ Boston Garden
April 12: Boston, MA @ Orpheum Theater
April 17: New York, NY @ Paramount Theater
October 1 and October 2: Mountain View, CA @ Shoreline Amphitheatre **(Bridge School Benefit)**

1995

January 14 and January 15: Washington, DC @ Constitution Hall **(Voters For Choice Benefit)**
February 5 and February 6: Seattle, WA @ Moore Theatre **(*billed as the Piss Bottle Men)**
February 8: Missoula, MT @ Adams Field House
February 18: Sendai-Shi, Japan @ Izumity 21
February 20: Chiyoda-Ku, Japan @ Budokan
February 21: Osaka, Japan @ Kosei Nenkin Kaikan
February 24: Taipei, China @ TICC
February 26: Manila, Philippines @ Folk Arts Theater
February 28: Bangkok, Thailand @ Hua Mark Indoor Stadium
March 3: Kallang, Singapore @ Singapore Indoor Stadium
March 6: Perth, Australia @ Perth Entertainment Centre
March 8: Adelaide, Australia @ Memorial Drive Tennis Centre
March 10 and March 11: Haymarket, Australia @ Sydney Entertainment Centre
March 14: Lyneham, Australia @ Exhibition Park
March 16 and March 17: Melbourne, Australia @ Flinders Park Tennis Centre
March 18: Melbourne, Australia @ Sidney Myers Music Bowl
March 21 and March 22: Brisbane, Australia @ Brisbane Entertainment Centre
March 24 and March 25: Auckland, New Zealand @ Mt Smart Stadium
June 16: Casper, WY @ Casper Events Centre
June 19 and June 20: Morrison, CO @ Red Rocks Amphitheatre
June 22: Sacramento, CA @ Cal Expo
June 24: San Francisco, CA @ Polo Fields
July 8 and July 9: Milwaukee, WI @ **Summerfest**
July 11: Chicago, IL @ Soldier Field
September 13: Phoenix, AZ @ Veterans Memorial Coliseum
September 14: Las Cruces, NM @ Pan Am Center
September 16: Austin, TX @ South Park Meadows
September 17: New Orleans, LA @ Tad Gormley Stadium
November 1 and November 2: Salt Lake City @ Delta Center
November 4: San Jose, CA @ Spartan Stadium
November 6 and November 7: San Diego, CA @ San Diego Sports Arena

1996

September 14: Seattle, WA @ The Showbox
September 16: Seattle, WA @ Key Arena
September 21: Toronto, ON, Canada @ Maple Leaf Gardens
September 22: Toledo, OH @ Savage Hall
September 24: Columbia, MD @ Merriweather Post Pavilion
September 26: Augusta, ME @ Civic Center Augusta
September 28 and September 29: New York, NY @ Downing Stadium, Randall's Island
October 1: Buffalo, NY @ Marine Midland Arena
October 2: Manchester, CT @ Dodge Music Center
October 4: Charlotte, NC @ Memorial Stadium
October 5: North Charleston, SC @ N. Charleston Coliseum
October 7: Ft. Lauderdale, FL @ F.L. Baseball Stadium
October 19 and October 20: Mountain View, CA @ Shoreline Amphitheatre **(Bridge School Benefit)**
October 24: Cork, Ireland @ Millstreet Arena
October 26: Dublin, Ireland @ The Point
October 28 and October 29: Wembley, England @ Wembley Arena
November 1: Warszawa, Poland @ The Torwar
November 3: Berlin, Germany @ Deutschlandhalle
November 4: Hamburg, Germany @ Sporthalle
November 6: Amsterdam, Netherlands @ Parkhal
November 7: Paris, France @ The Zenith
November 9: Zürich, Switzerland @ Hallenstadion
November 12: Rome, Italy @ Palaeur
November 13: Assago, Italy @ Forum Milan
November 15: Prague, Czech Republic @ Sports Hall Prague
November 17: Budapest, Hungary @ Sports Hall Budapest
November 19: Istanbul, Turkey @ World Trade Center
November 21: Barcelona, Spain @ Sports Palace
November 22: San Sebastián, Spain @ Anoeta Velodrome
November 24 and November 25: Lisbon, Portugal @ Cascais Pavilion

1997

November 12: Santa Cruz, CA @ The Catalyst **(*billed as The Honking Seals)**
November 14, November 15, November 18, and November 19: Oakland, CA @ Oakland-Alameda County Coliseum Stadium

1998

February 20 and February 21: Maui, HI @ Alexander M. Baldwin Amphitheatre
February 26: Wellington, New Zealand @ Queen's Wharf Events Center
February 28: Auckland, New Zealand @ Ericcson Stadium
March 2, March 3, and March 5: Parkville, Australia @ Melbourne Park
March 7: Adelaide, Australia @ Thebarton Oval
March 9, March 11, and March 12: Haymarket, Australia @ Sydney Entertainment Centre
March 14 and March 15: Brisbane, Australia @ Brisbane Entertainment Centre
March 19 and March 20: Perth, Australia @ Perth Entertainment Centre
May 7: Seattle, WA @ ARO.space **(*billed as Harvey Dent & The Caped Crusaders)**
June 20: Missoula, MT @ Washington-Grizzly Stadium
June 21: Park City, UT @ Wolf Mountain
June 23: Denver, CO @ Fiddler's Green Amphitheatre
June 24: Rapid City, SD @ Rushmore Plaza Civic Center
June 26 and June 27: East Troy, WI @ Alpine Valley Music Theatre
June 29: Chicago, IL @ United Center
June 30: Minneapolis, MN @ Target Center
July 2: Maryland Heights, MO @ Riverport Amphitheatre
July 3: Kansas City, MO @ Sandstone Amphitheatre
July 5: Dallas, TX @ Reunion Arena
July 7: Albuquerque, NM @ Tingley Coliseum
July 8: Phoenix, AZ @ Veterans Memorial Coliseum
July 10: San Diego, CA @ Viejas Arena
July 11: Las Vegas, NV @ Thomas and Mack Center
July 13 and July 14: Inglewood, CA @ Great Western Forum

July 16: Sacramento, CA @ Arco Arena
July 18: Portland, OR @ Rose Garden Arena
July 19: Vancouver, BC, Canada @ Pacific Coliseum
July 21 and July 22: Seattle, WA @ Memorial Stadium
August 17: Noblesville, IN @ Deer Creek Music Center
August 18: East Lansing, MI @ Breslin Center
August 20: Montreal, QC, Canada @ Molson Centre
August 22: Barrie, ON, Canada @ Molson Park
August 23: Auburn Hills, MI @ The Palace of Auburn Hills
August 25: Pittsburgh, PA @ Star Lake Amphitheater
August 26: Cuyahoga Falls, OH @ Blossom Music Center
August 28 and August 29: Camden, NJ @ Blockbuster Music Entertainment Center
August 31: Raleigh, NC @ Walnut Creek Amphitheatre
September 1: Atlanta, GA @ Lakewood Amphitheatre
September 3: Birmingham, AL @ BJCC Coliseum
September 4: Greenville, SC @ Bi-Lo Center
September 6: Knoxville, TN @ Thompson-Boling Arena
September 7: Virginia Beach, VA @ Virginia Beach Amphitheatre
September 8: East Rutherford, NJ @ Continental Arena
September 10 and September 11: New York, NY @ Madison Square Garden
September 13: Manchester, CT @ Dodge Music Center
September 15 and September 16: Norton, MA @ Great Woods Center
September 18: Columbia, MD @ Merriweather Post Pavilion
September 19: Washington, DC @ Constitution Hall **(Voters For Choice Benefit)**
September 22 and September 23: West Palm Beach, FL @ Coral Sky Amphitheatre
October 10: Seattle, WA @ Crocodile Café

1999
October 30 and October 31: Mountain View, CA @ Shoreline Amphitheatre **(Bridge School Benefit)**

2000
May 10: Bellingham, WA @ Mt. Baker Theatre
May 11: Vancouver, BC, Canada @ Commodore Ballroom
May 23: Lisbon, Portugal @ Restelo Stadium
May 25: Barcelona, Spain @ Palau St. Jordi Pavilion
May 26: San Sebastián, Spain @ Anoeta Velodrome
May 29, May 30: Wembley, England @ Wembley Arena
June 1: Dublin, Ireland @ The Point
June 3: Glasgow, Scotland @ S.E.C.C.
June 4: Manchester, England @ Manchester Evening News Arena
June 6: Cardiff, Wales @ Cardiff Arena
June 8: Paris, France @ Bercy
June 9: Köln, Germany @ **Rock am Ring**
June 11: Nord, Germany @ **Rock im Park**
June 12: Landgraaf, Netherlands @ **Pinkpop Festival**
June 14: Prague, Czech Republic @ Paegas Arena
June 15 and June 16: Katowice, Poland @ Spodek
June 18: Salzburg, Austria @ Residenzplatz
June 19: Ljubljana, Slovenia @ Hala Tivoli
June 20: Verona, Italy @ Arena di Verona
June 22: Assago, Italy @ Forum Milan
June 23: Zürich, Switzerland @ Hallenstadion
June 25: Berlin, Germany @ Wuhlheide
June 26: Hamburg, Germany @ Sporthalle
June 28: Stockholm, Sweden @ Sjohistoriska Museet
June 29: Oslo, Norway @ Spektrum
June 30: Copenhagen, Denmark @ **Roskilde Festival**
August 3: Virginia Beach, VA @ Virginia Beach Amphitheatre
August 4: Charlotte, NC @ Blockbuster Pavilion
August 6: Greensboro, NC @ Coliseum
August 7: Atlanta, GA @ Phillips Arena
August 9 and August 10: West Palm Beach, FL @ Mars Music Amphitheatre
August 12: Tampa, FL @ Ice Palace
August 14: New Orleans, LA @ UNO Lakefront Arena
August 15: Memphis, TN @ The Pyramid
August 17: Nashville, TN @ AmSouth Amphitheatre
August 18: Noblesville, IN @ Deer Creek Music Center
August 20: Cincinnati, OH @ Riverbend Music Center
August 21: Columbus, OH @ Polaris Amphitheatre
August 23, August 24, and August 25: Wantagh, NY @ Jones Beach Music Theatre
August 27: Saratoga Springs, NY @ Saratoga Performing Arts Center
August 29 and August 30: Mansfield, MA @ Tweeter Center
September 1 and September 2: Camden, NJ @ E-Centre
September 4: Columbia, MD @ Merriweather Post Pavilion
September 5: Pittsburgh, PA @ Post-Gazette Pavilion
October 4: Montreal, QC, Canada @ Molson Centre
October 5: Toronto, ON, Canada @ Air Canada Centre
October 7: Auburn Hills, MI @ The Palace of Auburn Hills
October 8: East Troy, WI @ Alpine Valley Music Theatre
October 9: Rosemont, IL @ Allstate Arena
October 11: Maryland Heights, MO @ Riverport Amphitheatre
October 12: Kansas City, MO @ Sandstone Amphitheatre
October 14 and October 15: The Woodlands, TX @ Cynthia Woods Mitchell Pavilion
October 17: Dallas, TX @ Smirnoff Music Centre
October 18: Lubbock, TX @ United Spirit Arena
October 20: Albuquerque, NM @ Mesa del Sol
October 21: Phoenix, AZ @ Desert Sky Pavilion
October 22: Las Vegas, NV @ MGM Grand **(10th Anniversary Show)**
October 24: Los Angeles, CA @ Greek Theatre
October 25: San Diego, CA @ San Diego Sports Arena
October 27: Fresno, CA @ Selland Arena
October 28: San Bernadino, CA @ Glen Helen Blockbuster
October 30: Sacramento, CA @ Sacramento Valley Amphitheatre
October 31: Mountain View, CA @ Shoreline Amphitheatre
November 2: Portland, OR @ Rose Garden Arena
November 3: Boise, ID @ Idaho Center
November 5 and November 6: Seattle, WA @ Key Arena

"OCEANS"

There was no time to waste at the dawn of 1992. A long year of grueling hard work (one hundred tour dates total, eighty-two of which came after *Ten* sessions wrapped) had paid off as interest in Pearl Jam and the emerging grunge scene was starting to manifest. The exposure of the Red Hot Chili Peppers tour drove radio to pay attention to Pearl Jam as stations started adding "Alive" to their rotations. Coupled with Nirvana's *Nevermind* going to No. 1 by January 1992, suddenly there was a total sea change for alt rock. Pearl Jam was keen to ride that wave and also start to use it for a greater purpose.

For Pearl Jam, music has often acted as a vehicle to drive other important motivations forward. As the website *Afterglow* perfectly surmised, the band has spent a good part of their career "turning early angst into ongoing activism."

OPPOSITE:
Pearl Jam performs at the University of London Union on February 28, 1992.

BELOW:
Mike McCready during a '90s-era performance.

Over the years, Pearl Jam has been incredibly committed to causes they care about, whether abortion rights, voting rights, environmental policy, mental health, education, the arts, or combating homelessness and gun violence—or personal causes, like the Crohns & Colitis Foundation of America, as Mike was diagnosed with the often debilitating disease. And they do so largely through the platform or proceeds of their live shows. To this day, Pearl Jam continues to contribute $5 from each ticket sale to their Vitalogy Foundation.

Songs have also been included on charitable compilations, like "Porch" on several tribute albums for abortion rights organizations and "Last Kiss" on an album that benefited victims of the Kosovo War. Charities Pearl Jam has partnered with over time have included Conservation International, Habitat For Humanity, HeadCount, Oceana, Red Cross, Rock the Vote, Sweet Relief Musicians Fund, and Vote For Change, among others.

The earliest inklings of the band's activism came on January 24, 1992 at the Hollywood Palladium when Pearl Jam was included on a bill for Rock For Choice. The series of concerts was started by L7 and music journalist Sue Cummings in 1991 and ran through 2001 with a mission to support abortion rights and women's right to choose.

> **Pearl Jam would be a part of several Rock For Choice benefit shows over time; the first, in 1992, came on the nineteenth anniversary of Roe v. Wade, and Eddie carried his thoughts on the topic over to several key moments that year.**

That famously included writing "Pro-Choice" on his arm during the *MTV Unplugged* episode in March and wearing a T-shirt with the image of a coat hanger during an appearance on *Saturday Night Live* in April. Eddie also wrote an op-ed for the November 1992 issue of *SPIN* magazine, which he scribed while on Pearl Jam's European tour.

In part, Eddie wrote, "This is not a game. This is not a religious pep rally. This is a woman's future. Roe v. Wade was decided 19 years ago and the fact that a well-organized group has come close to overturning it is raw proof that we do live in a democracy. But also the reason that any opposition must be equally as vocal. . . . Decide on the issues and vote—male or female—for this is not just a women's issue. It's human rights."

When Roe v. Wade was overturned in the United States in June 2022, Pearl Jam again voiced their support for women's right to choose. Mike joined the Women's March in San Francisco, and the band posted

OPPOSITE:
Eddie Vedder backstage during the Rock For Choice concert at The Hollywood Palladium in Los Angeles, California on January 24, 1992.

84   PEARL JAM LIVE!

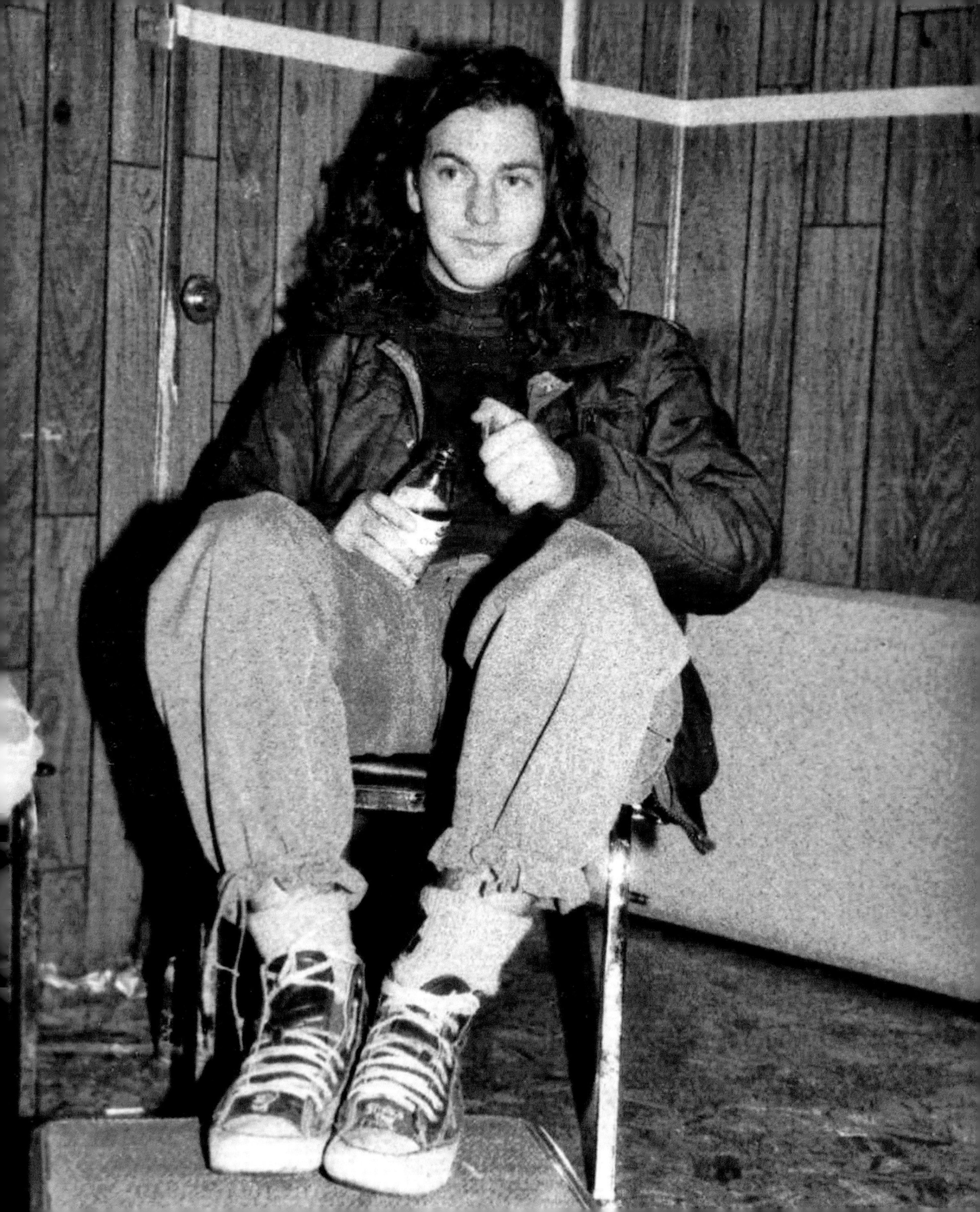

a statement to social media, one that Eddie also read aloud at a concert: "No one, not the government, not politicians, not the Supreme Court should prevent access to abortion, birth control, and contraceptives. People should have the freedom to choose. Today's decision impacts everyone and it will particularly affect poor women who can't afford to travel to access health care. We will stay active, we will not back down and we will never give up. Elections have consequences, please join us."

After the galvanizing moment at the Rock For Choice show on January 24, 1992, it felt like there wasn't anything Pearl Jam *couldn't* do—even take on the world. The band members packed their bags and prepared for their first international tour in February and March, descending upon the UK, France, Germany, Italy, the Netherlands, Denmark, Norway, Sweden, Spain, and Switzerland.

It was an interesting strategy by the band's team. *Ten* wasn't even distributed in Europe yet. Just three hundred people showed up on the very first night, at The Esplanade in Southend, England on February 3. Still, those who were in the know had found a copy of the album import and were singing along.

Eddie Vedder and Stone Gossard onstage at Melkweg in Amsterdam on February 12, 1992.

The next day, Pearl Jam headed to an in-studio performance for BBC2's *Late Show* where they debuted on TV for the very first time—and as many tuned into the segment, crowds at the European dates began to grow. Pearl Jam's gig at The Borderline in London that very same night sold out, with many fans turned away at the door. As Pearl Jam Concert Chronology noted, "Eddie and Dave did their best to counter the crowd's disappointment by spending most of the evening outside the club, handing out free CDs and autographs." Other dates soon started to follow suit, with demand outgrowing the small clubs that were originally booked and promoters often scrambling, unable to book other venues. Several of the gigs were broadcast on radio to reach a wider audience. The band also ran into sound issues, vocal issues (Eddie started losing his voice), and concerns over fans stagediving and injuring themselves.

Regardless, the inaugural European trek was a massively successful one and began a long tradition of Pearl Jam playing overseas. As *Rolling Stone* said in 2019, the initial European tour "was the start of a powerful relationship the Seattle band developed with audiences all across Europe." As an example, the magazine added, "When they last hit the road in 2018, they did 15 shows on the continent and a mere seven in America at just four stadiums. They took 2019 off (the first year of their career where they did zero shows) and now have 13 gigs booked in Europe and not a hint of anything in their home country."

> Some of Pearl Jam's other notable gigs on the initial international run included March 1 in the Netherlands, which marked the first time Eddie played guitar in a Pearl Jam show, and the finale in Munich, Germany on March 13 in which Pearl Jam offered a full, in-order album play of *Ten* for the first time.

It's only been repeated on one other occasion in the band's history thus far, on April 29, 2016 at the Wells Fargo Center in Philadelphia, to commemorate the band's tenth time selling out the venue.

Another pivotal date on that first European trek was February 19 at the Albani Music Club in Winterthur, Switzerland. Arriving at the venue and finding the stage much too small to fit all the instrumentation plus the five guys in the band, Pearl Jam diverted to plan B: a full acoustic show. Though they'd had some practice with the idea at recent record store appearances in New York and New Jersey in November '91 and at Paris's Virgin Megastore days prior, the full acoustic set no doubt helped inspire Pearl Jam's next move upon their return to the States: the infamous *MTV Unplugged* episode.

My Pearl Jam Moment

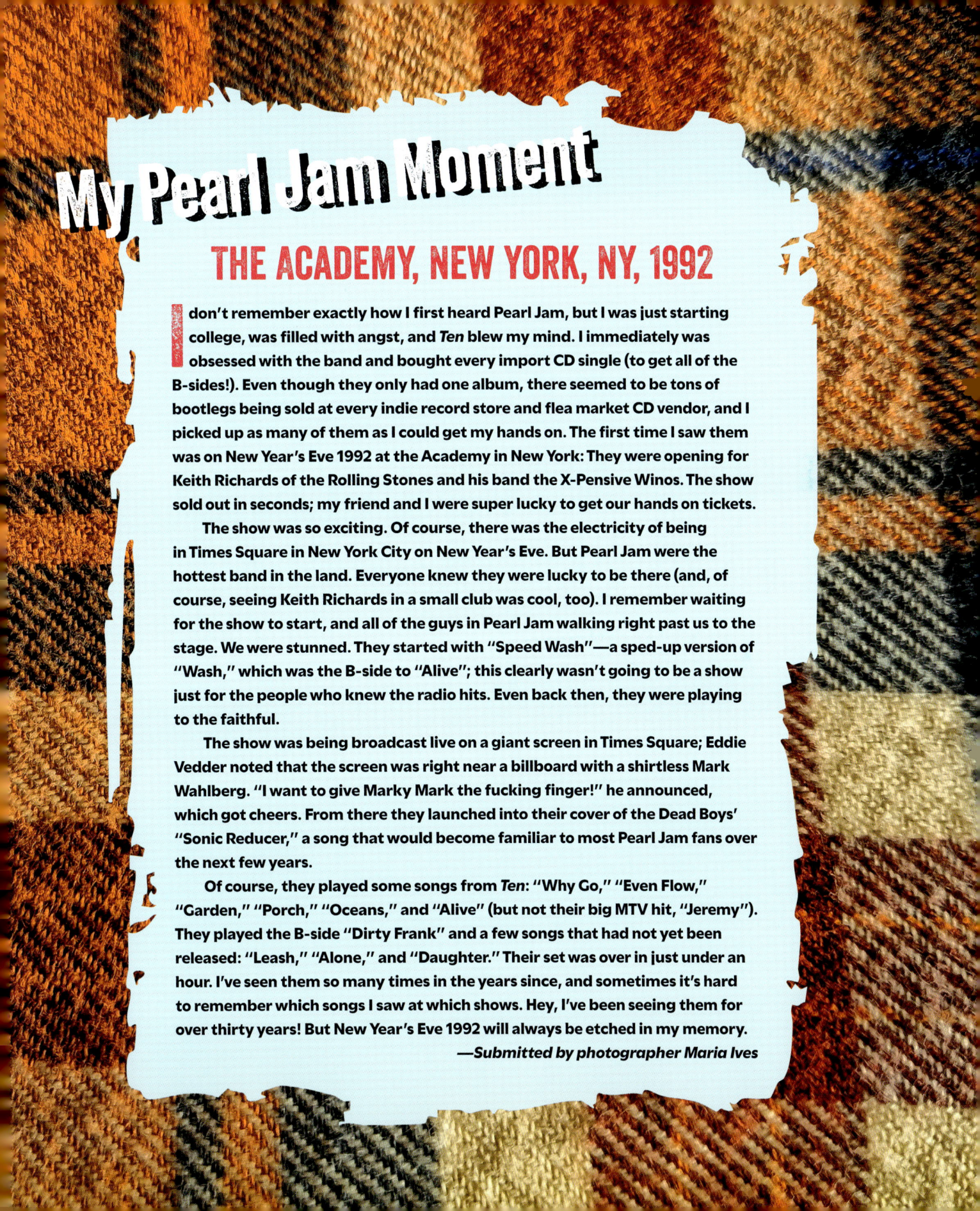

THE ACADEMY, NEW YORK, NY, 1992

I don't remember exactly how I first heard Pearl Jam, but I was just starting college, was filled with angst, and *Ten* blew my mind. I immediately was obsessed with the band and bought every import CD single (to get all of the B-sides!). Even though they only had one album, there seemed to be tons of bootlegs being sold at every indie record store and flea market CD vendor, and I picked up as many of them as I could get my hands on. The first time I saw them was on New Year's Eve 1992 at the Academy in New York: They were opening for Keith Richards of the Rolling Stones and his band the X-Pensive Winos. The show sold out in seconds; my friend and I were super lucky to get our hands on tickets.

The show was so exciting. Of course, there was the electricity of being in Times Square in New York City on New Year's Eve. But Pearl Jam were the hottest band in the land. Everyone knew they were lucky to be there (and, of course, seeing Keith Richards in a small club was cool, too). I remember waiting for the show to start, and all of the guys in Pearl Jam walking right past us to the stage. We were stunned. They started with "Speed Wash"—a sped-up version of "Wash," which was the B-side to "Alive"; this clearly wasn't going to be a show just for the people who knew the radio hits. Even back then, they were playing to the faithful.

The show was being broadcast live on a giant screen in Times Square; Eddie Vedder noted that the screen was right near a billboard with a shirtless Mark Wahlberg. "I want to give Marky Mark the fucking finger!" he announced, which got cheers. From there they launched into their cover of the Dead Boys' "Sonic Reducer," a song that would become familiar to most Pearl Jam fans over the next few years.

Of course, they played some songs from *Ten*: "Why Go," "Even Flow," "Garden," "Porch," "Oceans," and "Alive" (but not their big MTV hit, "Jeremy"). They played the B-side "Dirty Frank" and a few songs that had not yet been released: "Leash," "Alone," and "Daughter." Their set was over in just under an hour. I've seen them so many times in the years since, and sometimes it's hard to remember which songs I saw at which shows. Hey, I've been seeing them for over thirty years! But New Year's Eve 1992 will always be etched in my memory.

—Submitted by photographer Maria Ives

"Immortality"

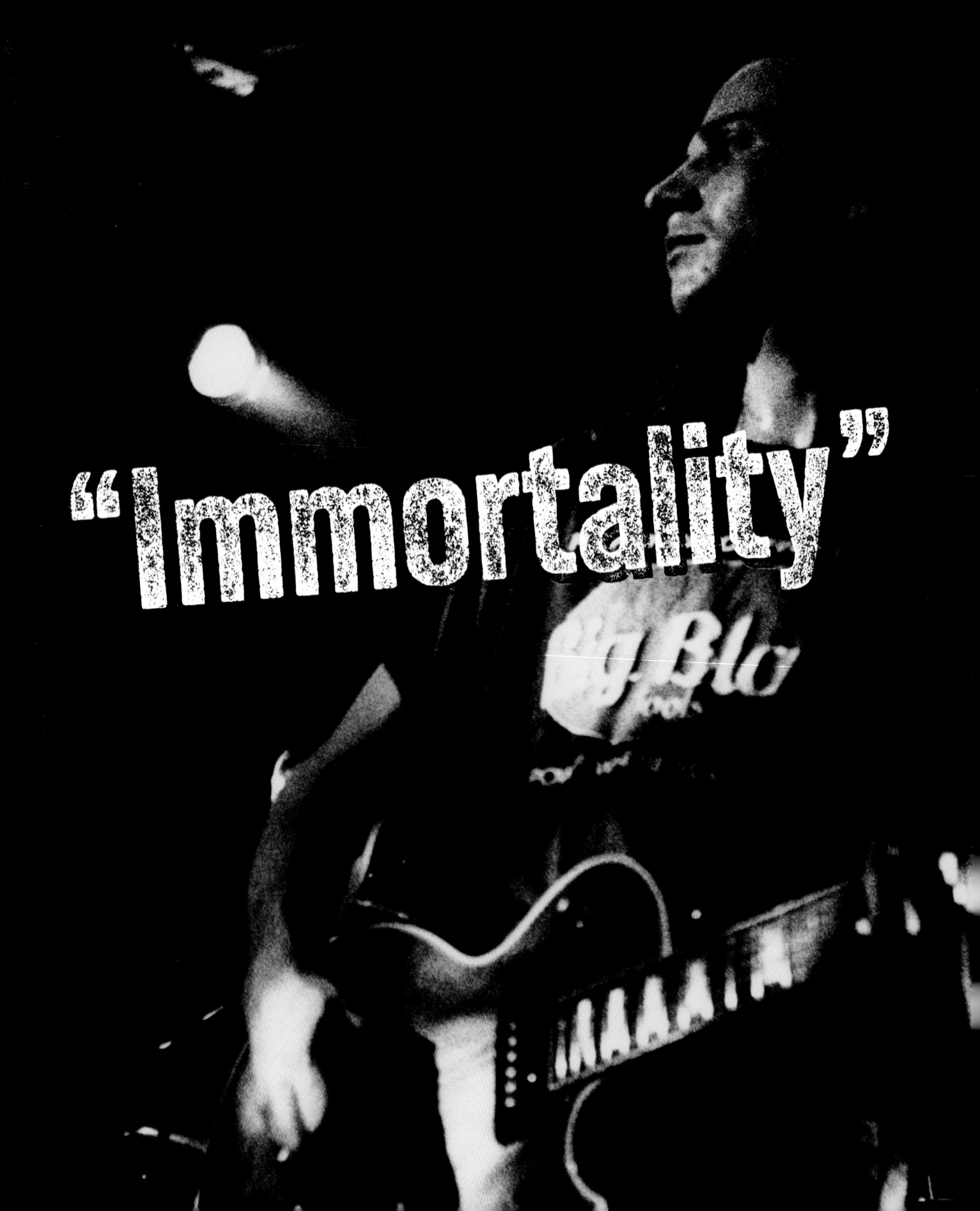

It was around midnight when filming for *MTV Unplugged* began on March 16, 1992. Pearl Jam, jet-lagged and road weary from a two-month European run, had barely been home three days when the band headed to the Kaufman Astoria Studios in New York (also the soundstage for *Sesame Street*) to unplug. This was MTV, after all, the zeitgeist of Gen X that could make or break careers. It was surprising that Pearl Jam was invited to appear on the show in the first place, and they graciously accepted.

At the time, Pearl Jam only had one single and video—"Alive"—circulating on the channel and radio. It was still a month until promotion for "Even Flow" and five months before "Jeremy" would surface. But *Unplugged* bookers were getting hip to the buzz around the band and the Seattle sound in general and took a chance on signing up Pearl Jam. Their episode even predated Nirvana, who would film their incredible *Unplugged* moment a year-and-a-half later in November 1993, while Alice In Chains would get their due in 1996. The three episodes have been, historically, some of the most revered *Unplugged* installments, and their album accompaniments have been some of the best-selling.

But still, it was a big risk giving such a new band such primetime space. To save face and ensure their bottom line, MTV bookers scheduled two other larger and guaranteed acts to film *Unplugged* episodes on the very same day: Boyz II Men and Mariah Carey.

According to one of the series directors, Joel Gallen, "For the most part, I think most people at MTV were pretty excited about having a Pearl Jam *Unplugged* episode, but... it might've been in their minds that, even if the Pearl Jam *Unplugged* didn't work, it wouldn't exactly be wasting production funds because we were doing the other two no matter what."

The line of eager fans waiting to get inside the studios on March 16 already was a good sign. "It was so cold that day and we had just had a snowstorm, so the Pearl Jam fans were waiting outside for hours in the freezing cold. When it was time for the show to actually start taping, they were enthusiastic and ready to go," Joel added, noting that the energy added to the buoyancy of the night.

It was actually Joel's first time directing an episode of *Unplugged*; to this point, he had worked as a producer, mostly on the VMAs, but he was a fan of Pearl Jam and threw his hat in the ring when he got the memo about their upcoming appearance. Joel shared in the interview with Grammy.com that, of all the closeups he's shot in his career, Eddie takes the cake. "There's no one better than Eddie Vedder. The energy and feeling and passion that you feel coming out of him when he's singing," he said. It could've also been the look of stress.

OPPOSITE:
Stone Gossard during a Pearl Jam performance at Melkweg in Amsterdam on December 2, 1992

IMMORTALITY 91

Pearl Jam filmed the episode under a precarious set of circumstances—not only sheer exhaustion but having to rent equipment. "We showed up, and instead of the Gibson Chet Atkins steel-string guitar I had ordered, they had a classical one there. It was getting late . . . and where can you rent stuff at that hour?" Stone recalled to *Guitar World*. "Luckily, we knew some people who were able to score us a couple more guitars, and it turned out fine."

Mike didn't even want to take the offer in the beginning. "I don't think anybody else was of this mindset, but I didn't really want to do it," he later told Cleveland.com. "I didn't think we were as good acoustically as we were electric. That's how I was thinking back then. . . and being a lead player, playing leads on acoustic for me was really fucking hard. It just didn't feel like the right thing to do, at that time." He added, "But, y'know, Ed rose to the challenge and we all did again. . . . I guess I was wrong."

If there was ever a moment for Eddie, Jeff, Stone, Mike, and Dave to shine in the early days of Pearl Jam, it was on *Unplugged*. The performance gave a whole new interpretation and appreciation for the songs on *Ten* and proved their weight as stripped-back opuses, too. Without amplification, pedals, or other distortion effects (though, still a full drum kit), there was a naked fury on "Black," an immediacy to "Porch" (the song where Eddie Sharpied PRO-CHOICE!!! on his arm and Jeff got off his stool to noodle around on the drum riser), and a harrowing quality to "Even Flow." Elsewhere in the performance, Pearl Jam dug out "Jeremy," "State Of Love And Trust," and "Alive," showing a tempered cohesiveness and visceral impunity that resonated with viewers.

"From a directing standpoint, I just had to try and put my cameras in the right place, anticipate the energy of the band, and react to the

Pearl Jam performs during their MTV Unplugged episode at Kaufman Astoria Studios in New York City on March 16, 1992.

moments they were creating," Joel shared, adding that Pearl Jam gave no clues during the rehearsal of what they would ultimately do during the taping, which made it even more "raw and sensational."

In particular, "Black" struck a chord. As Cameron Crowe summed it up in his 1993 *Rolling Stone* cover story, "It was simple, a guy sitting on a stool, ripping his heart out, drowning emotionally, right there in front of you." He called it a "galvanizing" moment for the band. Thereafter, letters addressed to Pearl Jam's Ten Club HQ almost doubled. As noted earlier, many of the messages were from fans in the grips of despair, on the brink of ending it all, until they saw Eddie sing. "Vedder answered many of the letters himself, sometimes leaving the band's office in a wreck," Cameron added in his piece.

During the *Unplugged* session, Pearl Jam also recorded "Oceans" and a cover of Neil Young's "Rockin' In The Free World," neither of which ever made it to air. "There just wasn't enough time for it. I mean, what song would you cut to put 'Rockin' In The Free World' in its place, that's the question," Joel surmised to Grammy.com. "We weren't going to get a full hour for such a new band, which would've been the only other option. Even Mariah Carey was still only getting a half-hour show at that point."

When Pearl Jam's episode of *MTV Unplugged* aired on May 13, 1992, it was also out of order from the actual in-studio performance. As author Ronen Givony wrote in his 2020 book, *Not For You: Pearl Jam And The Present Tense,* "the 'Unplugged' we'd been watching all these years was, in fact, a fraud." The televised version opened with "Even Flow," "Jeremy," "Alive," and "Black," while Pearl Jam' had actually played "Oceans" into "State Of Love And Trust," then "Alive," "Black," "Jeremy," "Even Flow," "Porch," and the Neil Young cover to end it. "In hindsight, it seems so obvious," Ronen added. "Of course, Pearl Jam knew better than to open with 'Even Flow' . . . or 'Jeremy' into 'Alive.'"

Fans did ultimately get to view the full, as-intended *Unplugged* performance when the band released it on YouTube in 2020. Given the COVID-19 pandemic at that time, the show provided solace and gained new significance. A year later, Pearl Jam also released the full performance on vinyl for the band's thirtieth anniversary.

But when MTV began airing Pearl Jam's *Unplugged* episode in May 1992, they never really stopped, and the band's visibility grew exponentially. The rush was helped by their first appearance on *Saturday Night Live* in April 1992 where Pearl Jam played "Porch" and "Alive," plus the kinetic video for "Even Flow" that launched the same month. But the biggest catalyst was the incredibly controversial video for "Jeremy" airing in August 1992 that had pundits on all sides talking. And then one giant 'Palooza really pushed things to the brink.

"Lightning BOLT"

In the summer of 1992, *Rolling Stone* tagged along on the Lollapalooza caravan, eventually publishing a wild exposé the following September that pondered, "Can Perry Farrell's traveling rock and roll circus change the world? Only time will tell." Thirty-some years later, time has shown that the festival not only was an experiment done right, forever changing live events in America, but was also the match that sparked Pearl Jam's explosion and helped mold them into the arena-dominating band of the future.

In the evolution of Pearl Jam, few moments stand out more than the summer of '92. And when the invitation came to play the second iteration of the emerging cultural beacon, everything the band had been doing up until that point prepared them to take the moment head on and completely run with it.

First was the fact that many of Pearl Jam's early 1992 North American dates were booked on college campuses, including Marquette University's Varsity Theatre, the Student Union Ballroom at UMass, the University of Maryland's Ritchie Coliseum, the Glenn Miller Ballroom at the University of Colorado, Legion Field at the University of Georgia, and the University of Kansas's Companile Hill, among others. Here, Pearl Jam was preaching to their choir, seeing eye-to-eye with students on the political issues, social issues, and overall disillusionment of the era.

Even back in the embryonic days of the Seattle scene, the college market was essential. KCMU, the student-run station of the University of Washington (evolving into the famous KEXP in the early 2000s) was a huge contributor. "For several years KCMU was ground central for the Seattle music scene. It was the only area radio station that regularly supported local bands, and, if its listenership was tiny, it was influential in breaking many bands," reported the *University of Washington Magazine*. "At times the station had more DJs than listeners, but it's no exaggeration to say that virtually every volunteer who had an air shift in the late '80s ended up getting a job in the music industry or playing some role in the Seattle scene." Among UW's famous alumni were the founders of Sub Pop, band manager Susan Silver, and even Soundgarden's Kim Thayil.

Into the '90s, much like the decades prior, college campuses were still also a prominent and important place to see many bands, especially emerging artists. "Many colleges and universities were then hosting one or two large concerts per year . . . sometimes catching artists on their way to explosive fame," said a report in *Marquette Today*, part of Milwaukee's Marquette University, where Pearl Jam played on March 27, 1992. One of the student organizers, Lisa Moore, remembered that date (and the fact that the seats in the theater were "a point of contention for the

OPPOSITE:
Jeff Ament onstage during a Pearl Jam gig in Rotterdam, the Netherlands on July 16, 1993.

LIGHTNING BOLT 95

Eddie Vedder crowd-surfing during Pearl Jam's appearance at the Pinkpop Festival in Landgraaf, the Netherlands on June 8, 1992.

band" since Pearl Jam didn't play sit-down venues). "They put on a hell of a show," she said. "And then it was like, three minutes later, we would have never been able to afford them."

A similar shift happened in Cleveland on April 2, when the band played a small club makeup gig (after postponing it for the Peppers/Pumpkins tour). "No one would have been surprised if Pearl Jam canceled. But the band didn't, setting up an event that those who witnessed will never forget," said a report on Cleveland.com. "The 12-song set would feature the energy and antics witnessed on now-iconic videos of Pearl Jam performing at huge festivals later that summer. Only, on this night, it was happening at a small club."

Before Lollapalooza, Pearl Jam also whet their appetite for festivals with an early summer run in Europe that saw them on the bill for Rock Am Ring in Nuremburg, Germany; In The Park in London; Go Bang! In Berlin; and the infamous Pinkpop in Landgraaf, the Netherlands, where Pearl Jam played to its largest crowd yet (fifty-five thousand) and Eddie famously cascaded a camera crane before flinging his body into the mass of people. The trek wrapped with Pearl Jam's first performance at Roskilde on June 26, a festival that would, of course, haunt them again in later years.

Just a few weeks later, Lollapalooza 1992 kicked off on July 18 and was a frenzied affair full of circus tricks, bungee jumping, the "Wheel of Safe Sex," a Cyber-bar offering "smart drinks," and an activist square, all gunning for young people's attention. Event co-founder Perry Farrell told MTV he intended it to be "a coffeehouse for the youth to discuss what's going on in their lifetimes." More like a freak show (they had the Jim Rose Circus, for chrissakes). Officially, Lollapalooza was dubbed "alternative rock's biggest roadshow," with co-founder Don Muller telling *Iowa Magazine*, "Music was exploding—that whole world was changing. It was a coming of age."

To appeal to that important demographic, Pearl Jam, along with Seattle friends Soundgarden, were two of the acts booked on the multi-day event, which at the time was still a touring operation. This was years before Lolla established roots in Chicago. The lineup offered Red Hot Chili Peppers, Ministry, Ice Cube, The Jesus and Mary Chain, and Lush. There was also a side stage offering everyone from Cypress Hill and Perry Farrell's Porno For Pyros to Rage Against The Machine and Stone Temple Pilots on varying dates. Some say it was the best lineup the festival has ever had in its thirty-some-year history. *Uproxx* said, it was the "most consequential in the festival's history." In fact, the magazine—which points out that Lolla was only supposed to happen in 1991, as a way for Jane's Addiction to bid adieu—claims the fest "endured because the sequel in 1992 was even better than the original."

Pearl Jam was booked as the second act on the bill, right after Lush, though time would prove that to be either a terrible or a great decision. As the band's star wattage grew into the spring and summer months of 1992, they could've easily played later in the day (and some found it incredibly odd the rock giants were taking the stage in daylight). Jeff told *Uproxx,* "A couple of weeks before the tour there was an opportunity for us to renegotiate, not just the money, but the time slot. But we were like, 'Nah, we don't want any added pressure to this situation.'" In hindsight, having them appear early was a boon as it brought in crowds early.

Pearl Jam (and Soundgarden) wound up on the lineup because they shared the same booking agents as Perry Farrell, who also happened to be Lolla co-founders Don Muller and Mark Geiger.

Richard Bienstock, journalist and co-author of the book *Lollapalooza: The Uncensored Story of Alternative Rock's Wildest Festival,* shared that "Don really wanted Pearl Jam on there. He knew that they were going to be a big deal. Don actually had been talking to the guys since the Mother Love Bone days, and he was originally going to sign Mother Love Bone [to his booking roster]. After all that transpired, Stone and Jeff started sending him tapes of their new band, Mookie Blaylock. And he loved it and signed Pearl Jam." Richard added that originally,

Pearl Jam during a Lollapalooza set in Scranton, Pennsylvania on August 15, 1992.

"Perry was not into it. He was not into having [Pearl Jam] there. And Don was just like, 'This is happening.'"

Perry revealed in a chat with KROQ that seeing the band live changed his opinion. "[Don] told me, there's one band I want you to see, this is my new band, please come and watch them with me. [Eddie] took a swan dive off a speaker stack like two stories high into the crowd and he won my heart."

At the time when the booking and billing of the lineup was happening, Richard estimated it would have still been 1991, so Pearl Jam "was given the slot they were deserving of at the time. . . . But it was clear right from the beginning of the summer that they had a real thing on their hands that they were gonna have to deal with."

Eddie was pumped to play Lollapalooza from the get-go. In a preview story with *SPIN*, he shared, "I'm just amazed that I went from a California surfer bum to a personality that thousands of people actually want to listen to. I plan to bring my Polaroid camera and hang out just talking to the crowd. It's like putting a finger on the pulse of what young America's doing. Pearl Jam's just a small piece of the big picture. Our participation is on a much bigger level."

He shared that sentiment again with *Rolling Stone* during their ground coverage of the '92 affair: "I'm telling you, I'm really proud to be part of this. We had a bad show yesterday, and the coolest part was realizing that it didn't fucking matter, because there was so much to do. You realize, 'Okay, so the bass guitar went out on two songs' or 'They couldn't hear my vocals—big fucking deal.' It's so much bigger than just individual bands."

Going with the flow and being in the moment paid off. Jeff Ament has said Lolla is one of Pearl Jam's fondest memories. "I don't know that we've ever had more fun on a tour," he told *Uproxx*.

The tight-knit relationship between Pearl Jam and Soundgarden—and Eddie and Chris—was growing on the Lolla trek, too, whether it was the infamous "bile beer" escapades they dragged each other into (we'll spare a rehashing of the details), or the mud charades in Ohio where the two frontmen joined the crowd and slid down soaked hills and wrestled in the wet dirt. Or just good old-fashioned jam sessions.

"There was a second stage at Lollapalooza, so Eddie and me worked up an acoustic set and got some space for the middle of the day," Chris told *SPIN*. "We got a golf cart and drove through the crowd to the stage, and it was like the Beatles. There were, like, a hundred people running and screaming and chasing the golf cart. It was the first time I realized what was happening with his band." There was another time, in Virginia, when Chris almost had to cover for Eddie in Pearl Jam's set after the singer missed his bus call the night prior and hitchhiked his way to the next venue. Eddie got to the stage just as Chris was about to belt out the first notes, and the two used the moment to launch into "Hunger Strike."

Chris Cornell performs with Soundgarden during Lollapalooza in Stanhope, New Jersey on August 12, 1992.

Many reviews of the era can't help but call out Pearl Jam's incendiary live show—and the antics of Eddie Vedder. "For many teenagers, this it not only their first Pearl Jam show but also their first experience at a rock festival, and the band's electrifying performances made a profound impression," said Pearl Jam Concert Chronology. Ticketholders clamored to get their chance to see the act that rivaled Jim Rose's Circus as a total freakshow of physics.

"The band had the entire venue bouncing along to the songs," said a reporter for the *Chicago Reader* who attended the Missouri date, recounting Eddie's leaps with great

SET LIST SPOTLIGHT

The Return to Lollapalooza
August 5, 2007, Grant Park, Chicago, IL

1. Why Go
2. Corduroy
3. Save You
4. Do The Evolution
5. Elderly Woman Behind The Counter In A Small Town
6. Severed Hand
7. Education
8. Even Flow
9. Given To Fly
10. World Wide Suicide
11. Lukin
12. Not For You
13. Daughter
14. State Of Love And Trust
15. Wasted Reprise
16. Alive

— ENCORE —

17. Better Man
18. Crazy Mary (Victoria Williams cover)
19. Life Wasted
20. Rearviewmirror

— ENCORE 2 —

21. No More (Eddie Vedder song) with Ben Harper
22. Rockin' In The Free World (Neil Young cover)

HIDDEN PEARL

The set was recorded for a live album, though the record doesn't include the performance of "No More" featuring special guest Ben Harper prefaced by a speech from an Iraq war veteran.

100 PEARL JAM LIVE!

Pearl Jam executes one of their notoriously physical performances during a Lollapalooza stop in 1992.

detail. "On the last number, Vedder, an inveterate stage diver, looked around for the best place from which to make his obligatory leap into the outstretched hands of the crowd. . . . The crowd started frothing at the mouth and clustered below Vedder in anticipation of his jump. But he didn't stop climbing; he continued to the top until he could, gingerly, reach out, grab hold, and swing himself up into the superstructure beneath the pavilion roof. . . . Vedder essentially had to do a high-wire act, walking across a surface narrow as a balance beam about half the way. Beneath him was sheer pandemonium: The crowd, to put it mildly, was going nuts; the remaining members of Pearl Jam kept blasting their way through some riff onstage; from backstage, this or that manager type kept bursting out, barking into a walkie-talkie, and disappearing. Up on the lawn, people could tell something was happening, but were a little less certain in their excitement—until Vedder, after five minutes or so, reached the back of the pavilion, poked his head out, and waved to the crowd, eliciting a roar that was probably heard in Saint Louis, about 10 miles [16 km] away. . . . That was the high point." It's been said that Eddie and Pearl Jam were banned from playing the Missouri venue for a while afterwards.

Eddie's risky antics were "a real concern," said Richard Bienstock. "The members of Pearl Jam talk about how frightened they were, and one of the guys we talked to in the book [about

LIGHTNING BOLT 101

Lollapalooza], the head rigger on the tour, had to be the one who basically followed [Eddie]. Partly just to make sure he was going to be okay. But also he had to grab the mic from him when he was trying to get down so that the mic didn't fall and become damaged because they were really expensive," Richard added. "These venue infrastructures, if you can call them that, were pretty rickety sometimes. They were putting them up and tearing them down day after day and many were nervous that [Eddie] was going to plummet to his death."

The other indirect issue Pearl Jam brought to Lolla was that it took time to get people through the ticketing entrance, and fans would snake the line waiting to get in and see the band of the moment. "Sometimes there would just be these masses of people that would start pushing toward the turnstiles trying to get in," Richard added. "It was a near riot because you had the bottleneck at the gates and then, once they got in, everybody just started stampeding down to the stage."

Rob Janicke described the pandemonium in an article recounting his Lolla '92 experience for *Generation Riff:* "Before I saw anything, I heard two sounds I'll never forget. First was the [aggressive guitar slide] intro to the song 'Even Flow' from the band's debut album, *Ten*. . . . Milliseconds after hearing that, another sound quickly emerged. I've never witnessed a real stampede of buffalo but if I had, I imagine it would sound something similar to what I heard that day in Stanhope, NJ." He added, "As Pearl Jam played the very first notes of its set, thousands of crazed, and as it turns out, very fast, fans came charging from behind us. I knew instantly that I had two choices . . . gather my stuff from the blanket and get out of the way, or leave it all behind and join these mad sprinters towards the stage. I chose to run with thousands of my newfound friends." The account adds to the belief that Pearl Jam's earliest fan community was forged at Lollapalooza.

> **Playing thirty-five dates from July to September 1992, Pearl Jam's involvement in Lollapalooza became paramount to their early success.**

"It was the biggest thing of the summer . . . that's all you were seeing on MTV, news updates from Lollapalooza," Richard said. "It was all people were talking about . . . and there was just so much attention focused on Pearl Jam in particular that summer. Not just even at the shows, but when you're watching MTV, you'd see Eddie walking around in that weird army helmet, he'd do sort of goofy MTV interviews, or was drinking the bile beer. They were just always on your TV." The band, too, could see the frenzy happening in real time, Richard said. "Being on a tour like Lollapalooza, it was very in front of their faces, they were seeing it in terms of the literal reaction of the crowds. And they were seeing it every day getting bigger and bigger and bigger."

My Pearl Jam Moment

LOLLAPALOOZA, EAST TROY, WI, 1992

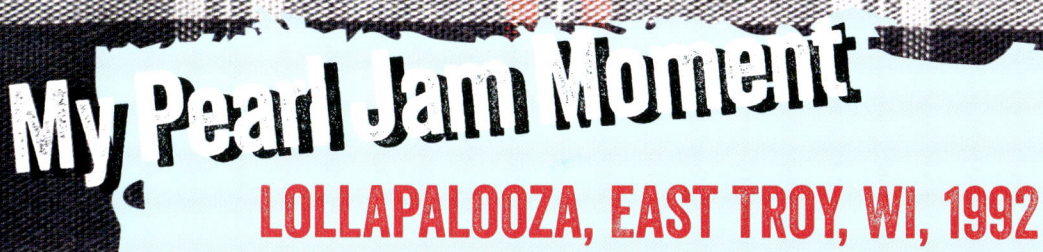

In 1992, I was a photo/film student at Columbia College Chicago and dating a girl named Angela who was studying fine art at The Art Institute. That year, we started vending at different festivals, starting with Mardi Gras in New Orleans and then, that summer, we had a small booth during Lollapalooza at the Alpine Valley show in Wisconsin.

Angela was the main talent here, and it was really her business, which sold hand-made crystal necklaces and a variety of metalwork jewelry. I, on the other hand, was mostly the driver, the assistant that made Fimo clay psychedelic mushroom necklaces and the occasional tie-dye T-shirt.

Our booth wasn't too far off from the main gate at the festival, a pretty good location in theory, but we got a little lost in the mix being located right near one of the smaller stages. One of the performers that day was the Jim Rose Circus sideshow, a modern-day version of the old carnival freak shows. During my break, I started watching the show, when a random guy walked up and we started chatting.

The act on stage at the time was Matt "The Tube" Crowley, who would invite audience members to drink bile beer from his stomach. When they asked for volunteers, the stranger said, "Hey, you want to do this with me?" I looked at him like he had two heads, he gave me a shrug, and proceeded to walk on stage. I watched in horror as he drank that nasty concoction without hesitation. It was only later, when Pearl Jam hit the stage, that I realized the stranger I was talking to was in fact their lead singer, Eddie Vedder.

—Submitted by photographer Barry Brecheisen

My Pearl Jam Moment

LOLLAPALOOZA, TINLEY PARK, IL, 1992

My unforgettable Pearl Jam moment, and it was only a moment, happened at Lollapalooza 1992 at Tinley Park's World Music Theatre.

My radio station, 93XRT, arranged for my colleague Johnny Mars and I to act as carnival barkers for some of the midway attractions. I hosted the "Safe Sex Wheel of Fortune," bringing people up to spin the wheel and land on various STDs to spread not disease but awareness.

Johnny and I also acted as emcees on the main stage, making announcements and introducing some of the bands. It was pretty cool to have All Access credentials for such a historic event. I don't think we felt the history at the time. We were just having fun.

If you look up the Lolla lineup for that year now, you'll sometimes see Pearl Jam listed at number two, right after Red Hot Chili Peppers and before Soundgarden, Ministry, The Jesus and Mary Chain, Ice Cube, and Lush. Fact is, Pearl Jam's slot was early in the afternoon, just after the first band Lush.

Their debut album, *Ten*, had been released almost exactly one year to the day, and although the album took a while to really catch on with alt-rock fans, the groundswell had been building. I remember Johnny and I camped ourselves on the side of the stage waiting for the band. Because it was so early, many pavilion ticketholders had yet to show. Far away from the stage, the lawn was totally packed already.

As Johnny and I stood there chatting about this, I saw some offstage movement. To our right, just behind the backdrop, the members of Pearl Jam were getting ready to hit the stage. They were all dressed in the Seattle Grunge uniform of the day: cargo shorts, Docs, flannels, backward baseball caps.

They formed a tight circle. You've seen the photo from *Ten*: arms raised with hands meeting at the top. It was like a huddle before the big game. A pre-show prayer perhaps. Or whatever words that psyched themselves to take the stage.

They all shouted some sort of cheer in unison, lowered their arms and stepped away to reveal what they were grouped around: a life-sized cardboard cutout image of Michael Jordan. To pump themselves up, they took inspiration from number 23. I'm not sure if the cardboard MJ traveled with the band, but in Chicago, he gave them the boost to destroy the stage that day. Eddie encouraged fans to come down from the lawn to fill the space at the front of the stage, just before they launched into "Even Flow." Those first few rows never stood a chance.

—*Submitted by Marty Lennartz, on-air personality at Chicago's WXRT*

This swell of attention was extrapolated by a few other key milestones: The provocative video for "Jeremy" debuted on August 1, 1992; *Ten* shot to No. 2 on the *Billboard* charts on August 22, 1992; and the Seattle-centric movie *Singles* hit theaters on September 18, 1992, three months after the soundtrack was released on June 30, and already became a hot commodity.

In fact, it took the explosion of grunge and Pearl Jam to finally get Warner Bros. to release the movie. As Cameron Crowe told *Rolling Stone*, "The Seattle explosion happened after we finished the movie [in May 1991]. Warner Brothers hadn't wanted to put the movie out. They didn't get it; we had to pretty much beg them to release it. And then Nirvana hit, and they said, 'Oh, OK, can we call the movie *Come As You Are*?' And we said, 'No, it's not called *Come As You Are*.' . . . And then finally I think their kids were telling them, 'You have Pearl Jam in a movie, and you're not putting the movie out?!?'" *Singles* was so influential in the long run, its concept was allegedly loosely poached by two famous TV showrunners.

Pearl Jam with filmmaker Cameron Crowe at the Toronto International Film Festival in 2011.

"I get a call from the Warner Brothers television department and they say, 'You know, we want to make a TV show out of *Singles*. We really like this idea of these young kids who live together and work in a coffee shop.' And I said, 'No. I don't want to make a TV show out of it,'" Cameron added in the *Rolling Stone* article. "[They said] 'Well, we may do it anyway.' Months and months go by and this item comes out in The Hollywood Reporter that says *Singles* is set to become a TV show, from David Crane and Marta Kaufman—the people who ended up doing *Friends*. . . . In my mind, at least, you can partially draw a line from the genesis of *Friends* to our little Seattle film." Ironically enough, "Yellow Ledbetter" is featured in the final episode of the series.

By the end of 1992, things were happening at a rapid pace as Pearl Jam helped usher in a whole cultural movement—but it wasn't necessarily the attention they asked for . . . or wanted.

LIGHTNING BOLT 105

"DISSIDENT"

Pearl Jam's career started ascending so quickly from '92 to '93 that they could barely see the horizon below them anymore—and they desperately needed to find some grounding. "Pearl Jam had been designed for a slow build. Instead, they were strapped to the rocket," Cameron Crowe shared in his 1993 *Rolling Stone* profile.

Things started to shift on June 25, 1992, when the band played Stockholm, Sweden and were victims of a callous theft. Fans found a way to break into the band's dressing room and walked away with some of Eddie's journals. "The theft weighed on him; it felt like a breach of trust, a bad omen," Cameron added. "For Vedder, it was a metaphor for the growing success of Pearl Jam." And he wanted to pump the brakes. In fact, Pearl Jam wanted to go in reverse.

In the background, there was also the situation with "Jeremy" and the reception to the music video that was casting a shadow. It was the first time Pearl Jam went out of their comfort zone to make a video that had a true concept, unlike "Alive" and "Even Flow" both taken from live footage, done in one take. "We're not actors," Eddie defiantly declared in a 1992 video interview filmed the day of the "Jeremy" shoot.

In Eddie's humble opinion, a big budget video was a total buzzkill from the music-listening experience he always held so dear. "I think that when music videos first came out it was an interesting thing. . . . Before that, you'd listen to songs with headphones on, listening in a bean bag chair with your eyes closed, and you'd come up with your own visions. And you'd see these things for the song, that came from within. . . . [Videos] rob that," he added.

For the "Jeremy" video, the direct interpretation of the song's lyrics and some unfortunate editing by MTV was a huge tipping point. While the band trusted director Mark Pellington—they were "blown away" by the Public Enemy "Shut 'Em Down" video he crafted in 1991—what was shown on MTV for the *Ten* song treatment was a bit of a bastardized version of what they all had intended, director included.

"I think Pearl Jam was very, very upset that this piece about an alienated kid who killed himself was taken to be this glorified piece about a guy who shoots his classmates," Mark told *The New Yorker*, referring to the way MTV spliced the piece to remove the image of the gun at the end. The ensuing blood spatter on the classmates made viewers infer it was a horrific mass shooting, which was not in line with the real-life story the song is based upon.

Fast forward to 2020, the band used the basis of the "Jeremy" video to push forward their hard stance on gun control in honor of National Gun Violence Awareness Day. They released the fully uncensored video for the first time, showing the actor (Trevor Wilson) placing the barrel inside his mouth. "The increase in gun violence since the debut of 'Jeremy' is staggering," the band said in

OPPOSITE:
Eddie Vedder and Jeff Ament performing in Rotterdam, the Netherlands on July 16, 1993.

Eddie Vedder arriving at the 1992 MTV VMAs in Los Angeles, California on September 9, 1992.

a press release. "We have released the uncensored version of the video which was unavailable in 1992 with TV censorship laws. We can prevent gun deaths whether mass shootings, deaths of despair, law enforcement, or accidental."

The outcome of the video back in '92 and '93 only corroborated Pearl Jam's initial instincts that scripted music videos were a roadblock for them. After "Jeremy," they refused to make another one for six years. They also tried to push back on MTV's growing requests as they started to grow untrusting of the channel.

First was at the 1992 VMAs on September 9 when Pearl Jam was insistent on scrapping a performance of "Jeremy" for a cover of the Dead Boys' "Sonic Reducer," which they had been performing live all tour. But eventually Pearl Jam buckled under the pressure and played "Jeremy" for the telecast. The very next night they got their comeuppance as the band laid siege on MTV's *Singles Premiere Party*. Apparently under some kind of influence, Pearl Jam purposely bloopered songs as Eddie tore down stage draping and scaffolding and screamed "Fuck MTV" into the cameras. He was nearly arrested and the showcase had to be heavily edited for TV.

"That was the birth of 'no,'" Stone shared in the *Pearl Jam Twenty* documentary. "It was really evident that they would just want you to do more."

MTV host Riki Rachtman remembers the pushback era well, and it arguably started even earlier, like that time he had Eddie and Mike on *Headbangers Ball* in 1991 when a distracted Eddie kept writing Fugazi on his arm in black marker. "It seemed to me that Eddie Vedder didn't want to be there. Now, I already dealt with that with Nirvana. My opinion was, if you don't want to be on *Headbangers Ball*, don't be on the *Headbangers Ball*. There's a lot of bands that do," Riki shared in an interview for this book, adding that booking Pearl Jam was not his doing. "I had nothing to do with one single video or interview on *Headbangers Ball* in my whole life. On my birthday, they said I could pick a video and it was Motorhead, which they would've played anyway."

108 PEARL JAM LIVE!

However, a sweet moment between Riki and Eddie came after they wrapped filming of the episode. "He gave me a little figurine he made that was me with a leather jacket on that said 'Cathouse' on the back and it's holding an MTV mic cube. When you turn it over, it says 'love Pearl Jam.'" Riki currently keeps it on display in a cabinet next to Dio and Motorhead memorabilia.

It's a thing Eddie would do in those very early days, as Stone told *Uncut* magazine. "We would fly [Vedder] up here [to Seattle], and on plane trips he would make little art projects on the plane, and he would give them to you. I was used to hanging out with . . . drunk, fucking, guys. You don't give each other a gift of a poem and a picture you drew. That sweetness, I don't even think I understood. Now I thank god for somebody as thoughtful and humble as that."

But back to MTV. Riki believes there's a strong rationale for not biting the hand that feeds: "People can shit on MTV as much as they want. But the truth is, as great as they are, if it wasn't for that 'Jeremy' video, they probably wouldn't have been as big as they are. It was powerful."

Pearl Jam's first true denial started with "Black," which Stone told *SPIN* was a "sore subject." Many at Epic were insistent that the band release it as the next single and Pearl Jam flat out refused. Eddie recalled in the *Rolling Stone* '93 cover story that executives told him the song was "bigger than 'Jeremy,' bigger than you or me."

"Some songs just aren't meant to be played between Hit No. 2 and Hit No. 3," he added. "You start doing those things, you'll crush it. That's not why we wrote songs. We didn't write to make hits. . . . I don't want to be a part of it. I don't think the band wants to be part of it."

Radio moved forward anyway, putting "Black" into rotation and kicking it up to No. 3 on *Billboard*'s Mainstream Rock Charts. It's said that Eddie even tried

The figurine Eddie Vedder made for MTV host Riki Rachtman.

to call radio stations to get it removed. It felt like nothing was in their control. Not even how they were perceived—either by media like *Entertainment Weekly* and *NME*, who bashed Pearl Jam's *Ten* as a rip-off of bands like Nirvana and Alice In Chains, or by bands like Nirvana (really Kurt Cobain) who thought Pearl Jam was a sellout, too.

Prominent Seattle journalist Charles R. Cross shed light on the situation for *The Seattle Times:* "They were criticized by Kurt Cobain and others as careerists, but every band in town wanted success. For some reason, the populism of Pearl Jam—writing anthemic rock, striving to be a band that gets on the radio—these were things that, in Seattle, were not the way people acted. You were supposed to play a bunch of shows nobody saw, release three or four crappy singles on alternative labels and not be a success, and THEN break through. Pearl Jam didn't follow those rules."

Yet, the ironic part is that both Nirvana *and* Pearl Jam were fighting back against the onslaught of fame—one out of principle and the latter as a defense mechanism. As *Los Angeles Times* put it, "they felt both unworthy of their fame and a bit embarrassed by it." For Pearl Jam, "no" became their go-to response.

"We turned down inaugurals, TV specials, stadium tours, every kind of merchandise you can think of," manager Kelly Curtis told *SPIN*. "I got a call from Calvin Klein, wanting Eddie to be in an ad. I learned how to say no really well. I was proud of the band, proud of their stances."

Neil Young and Pearl Jam perform onstage in Belgium on August 25, 1995.

Pearl Jam's staunchness would carry over into the making of sophomore album *Vs.*, a process in which the joy and excitement of making *Ten* turned into more pressure and a growing uneasiness. "The picture of the sheep on the cover . . . at least semi-represented how we felt at the time," Jeff, who photographed the image, has said. "As Prince would put it, we were slaves."

After winding up the 1992 tour—including a free Drop in the Park concert in Seattle (an effort to get young people registered to vote in the upcoming election), several Hawai'i dates, the band's first-ever Bridge School Benefit with Neil Young, and a New Year's Eve date opening for Keith Richards—Pearl Jam headed back into the studio in February and March 1993 to begin laying down the new album, *Vs.*

With *Vs.*, it was Pearl Jam's first time working with producer Brendan O'Brien, who would become a trusted resource in the years to come. Brendan had mixed the Temple of the Dog album and had engineered Red Hot Chili Peppers' *Blood Sugar Sex Magik,* and Pearl Jam admired his guiding hands on making those iconic records. The band first called on him to remix the "Jeremy" audio for the accompanying music video, and when it went well, they flew Brendan out to Nuremburg, Germany for a meeting to discuss helming *Ten*'s follow-up. In an interview with music figurehead Rick Beato, Brendan recalls, out of all the guys, Eddie initially gave him pushback. "On the first couple records, Eddie was hard on me, he was not easy to get next to." Sensing this, Stone joked with Brendan, "You must really want this job."

From the get-go, it was a bit of a tenuous situation making *Vs.*, at least where extraneous matters were concerned—the band didn't want to deal with hearing about interviews they had to do or be tasked with picking singles. Eddie questioned whether "Rearviewmirror" was "too catchy." In the song "Animal," they put in the loaded line about "five against one" (one being the omnipresent industry they kept fighting against) and almost made it the album title. Of course, it ended up just being abbreviated to the similarly pungent *Vs.* at the final hour. Pearl Jam also bucked the angsty rocker visage that was branded on them and included softer acoustic numbers "Daughter" and "Elderly Woman Behind The Counter In A Small Town." They didn't include "Better Man" (though it would resurface on *Vitalogy*) because it was being positioned by the powers that be as a radio hit and the band were fully shunning the idea of being seen as commercialized pawns.

"I think our band, it's a small foreign film, it's not a blockbuster American movie. It's not *Terminator 2*, you know, we never wanted to be," Eddie shared in archival video footage from 1993. Led by Eddie's resoluteness, Pearl Jam were backpedaling on anything that reeked of

Producer Brendan O'Brien and Stone Gossard onstage together at the Ohana Festival at California's Doheny State Beach on September 29, 2024.

fame and corporate manipulation. They wanted a modicum of success of course, but not all the baggage that came with it. As Cameron Crowe posited in his *Rolling Stone* profile, *Vs.* was "the band's turf statement, a personal declaration of the importance of music over idolatry." The band has also been quite explicit over the years about how they were always focused on the long haul and not crashing and burning in the beginning. They had incredible foresight on the matter, which no doubt has been a big component of their thirty-five-year longevity.

"At that point we had taken ourselves out of working with MTV . . . we were trying to control our situation to one where we felt was sustainable," Eddie told Howard Stern in a 2024 interview about his thoughts on the concept of radio hits. "Our concern was music, our concern was what was the third, or fourth, or fifth record going to sound like. Or the twelfth record. I think we were protecting even more than ourselves, I think we were trying to protect the music and our band."

After churning out "Leash" (a song they developed on tour) and early new tracks "Go," "Rats," and "Blood" for *Vs.*, Eddie was also getting thwarted by writer's block and needed to return to nature to get his bearings. This time, the crashing surf waves he once rode to write the early material of *Ten* were replaced by long hikes and sleeping in his truck near the Bay Area music studio The Site where the band worked and lived for two months.

Eddie has, over time, called *Vs.* the album he "least enjoyed" making. As he told Howard Stern in 2020, "You kind of knew there was an audience there and that's when I felt a little pressure: Could I say this or what would they think about me or think it's about me?" He added that "looking back on those times, I wish I would've handled a few things differently . . . [but] my instincts were saying this is not okay what's happening. We got in a band to be our own boss and be a gang and make our own decisions . . . it was a little hard to handle, but I think that's because we were coming at it as real people."

For *Vs.*, the band tapped into that down-to-earth approach, working on songs one by one with the full ensemble contributing each of their parts at the same time, so it became akin to the live setting—an environment where Pearl Jam has always felt most comfortable.

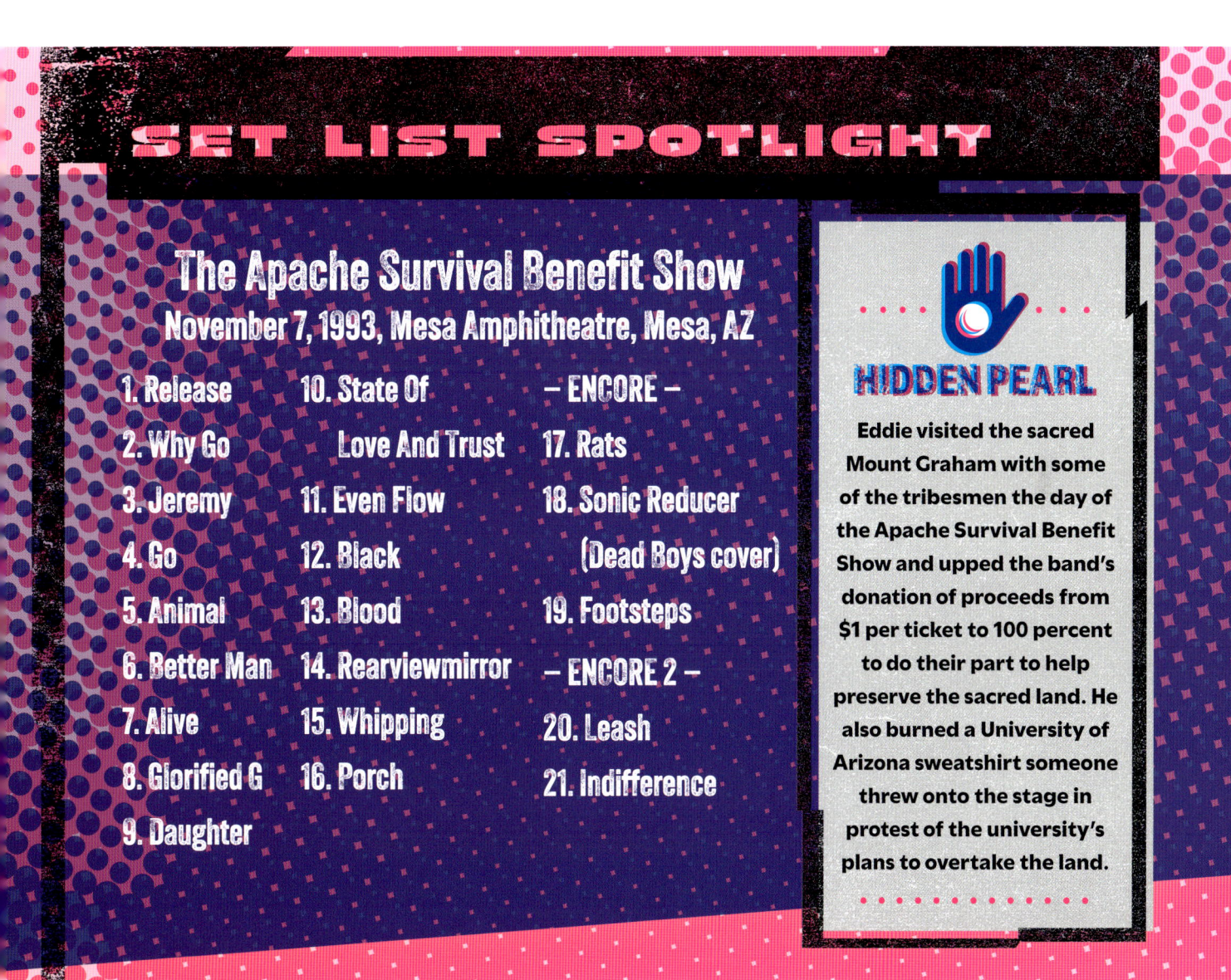

SET LIST SPOTLIGHT

The Apache Survival Benefit Show
November 7, 1993, Mesa Amphitheatre, Mesa, AZ

1. Release
2. Why Go
3. Jeremy
4. Go
5. Animal
6. Better Man
7. Alive
8. Glorified G
9. Daughter
10. State Of Love And Trust
11. Even Flow
12. Black
13. Blood
14. Rearviewmirror
15. Whipping
16. Porch

— ENCORE —

17. Rats
18. Sonic Reducer (Dead Boys cover)
19. Footsteps

— ENCORE 2 —

20. Leash
21. Indifference

HIDDEN PEARL

Eddie visited the sacred Mount Graham with some of the tribesmen the day of the Apache Survival Benefit Show and upped the band's donation of proceeds from $1 per ticket to 100 percent to do their part to help preserve the sacred land. He also burned a University of Arizona sweatshirt someone threw onto the stage in protest of the university's plans to overtake the land.

Brendan O'Brien, only thirty-one at the time, was a near contemporary of the band and found ways to keep them engaged, in spite of the volatility fomenting in the background. First, he had them meet every morning to discuss the day's agenda and then engaged the band in a game of softball as a "warm-up." Some of the songs were also written in the moment. One of them was "Go," which *Rolling Stone* reported developed around a campfire one night when drummer Dave picked up an acoustic guitar and just started strumming and organically came up with the riff. "Glorified G" also was inspired by Dave, mockingly, as a direct reaction to the others' learning the drummer had purchased two firearms; sensing disdain, Dave tried to pass them off as "glorified pellet guns." The band's strong social-political stances reared their head on other songs like "W.M.A.," about police brutality against people of color, "Daughter" about child neglect and abuse, "Dissident" about political outliers, and "Rats" about, well, the downfall of humanity.

The topics were heavy, whether symptomatic of the state of the band or the state of Eddie's mind about the world, and the comfort of the black cloud compelled fans to buy *Vs.* when it came out October 19, 1993. In the first week alone, *Vs.* sold more than 950,000 copies, which set a record at the time and unseated the previous victor, Guns N' Roses and their 1991 album *Use Your Illusion II*. *Vs.* also shot up the *Billboard* 200 chart, taking the No. 1 spot for five consecutive weeks. Eventually it would be certified 7x platinum by the RIAA® for selling seven million copies. Reviews were also positive, with *The New York Times* saying the band "broadened its music" on *Vs.* and *Rolling Stone* declaring it "topped the debut." *AllMusic* also hailed it some of the band's "best work."

The material would be nominated in three categories for the 1995 Grammy cycle, including Best Rock Album, Best Rock Performance by a Duo or Group with Vocal for "Daughter," and Best Hard Rock Performance for "Go." Pearl Jam didn't win any trophies; that would come a year later, and their reaction to the win would again show their contrarian nature.

This period of Pearl Jam was a new phase, a total blackout on media (no MTV videos, barely any interviews, no TV at all except a return to the MTV VMAs in September 1993 and *Saturday Night Live* in April 1994, shortly after the death of Kurt Cobain).

> **The band still toured during this time, of course, including a run of dates in Europe and a few in the Pacific Northwest with Neil Young in the second half of 1993 that became highly influential.**

There were also European dates opening for U2 in 1993 and two dates in Mesa, Arizona that November to benefit the San Carlos Apache, who were in a battle to preserve the sacred site Mount Graham.

Guitar World reported that Eddie spat on a fan who had been harassing him. "I just wanted you to know what it felt like . . . you know, the Indians around here have been spat on every day for 400 years," the magazine reported him as saying. Stone divulged to the reporter more about the motivation for doing the shows at a time when they truly could play just about anywhere: "We just need to stay sane and balanced, and that means doing things that feel right to us, not what the media or whatever expects or demands."

Mike McCready and Eddie Vedder with Neil Young at the 24th Annual Bridge School Benefit Concert in Mountain View, California on October 23, 2010.

By the time 1994 rolled around, Pearl Jam was on an all-out rampage against "the man" when it came to their music and their shows. The band demanded huge chunks of tickets to be set aside for students at various stops along the way, and at the AT&T Amphitheatre in Miami on March 28, 1994, the band "wanted to maintain its no-corporate-sponsorship policy and, at the 11th hour, refused to play unless the AT&T logos around the amphitheater were covered up," according to Pearl Jam Concert Chronology.

The fan site also noted that "Not For You" had a special dedication that night: namely, to "all those fuckers who were charging more than $18 for your fucking ticket." In less than two months' time, this would become the hill Pearl Jam proverbially was prepared to die on. They demanded their summer 1994 concert be priced at no more than $18 a pop, a way to bring music directly to the fans at a price that was equitable and would also prevent scalpers and corporate profits. When there was pushback, the band kept up their dukes and attempted to take on the biggest music corporation of all: Ticketmaster.

DISSIDENT

My Pearl Jam Moment

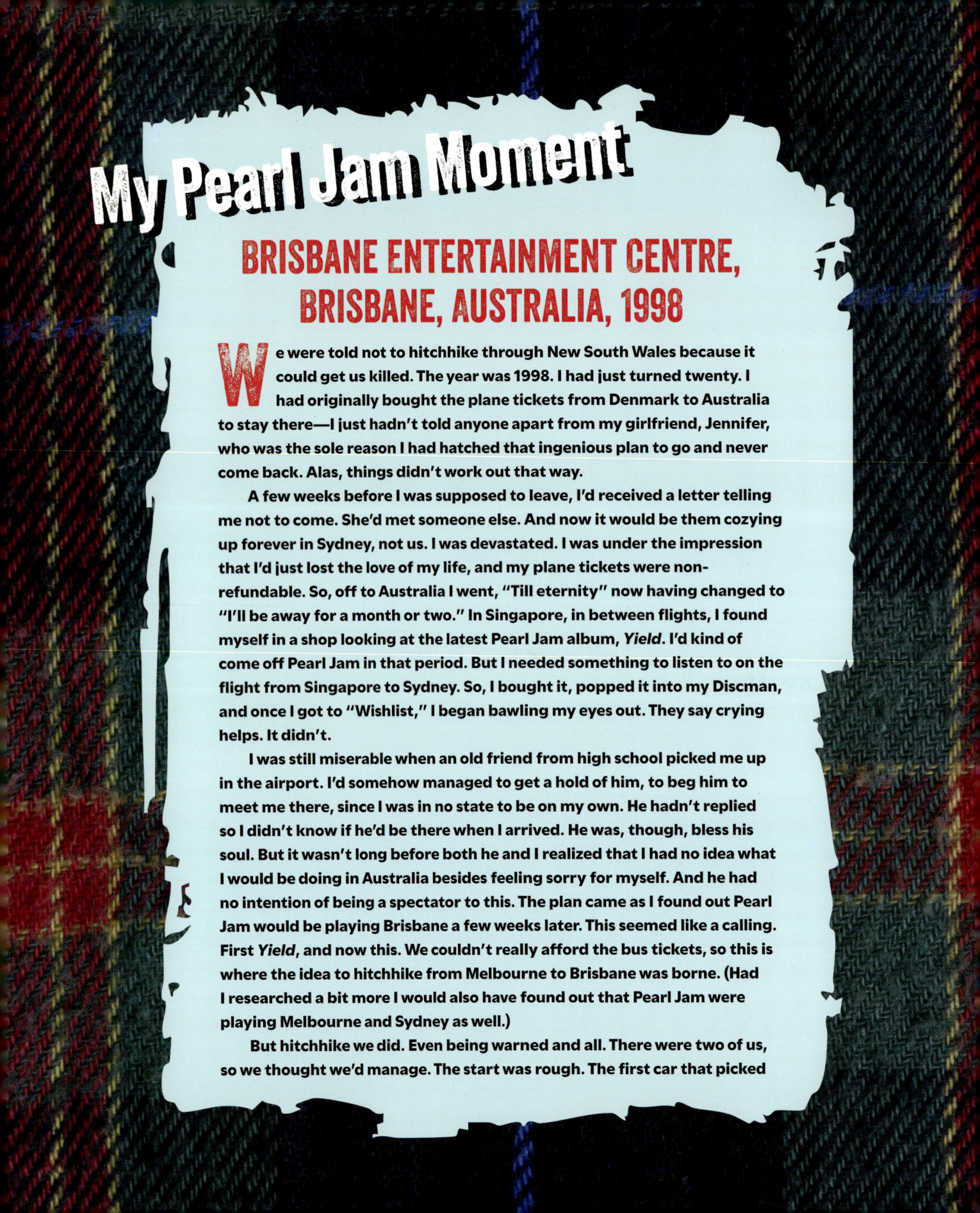

BRISBANE ENTERTAINMENT CENTRE, BRISBANE, AUSTRALIA, 1998

We were told not to hitchhike through New South Wales because it could get us killed. The year was 1998. I had just turned twenty. I had originally bought the plane tickets from Denmark to Australia to stay there—I just hadn't told anyone apart from my girlfriend, Jennifer, who was the sole reason I had hatched that ingenious plan to go and never come back. Alas, things didn't work out that way.

A few weeks before I was supposed to leave, I'd received a letter telling me not to come. She'd met someone else. And now it would be them cozying up forever in Sydney, not us. I was devastated. I was under the impression that I'd just lost the love of my life, and my plane tickets were non-refundable. So, off to Australia I went, "Till eternity" now having changed to "I'll be away for a month or two." In Singapore, in between flights, I found myself in a shop looking at the latest Pearl Jam album, *Yield*. I'd kind of come off Pearl Jam in that period. But I needed something to listen to on the flight from Singapore to Sydney. So, I bought it, popped it into my Discman, and once I got to "Wishlist," I began bawling my eyes out. They say crying helps. It didn't.

I was still miserable when an old friend from high school picked me up in the airport. I'd somehow managed to get a hold of him, to beg him to meet me there, since I was in no state to be on my own. He hadn't replied so I didn't know if he'd be there when I arrived. He was, though, bless his soul. But it wasn't long before both he and I realized that I had no idea what I would be doing in Australia besides feeling sorry for myself. And he had no intention of being a spectator to this. The plan came as I found out Pearl Jam would be playing Brisbane a few weeks later. This seemed like a calling. First *Yield*, and now this. We couldn't really afford the bus tickets, so this is where the idea to hitchhike from Melbourne to Brisbane was borne. (Had I researched a bit more I would also have found out that Pearl Jam were playing Melbourne and Sydney as well.)

But hitchhike we did. Even being warned and all. There were two of us, so we thought we'd manage. The start was rough. The first car that picked us up was going in the wrong direction and made a U-turn on a heavily trafficked road, brakes screeching, to get us in the car, and drove us thirty minutes at the speed of light, while shouting about how busy he was. He kicked us off at the roadside just outside Melbourne, before speeding off again. But before we had a chance to question the sanity of this whole hitchhiking endeavor, another car stopped. It was a man going to see his mother somewhere close to Sydney. He could easily take us along. Only caveat, we needed to take a detour, two hours in the wrong direction for all of us, to taste the best meat pies in Australia. This of course could also be an invitation to Serial Killer town. The pies were good. Perhaps not "two hours in the wrong direction and two hours back" good, but maybe this man just really did not want to go see his mum. He dropped us off halfway to Newcastle.

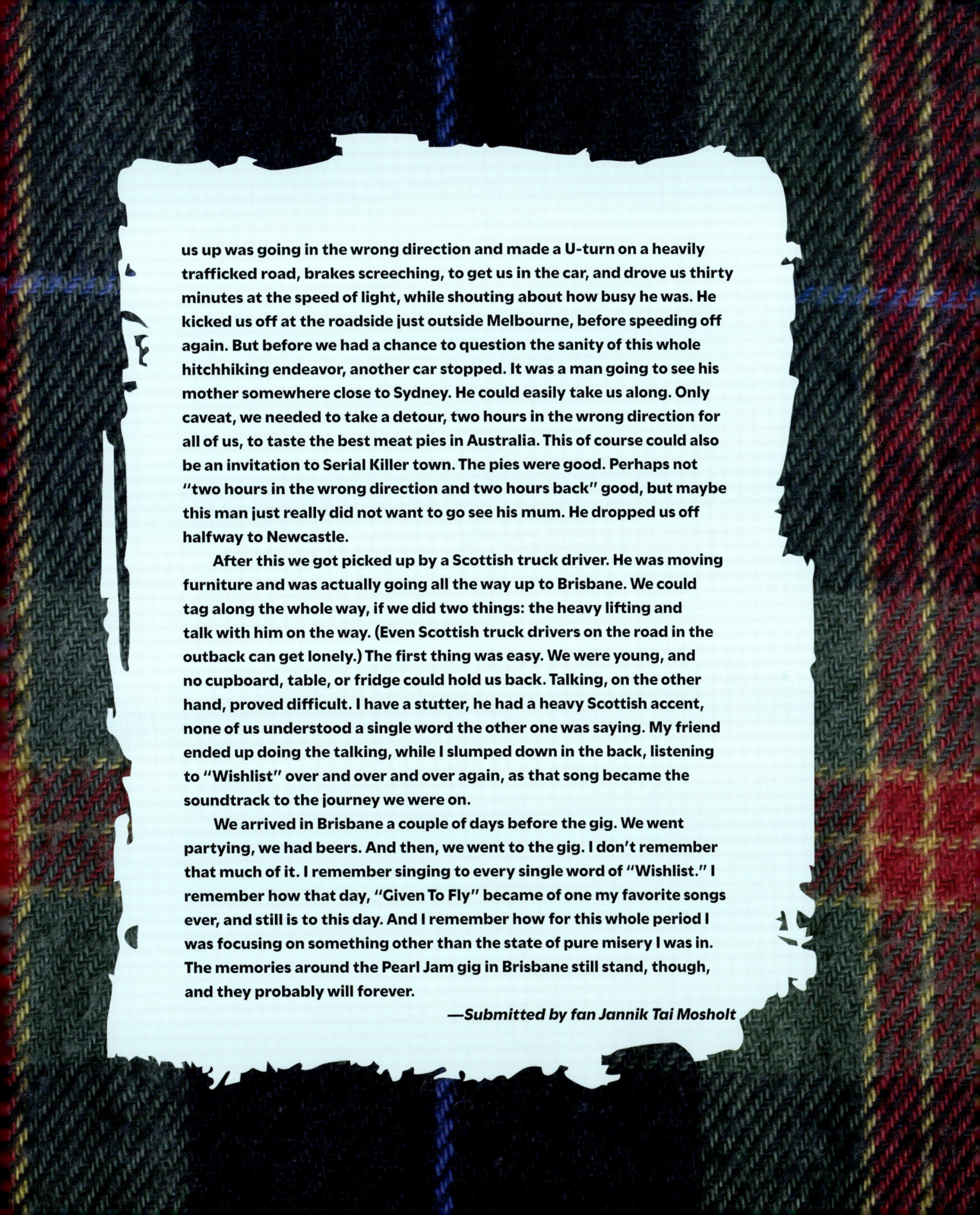

After this we got picked up by a Scottish truck driver. He was moving furniture and was actually going all the way up to Brisbane. We could tag along the whole way, if we did two things: the heavy lifting and talk with him on the way. (Even Scottish truck drivers on the road in the outback can get lonely.) The first thing was easy. We were young, and no cupboard, table, or fridge could hold us back. Talking, on the other hand, proved difficult. I have a stutter, he had a heavy Scottish accent, none of us understood a single word the other one was saying. My friend ended up doing the talking, while I slumped down in the back, listening to "Wishlist" over and over and over again, as that song became the soundtrack to the journey we were on.

We arrived in Brisbane a couple of days before the gig. We went partying, we had beers. And then, we went to the gig. I don't remember that much of it. I remember singing to every single word of "Wishlist." I remember how that day, "Given To Fly" became of one my favorite songs ever, and still is to this day. And I remember how for this whole period I was focusing on something other than the state of pure misery I was in. The memories around the Pearl Jam gig in Brisbane still stand, though, and they probably will forever.

—*Submitted by fan Jannik Tai Mosholt*

"Not For YOU"

On May 6, 1994, it was war. One of the biggest rock bands of the era was taking on one of the biggest giants in the music industry, and the ongoing tit for tat was better than most pay-per-view specials. With the lodging of a formal complaint with the US Justice Department on that date in May, the unprecedented battle of Pearl Jam vs. Ticketmaster took off, eventually bringing two of the band members to Capitol Hill to present their case.

OPPOSITE:
Eddie Vedder onstage at Neil Young's annual Bridge School Benefit concert in Mountain View, California, October 1994.

At the heart of the debate, reported the *Los Angeles Times*'s Chuck Phillips, who covered the case in many articles, was the band's belief that Ticketmaster "exercises a national monopoly over ticket distribution and used its influence with promoters to boycott Pearl Jam's planned low-priced tour this summer."

Pearl Jam had wanted any venues they played on the planned summer trek to meet three conditions: One, to lower their concert prices to a below-standard fee of just $18 per ticket (well below the market rate of $30-plus). Two, to ensure service fees were relegated to a $1.80 maximum and that the fee amount was clearly represented on the ticket. And three, to have Ticketmaster abstain from adding any additional promotions to the face or backside of the paper ticket.

On the previous *Vs.* tour run, from October 1993 to April 1994, Pearl Jam had charged $18 a ticket and wanted to keep that price point in place. And even though they were not successful in lowering ticket fees, they tried to keep merch prices down and asked venues to accept a smaller commission to do so. *Seattle Weekly* reported that the band lost an estimated $2 million in revenue from that decision. But it was never about the money for Pearl Jam.

"We swore when we formed this band that if we ever got successful, we would make sure we did something to keep our concert prices down," Stone told reporter Chuck Phillips, and Pearl Jam kept to their word, becoming vanguards in the fight against corporate greed.

The animosity between Pearl Jam and Ticketmaster had been brewing well before it came to a head in the courts. The first strike came in September 1992, when Pearl Jam staged a free show called Drop in the Park in their hometown of Seattle to express their gratitude for the people and place that had helped them become a massive act in the American music scene. The event was also a vehicle to encourage the crowd of thirty thousand that arrived at Magnuson Park to register to vote, with the 1992 presidential election just a couple of months away.

> **Upon finding out that Ticketmaster was going to charge a $1 service fee per ticket for the gratis event, the band was incensed and found a way to work around the company to get fans into the gig.**

NOT FOR YOU

Kurt Cobain onstage with Nirvana in Modena, Italy on February 21, 1994.

A large point of contention developed with scheduled charity shows in Chicago in March 1994, when Pearl Jam again realized Ticketmaster had "slipped in" extra service fees. There were also disagreements over agreed-upon charitable donations from proceeds of Pearl Jam ticket sales. But the biggest blow came when the band alleged that Ticketmaster used its influence in the marketplace and coordination with a lion's share of venues (they controlled "at least 90 percent of the American ticket market," said *Seattle Weekly*) to effectively get their summer 1994 tour boycotted.

In essence, internal notes revealed that Ticketmaster threatened lawsuits against any venues that didn't abide by the "exclusive agreements" they had with the ticketing company. Feeling bullied into complicity, Pearl Jam started looking into their options, hoping to explore other ways to distribute tickets and offer more choice in the marketplace. *Seattle Weekly* reported the band "started out with a New York concert for which it sold tickets through radio stations, and a Detroit-area concert where it sold tickets through a lottery." For the Detroit venue, Ticketmaster went as far as to shut off ticketing machines to impede distribution.

Pearl Jam also attempted to go rogue for the summer 1994 tour and build their own sites on open land or at independent outdoor venues not linked with Ticketmaster. But with little time to do things right, that plan brought liabilities for the health and safety of fans and the band, not to mention how time-consuming the effort was. To further complicate matters, Kurt Cobain died by suicide on April 8, 1994, at the same time Pearl Jam was embroiled in the Ticketmaster melee.

"Kurt died right at the point when Pearl Jam was encountering all these complications with putting together the tour," manager Kelly Curtis told the *Los Angeles Times*. "Coupled with everything else that was going on, it just about knocked the wind out of the band." With all the extraneous factors at play, and the negativity looming over the touring scenario, Pearl Jam eventually killed the idea of a DIY summer tour. They attempted it again in 1995 with a run of dates to promote *Vitalogy*, only partnering with non-Ticketmaster entities in their quest to make concerts more equitable and playing some bizarre locales like ski resorts and fairgrounds.

Keeping up the practice became a huge challenge in the long haul and, after more canceled dates in 1995 (due to exhaustion and illness) and focusing on international touring in the ensuing years, eventually Pearl Jam was forced to resume their working relationship with Ticketmaster in the United States, beginning in 1998.

"It was getting in the way of making music and playing live shows," Eddie told *Classic Rock*. "When we tried to do the tour all on our own, we spent more time on where to put the portaloos than when it came to the set list. You couldn't think straight for j-link fences and barricades and safety issues and how many roads in, how many roads out, parking." There was also the issue of counterfeit tickets to contend with. As Eddie added, "We had to bring the focus back to music and playing."

But not before they had their words in court. *Rolling Stone* reported that, at the prompting of the Department of Justice, Pearl Jam filed the legal complaint in May 1994 to spawn a federal investigation. Part of the claim, per a report in *SPIN* magazine, purported that "the company's 1991 buyout of Ticketron resulted in a Ticketmaster monopoly over ticket distribution in the country's arenas and stadiums." Ticketmaster CEO Fred Rosen, through a spokesperson, claimed the move was a smoke and mirrors show that allowed Pearl Jam to effectively promote their upcoming new album (*Vitalogy*) by getting their name in the press.

On June 30, 1994, Stone and Jeff headed to Capitol Hill to appear before the House subcommittee on Information, Justice, Transportation, and Agriculture. They were joined in the effort by managers and representatives for additional bands like Aerosmith and R.E.M. During the hearing, the Pearl Jam members also said that Garth Brooks, Neil Young, and the Grateful Dead had voiced their support of taking Ticketmaster to task, though Pearl Jam was the most forthright in the battle, continuing the fight in the months and years after most bands gave up and resumed working with the ticketing company.

SET LIST SPOTLIGHT

The Day Kurt Died
April 8, 1994, Patriot Center, Fairfax, VA

1. Release
2. Go
3. Animal
4. Dissident
5. Why Go
6. Deep
7. Jeremy
8. Daughter
9. Even Flow
10. Breath
11. State Of Love And Trust
12. Footsteps
13. Black
14. Alive
15. Porch

— ENCORE 1 —

16. Rearviewmirror
17. Corduroy
18. Not For You
19. Elderly Woman Behind The Counter In A Small Town

— ENCORE 2 —

20. Blood
21. Indifference

— ENCORE 3 —

22. Rockin' In The Free World (Neil Young cover)

HIDDEN PEARL

Right before "Porch," Eddie shared some words about Kurt Cobain's passing, saying in part, "Sometimes, whether you like it or not, people elevate you, you know . . . It's real easy to fall . . . but I don't think any of us would be in this room tonight if it weren't for Kurt Cobain."

"All the members of Pearl Jam remember what it's like to be young and not have a lot of money. Many Pearl Jam fans are teenagers who do not have the money to pay $30 or more that's often charged for tickets today," Stone said in his sworn testimony, which was widely aired on news networks and MTV. "It is well known in our industry that some portion of service charges Ticketmaster collects on its sale of tickets is distributed back to the promoters and the venues. It is this incestuous relationship and the lack of any national competition for Ticketmaster that has created the situation we are dealing with today."

He added, "As a result, our band, which is concerned about trying to keep the price of its tickets low, will almost always be in conflict with Ticketmaster."

Ticketmaster CEO Fred Rosen also appeared on Capitol Hill that day, to assert that the company was trying to compromise with Pearl Jam (reducing service fees to around $2.50 rather than the $4–$8 they normally charged per ticket, though still not hitting the $1.80 mark Pearl Jam requested) and to claim the ticketing company made "pennies on the dollar" in revenue from those fees.

Jeff Ament and Stone Gossard appear on Capitol Hill in Washington, DC to testify before a House Government Operations subcommittee on June 30, 1994.

NOT FOR YOU

R.E.M., who also took up the fight against Ticketmaster, make an appearance at the MTV VMAs in New York City on September 8, 1994.

Although several representatives on the House committee reacted favorably to Pearl Jam's point of view, and fans championed the band's protective nature, ultimately the case was dropped in July. Said *SPIN*, "Analysts believe that because venue owners and promoters willingly entered into the exclusive contracts, the Justice Department had no choice but to clear Ticketmaster." Jeff would later say that he felt "the Department of Justice used us to look hip. Stone and I spent a week with our lawyer, John Hoyt; he was drilling us with serious questions that we were [supposedly] going to get asked, and then it didn't feel like we got to utilize any of it. It made me a lot more cynical about what goes on with the government."

Of course, years later, Taylor Swift and her legion of Swifties attempted to bring down Ticketmaster again in November 2022 with similar allegations of a monopoly and unfair ticketing practices. It came after a disastrous on-sale event for her Eras Tour in which fans were left scrambling after being locked out of the site or frozen in a queue, only to find that scalpers had secured tickets and already reposted them for sale at exorbitant prices. The Department of Justice again became involved as several Congresspeople pushed for a look at the tenets of the merger between Ticketmaster and Live Nation in 2010 and how it may be negatively affecting consumers. As of publication, the issue is ongoing. But when news broke of the Swifties' swift action against the ticketing company, many couldn't help but remember when Pearl Jam did it first.

My Pearl Jam Moment

RANDALL'S ISLAND, NEW YORK, NY, 1996

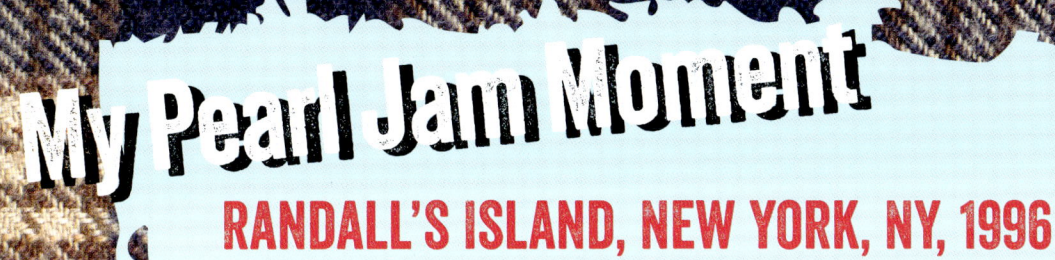

September 29, 1996. It's a Sunday, and I'm a naive teenager dropped off in the open fields and parking lots of Randall's Island in New York at 11 a.m. Seeing Pearl Jam for the first time, just one month after the release of *No Code*, it was also my first true live music experience. I felt everything.

After waiting for the gates (aka ropes) to open, we made it to the front of the pit where we would wait another four hours. I don't recall a drop of food, and the only hydration was from shared water hoses, thanks to security. It was all adrenaline.

The Fastbacks and Ben Harper set the night off beautifully. There was something about the skyline at Randall's Island that evening that blanketed the space like nothing else I have ever seen. Even though the pit got rough, and us kids had to be taken out before Pearl Jam started, there was still a campfire serenity to the atmosphere.

Just prior to that, there was an overwhelming roar—when the band first took the stage—that would ultimately have an everlasting impact on me. Someone flicked the switch and just like that the lights were down. I have always loved how Pearl Jam ascends in the dark, and often rolls right into the opening song.

Seattle had seemed like a place so far away. Then, a cross-country wave came to glide us toward each other, all over the common bond of music.

A gentle opening of "Sometimes" would be the first Pearl Jam song I ever saw live. An astounding thirty-one additional songs would follow, creating an evening that still holds a strong place in the history of this legendary touring band.

Perhaps Eddie Vedder felt the same rock 'n' roll campfire vibes, because during an epic "Porch" speech, he lit a cork and used the ashes to complement the emotion of his words.

This first Pearl Jam concert included one other most-special component: My cousin, compadre, and tour-mate! Over the past twenty-eight years, we've gone on to see forty-three additional PJ shows together across North America. We've met people from all over the world. Together, we sing our lungs out 'til the sound fills the room.

In fact, we just had the chance to do this again, two months ago in Boston. Coincidentally, there was something about these shows (the moon!) that reminded me of how that first 1996 show felt—where we all walked away with a piece of the glowing embers still lit inside of us.

I recall that Eddie said in 1996, "Still here from last night?" prior to launching into "Sometimes." And in many ways standing among the waves of Ten Clubbers at Fenway in 2024, it felt like the appropriate time to answer that question with a resounding "yes!"

—*Submitted by Jeff Gorra, founder of Artist Waves*

29

"Force of NATURE"

For a time in the early '90s, Eddie wore a helmet. "I went through this fucking yearlong period where I wore helmets all the time. It was like army helmets that I'd find . . . It was this kind of analogy, like I need a helmet," he told *Rolling Stone*'s Brian Hiatt. There's plenty of photo evidence (it started sometime during Lollapalooza), and some hysterical stories like the time Eddie was sleeping in the combat gear in his hotel room, got locked out, and had to wait shirtless in a long line at the front desk looking like "Tarzan goes to Vietnam."

Eddie truly was in battle mode, and the helmet was symbolic of not only fighting against the system but also defending himself against fame.

"For Eddie, it must have been hell, because he could not do a thing," Kelly Curtis told *SPIN*. "He had crazy stalkers, people threatening to kill themselves, set his house on fire. It made him miserable."

The godliness really picked up after Kurt Cobain died in April 1994. "When I first found out, I was in a hotel room in Washington, DC, and I just tore the place to shreds," Eddie told *Los Angeles Times* just a few weeks later. "Then I just kind of sat in the rubble, which somehow felt right . . . like my world at the moment."

> **Pearl Jam barely had a moment to process the loss and the tragic way in which Kurt Cobain left the world. The day his body was found, Pearl Jam still went on with their planned show in Virginia.**

The next day they visited the White House and took a meeting with President Bill Clinton, who asked the band's opinion on whether he should offer a national address about the Nirvana frontman and the topic of suicide. Eddie swayed him not to, fearing fans were still too fragile. Two days later, they were doing a three-night stand in Boston, and within another few days, they had to try to put on a brave face to play *Saturday Night Live*.

If Eddie wasn't already feeling the suffocating pressures as a frontman branded like a Christ-like savior for a generation of lost disciples, he sure was now. Eddie struggled with—if not also resented—the position, especially as the one member in Pearl Jam who was automatically relegated to it.

Eddie also, frankly, didn't understand it. He was flawed just like everyone else, and not the person to hitch ideals to. "People think you are this grand person who has all their shit together because you are able to put your feelings into some songs," he told *Los Angeles Times*. "They write letters and come to the shows and even to the house, hoping we can fix everything

OPPOSITE:
Eddie Vedder in his signature helmet during the MTV VMAs in Los Angeles, California, September 9, 1992.

for them. But we can't . . . because we don't have all our shit together either. What they don't understand is that you can't save somebody from drowning if you're treading water yourself."

Pearl Jam never planned for *Ten* and *Vs.* to be the manifestos for a downtrodden generation. Yet, young fans toiling in their own discontent found comfort in them all the same. "There's a feeling of burnout in the culture at large," author Simon Reynolds said in his book *Blissed Out* about youth in the '90s. "Kids are depressed about the future."

In the music time continuum, grunge came after riotous punk and ahead of basket case emo and borrowed or fostered tentacles of each. It was anti-establishment yet also unabashedly emotional, and it was just what scores of young people needed to hear when pop music's unattainable standards fell flat and hair metal's Aqua Net started to lose its grip. Though Riki Rachtman, for one, is a firm believer that grunge acts didn't kill metal, as they are often dogged as being responsible for.

"[Metal] bands that had a small window of opportunity died. . . . There's no way they could have lasted forever," he asserted. "But here's what nobody has figured out and I don't know why nobody has come up with this conclusion. If something is killed by something else, it means that it was stronger and more powerful. So to say grunge killed metal? That's not the music's fault. It's the fans. And heavy metal has always been strong. Slayer never stopped playing. Megadeth never stopped playing. How come nobody says that grunge killed Megadeth? How come nobody says grunge killed Metallica? . . . Things always change. And it was just time until another form of rock 'n' roll came in."

When Nirvana's "Smells Like Teen Spirit" came out of the gates in 1991, it was like a bat signal to young people—and a megaphone for all they had been saying. And as interest grew, and record sales accumulated, it became a free-for-all as bands and brands tried to capitalize on the "the next big thing."

"The most trouble I ever got into on MTV was in 1995 when we had Stone Temple Pilots on, and I thought that Stone Temple Pilots were trying to rip off Eddie Vedder and Pearl Jam," Riki Rachtman remembered. "And I said it, and it was not long after that I had to call [Scott] Weiland and apologize. And it was not long after that that I was fired."

Everything was a total knee-jerk reaction at that time. And there was a suffocating amount of exposure. In a study for Tarleton State University, author Paul Edgerton Stafford covered the media feeding frenzy and found that "from 1992 through 1994, grunge bands were mentioned or featured on the cover of *Rolling Stone* 33 times."

As a result, the movement lost some of its innocence and purity, with greedy parties not totally understanding what "grunge" was or who it was for. When Marc Jacobs designed a "grunge line" for high-end fashion house Perry Ellis's spring 1993 collection, did the label really think kids who liked Nirvana and Pearl Jam would want, or could afford, $500 flannels? Kurt Cobain was the literal mascot of dustbin thrift stores. The collection tanked and the designer was fired.

When *The New York Times* posted the ridiculous "Grunge: A Success Story" article in November 1992, did editors really think Gen X would read it? If they did, they laughed at it, especially the "grunge vocabulary" at the end of the piece, which was submitted as a joke by Megan Jasper, a twenty-five-year-old who worked for Sub Pop. No, "Swingin' On The Flippity-Flop" did not mean "Hanging Out."

When Andy Rooney broadcast his incredibly tone-deaf *60 Minutes* piece after Kurt's death in April 1994, did he think young people would agree with

Nirvana's Kurt Cobain, Dave Grohl, and Krist Novoselic onstage circa 1993.

Kurt Cobain at the Rock For Choice Benefit at the Palace Theater in Hollywood, California on October 25, 1991.

him? "A lot of people would like to have the years left that he threw away," Andy said in part. "What's all this nonsense about how terrible life is? . . . What would all these young people be doing if they had real problems like a Depression, World War II, or Vietnam?" In today's speak, that would be met with a hearty, "Okay, Boomer."

Whether diminishing young people's pain or trying to capitalize on it, the motivations were as transparent as the holes in jeans that the elders made so much fun of. And the more they pushed the topic in a disingenuous way, the more young people clung to the auteurs they knew understood them: namely, Eddie and Kurt. But, the two came at the position very differently, and it often resulted in the pair being pitted against each other in the media. What makes better headlines than a rivalry?

"I think that any of our comments, or any of Nirvana's comments, were probably based on being asked over and over about each other," Jeff told *Uncut* magazine. Kurt hated being in the same conversations as Pearl Jam. As *Los Angeles Times* summarized, Kurt "often ridiculed [Pearl Jam], arguing that [the band] lacked the underground purity of Nirvana—that it was simply an old-line commercial rock band in grunge clothing." Kurt even once called Pearl Jam "corporate puppets that are just trying to jump on the alternative bandwagon."

It was a difference in ethos, for sure. But was it personal? Probably not. There was that moment at the 1992 VMAs when Kurt and Eddie are seen in a slow dance underneath the stage. Around that time, Kurt also declared to a reporter, "I'm not going to do that anymore," regarding panning Pearl Jam. "It hurts Eddie and he's a good guy."

Both frontmen also found common ground in their mutual agreement that neither Pearl Jam nor Nirvana would participate in a planned *TIME* magazine feature for late 1993. "I didn't see being on the cover of *TIME* as an accomplishment for the band," Eddie told *Los Angeles Times*. "I was afraid it might be a nail in the coffin." *TIME* did it anyway.

"All The Rage," read the cover, next to a photo of Eddie bellowing into a microphone. "Angry young rockers like Pearl Jam give voice to the passions and fears of a generation," was the subhead. Inside the pages of the magazine, the writer, Christopher John Farley, declared Eddie was "rock's newest demigod" and yet criticized the reactions to the crossroads that grunge music found itself at in 1993 when dealt with the fame card.

In a chat with *American Songwriter*, Christopher John Farley claimed both Kurt and Eddie "wanted the attention, and didn't want to have the

Eddie Vedder onstage at the Chicago Stadium in Chicago, Illinois on March 10, 1994.

FORCE OF NATURE 131

attention. They didn't want to be seen as selling out," adding, "Back then, part of the power of *TIME* was synthesizing the cultural moment and reducing it to a single face. I wanted the face to be Nirvana, but their handlers had played a little bit coy as to whether they would talk to me."

It was a slimy move by *TIME* and one that only disenfranchised Eddie further from the spotlight. "Maybe I wasn't ready for attention to be placed on me, you know?" he told *SPIN*. "I never knew that someone could put you on the cover of a magazine without asking you, that they could sell magazines and make money and you didn't have a copyright on your face or something."

Eddie sought solace and advice from those who had been there before him, asking tour mates like Henry Rollins and Bono and idols like Pete Townshend (who he finally met in 1993) for any guidance on how to handle the situation.

"I just said to him, 'Drink your carrot juice, breathe deep, have fun, and don't do what you don't want to,'" Henry Rollins told *Rolling Stone* regarding his advice to Eddie.

"Anyone in their right mind would do [what Pearl Jam have done]; this is actually how to have a life, how to keep your dignity," Bono recounted to *SPIN*. Pete Townshend recalled, "I spent an hour with him. . . . I can't remember what I said. Probably something about just accepting who he

Eddie Vedder and Pete Townshend perform together in a benefit show at the House of Blues in Chicago, Illinois on July 29, 1999.

obviously was—a new rock star. I think maybe he could see the new rock 'n' roll rules of his life being rewritten, and he didn't like them."

Still, even with the support of music elite, Kurt's biting words and the unrelenting spotlight seeped through the cracks and into the psyches of Pearl Jam members. "I think [Kurt] raised our bar. By him being critical of us, I think we said, 'Well, that's what he says about us—what are we going to do?'" Stone shared with *Uncut*, conceding, "I think we made tougher records, and I think we thought about everything in the light of 'Are we doing this because we like it? Or are we doing it because we're sellouts?'"

As Pearl Jam went into the studio for *Vs.* in early 1993 and then for *Vitalogy* soon after in early 1994, that mindset was heavy. But not everyone was on the same page. Dave Abbruzzese wanted to go big with opportunities or go home. Even Mike McCready was questioning the abrupt halt with media and exposure. "The idea of pulling back at the height of our popularity was not exciting to me at the time," Mike told *The Daily Record*. "I wanted to continue to ride it and play the game, to do videos and go on tour, not throw away this great opportunity." Yet, in hindsight, it was for the best that it all transpired the way it did. "That's probably 90 percent of the reason that we're still a band," Jeff told *Uncut*.

Still, when the *Vitalogy* sessions started to take shape, it wasn't exactly a happy period. "It was the most stressful and unnerving time," Stone told *SPIN*. "I was going out of my mind. The band has never been more successful, but we can't all be in a room together." Returning producer Brendan O'Brien added, "*Vitalogy* was a little strained. I'm being polite—there was some imploding going on."

The band, in fact, almost broke up. The tensions led Mike to spiral with drugs and alcohol, the guitarist eventually checking himself into rehab ahead of the release. Stone considered walking. Eddie and Dave flat out stopped speaking to each other. Jeff focused his energy on art. And Eddie was keen to control everything, from song selection to tempos to signing himself up as the third guitarist. The frontman tried to explain his rationale to Cameron Crowe later on: "To be honest, I think that I felt that anything we put out was highly representative of me and because I was kind of becoming the most recognizable guy in the group, I needed to be more represented musically. And if that meant me creating the songs that were going to accomplish that, then I had to do it."

> ***Vitalogy*** **was a true road record, created along tour stops during late 1993 into 1994, before Pearl Jam canceled that planned summer tour.**

Sessions started at Kingsway Studio in New Orleans and ended at the famed Bad Animals in Seattle with stops at Atlanta's Southern Tracks, in Brendan O'Brien's hometown. "They were on the road so I just followed them around," Brendan told Rick Beato. In fact, "Better Man" was recorded live at the Fox Theater in Atlanta over two show days: April 2 and 3, 1994. The drums, bass, and Mike's guitar playing were all taken from those live recordings, according to Brendan. The producer also claimed in the interview that the song's psychedelic guitar intro was planned for another track (he didn't divulge which one), but it was added to "Better Man" in an effort to make it less 'poppy' and appease Eddie's qualms.

In many ways, *Vitalogy* was more experimental for the band, as they added in elements of punk ("Spin The Black Circle," "Satan's Bed," "Whipping"), funk ("Pry, To"), slow burners ("Nothingman"), and the avant garde ("Bugs").

Song topics also ranged in tone, from continuing to rail against the system on "Not For You" and "Corduroy," to devastating breakups on "Nothingman," a love ode to vinyl on "Spin The Black Circle," and a debilitating case of poison oak on "Bugs." (The band wouldn't play the latter live for fifteen years, until 2009 on a whim at a Halloween show.)

There are some other interesting departures on *Vitalogy:* One, there were no showboating guitar solos (which may have been as much about Mike's struggles at the time as it was Eddie taking over the reins) and there were three drummers. During sessions for "Satan's Bed," Dave was having his tonsils removed and his tech Jimmy Shoaf filled in and got the credit. One of the final songs to be recorded, "Hey Foxymophandlemama, That's Me" also features Jack Irons, Dave's replacement on the kit, who came in near the completion of the album.

It's been said that *Vitalogy* was ready to go in the first half of 1994 but was delayed due to the band's feud with Ticketmaster. But when it was released on November 22, 1994, demand helped it move units. *Vitalogy* sold 877,000 copies in its initial seven days on the market and became the second-fastest selling album of all time, second only to *Vs*. It reached No. 1 on the *Billboard 200* chart by December and would go on to be certified 5x platinum by the RIAA® for sales of five million in the States. It was also nominated for three Grammys in 1996, for Best Rock Album, Album Of The Year, and Best Hard Rock Performance for "Spin The Black Circle." Pearl Jam won the latter award, besting fellow nominees Red Hot Chili Peppers, Alice In Chains, Primus, and Van Halen.

When Pearl Jam's name was called, however, none of the members looked too pleased, taking a long time to get up from their seats and forgoing the obligatory hugs and kisses with their partners. Eddie's speech was likewise lukewarm: "We just came to relax. I just wanted to watch the show. I hate to start off with a bang. I'm going to say something typically me on behalf of all of us. I don't know what this means. I don't think it means anything. That's just how I feel." A round of slow claps could be heard in the theater. "Thanks, I guess." Stone and Mike got a few words in, respectively thanking Dave Abbruzzese and the "Seattle faction," with a special shout out to Alice In Chains.

Eddie Vedder backstage at the 38th annual Grammy Awards in Los Angeles, California on February 28, 1996.

Vitalogy's bigger legacy, however, was that "it clearly divides [Pearl Jam's] story between their first two full-length records that turned them into stars and the following, more experimental ones, that gradually took them away from the spotlight," noted The Year Grunge Broke in a post on Facebook.

"There's going to be a point where it'll revert back to the way that it was," Jeff told *Rolling Stone,* trying to put a positive spin on the situation. "We'll get through this whole period right now. We'll get back out there playing. We'll get back to actually being five guys who want to work it out together." It wasn't that long until Jeff's prophecy came true, thanks in large part to some needed intervention.

FORCE OF NATURE 135

"Quick ESCAPE"

If Pearl Jam was going to have any mentor over the course of their career, it only made sense that it would be Neil Young. He's long been regarded as the original "godfather of grunge," as a 1991 issue of *Pulse Magazine* first stated. The article credits the distorted guitars on Neil and Crazy Horse's 1979 album *Rust Never Sleeps* as well as Neil's anti-authoritarian stance on a number of issues—from farmers/workers' rights to environmental causes and women's right to choose—as rationale. In many ways, Neil was a natural elder for bands like Pearl Jam and Nirvana. Kurt even pilfered Neil's "it's better to burn out than fade away" lyric for his suicide note.

Before Pearl Jam did, Neil battled it out with MTV in 1988, scolding the station for refusing to air his video "This Note's For You," his rail against the corporate takeover of music and art. "MTV, you spineless twerps. You refuse to play 'This Note's For You' because you're afraid to offend your sponsors," Neil shared in an open letter. "What does the 'M' in MTV stand for: music or money? Long live rock and roll." Given the uproar, MTV reversed their decision. It's not that far-fetched to think Pearl Jam would get their idea for "Not For You" from "This Note's For You."

Pearl Jam lovingly called him "Uncle Neil," and over the years, the relationship became quite familial. The two camps planned to induct each other into the Rock & Roll Hall of Fame (Pearl Jam did so on behalf of Neil in 1995, and Neil was set to repay the honor in 2017, though he fell ill and was ultimately replaced by David Letterman). "He's taught us a lot as a band about dignity and commitment and playing in the moment," Eddie shared in his speech in '95. Pearl Jam's bootleg collection could stand up against Neil's archives. And when Eddie became gravely ill at a show in 1995, who else but Neil Young would jump in to take over? It's what any good uncle would do.

> **Pearl Jam has routinely offered up a cover of Neil's "Rockin' In The Free World" over the course of their thirty-five-year live career—to date, nearly three hundred and fifty times—and, on some occasions, Neil has jumped in, including at the 1993 MTV VMAs.**

The friendship started brewing in October 1992 when Neil, Eddie, and Mike all appeared at a special thirtieth anniversary celebration of Bob Dylan at Madison Square Garden in New York City. Within weeks, Pearl Jam was participating in one of Neil's annual Bridge School Benefit concerts that raise funding for the educational institute for children with speech and

OPPOSITE:
Eddie Vedder and Neil Young perform at the Rock & Roll Hall of Fame when Neil was inducted on January 11, 1995.

Pearl Jam and Neil Young perform together during the 1993 MTV VMAs in Los Angeles, California on September 3, 1993.

physical impairments. Either the full band or individual members of Pearl Jam have performed in fourteen editions of the event, beginning with their first appearance in 1992, before the last concert was held in 2016.

"[Neil] took our whole band under his wing, I guess it was right around that second record," Eddie told Howard Stern in an appearance on the radio host's show in 2020. He remembered that there was one time Neil sensed the growing divide in the band and had a pep talk with Eddie to sway him from making any drastic moves, like going solo. As Eddie recalled, Neil told him, "Hey, just so you know, there might be some people that'll try to pull you away from this group, but you guys, the sum is greater than the parts. Remember that."

Pearl Jam and Uncle Neil grew even closer in 1993 when the Seattle band opened for their rock hero on dates in Europe and the Pacific Northwest; by 1995, they were teaming up on more meaningful benefit shows like a new edition of the Voters for Choice concert in DC. The January show was also notable for being the debut of Jack Irons. Eddie had some words for the occasion, upon hearing boos from the crowd when they realized Dave Abbruzzese wasn't there: "Jack Irons saved the life of this band, so thank him," the singer vehemently claimed.

> *Rolling Stone*'s coverage of the night claimed the band came off so tight and cohesive "they sounded better than almost any band on earth," adding they were "so complete, so compelling, and so intoxicating that it could turn any fan into a fanatic."

Neil Young was one of them. Like so many others over time, he was gripped by Pearl Jam's live show, especially when the instrumental backbone of Pearl Jam teamed up with him on a performance of "Act of Love." Neil was so blown away by the collaboration, he invited Pearl Jam to back him up on a new album called *Mirror Ball*.

Speaking of the "Act of Love" collaboration, Neil told *MOJO* magazine, "I decided there and then to record with them as soon as possible." Neil recalled he initially only booked two sessions with Pearl Jam, traveling up to Bad Animals Studio in Seattle and working with Pearl Jam's go-to producer Brendan O'Brien as a "challenge" to his own recording process. But as sessions turned fruitful, Neil took it further. "Recording *Mirror Ball* was like audio verité . . . I was just conscious of this big smoldering mass of sound," the icon added.

Mirror Ball was released on August 7, 1995, although Pearl Jam wasn't able to be credited on the album due to conflicting label contracts (Neil was on Reprise while Pearl Jam was on Epic). Individual members were named for their contributions, however. The original works Eddie wrote during the tail end of the sessions—"I Got Id" and "Long Road"—also couldn't be included on the *Mirror Ball* album for the same reason but were instead reserved for Pearl Jam's December 1995 *Merkin Ball* EP. Likewise, Neil was credited on that EP for guitar, vocals, and pump organ.

After the release of *Mirror Ball*, Pearl Jam got the opportunity of a lifetime to join Neil for eleven dates in Europe to promote the album. "It was a dream come true," Mike told *Daily Record*. Eddie didn't join, explained by his "pretty intense stalker problem" at the time, but Brendan O'Brien did, contributing keyboards. Brendan added keys to Pearl Jam's sets for a number of years, before Boom Gaspar joined in 2002.

Stone told *SPIN* that working with Neil on *Mirror Ball* "came at a time when we needed it, Neil thought we were a band that would be good to make a record with. He probably felt sorry for us [but] he made it all right for us to be who we were." In the same article, Eddie said, "Everything he taught us at the time resonated. . . . We needed a North Star and a bit of a compass, and he provided both."

Neil Young and Eddie Vedder backstage at the 1993 MTV VMAs in Los Angeles, California on September 3, 1993.

On June 24, 1995, Neil would save the band yet again. Pearl Jam was back to playing live after the Ticketmaster fracas, now coordinating with newcomer ticketing agency E.T.M. Entertainment Network. But another stroke of ill-timed misfortune came when Eddie suffered a debilitating case of food poisoning on that date. After spending hours in the ER, Eddie proceeded to try to start the show at San Francisco's Polo Field but could only make it through seven songs. "I think that might be it from me for a while," he told the crowd.

Uncle Neil was waiting in the wings as the band had planned to premiere a few songs from the *Mirror Ball* album, and the veteran rocker stepped in to help steer the show. The throng of fifty thousand fans was none too pleased and others started spreading false information about the "real" cause of Eddie's malaise. "After Vedder's remarks about a hospital visit Saturday, rumors spread that he had suffered a drug overdose, but both Vedder and people who work with Pearl Jam have repeatedly insisted that he does not have a drug problem," *Los Angeles*

Times reported in their coverage. That night it was decided to reschedule the remaining dates and regroup. "After that show, Neil said, 'You know what, if it doesn't feel right, go home,'" manager Kelly Curtis told *SPIN*. "And the band looked at each other and said you know what, we feel like going home."

> **By mid-July 1995, Pearl Jam did come back for a few dates, two at Summerfest and one at Chicago's Soldier Field, where they broadcast their set live for the first time, allowing it to be played on the PA outside the stadium as well as on some local radio stations.**

It was the dawn of Pearl Jam's Monkeywrench Radio brand; during 1995, the band would go further in broadcasting additional concert dates.

The concept for Monkeywrench Radio evolved from two events earlier in 1995: One was staging Self-Pollution Radio in January, where Pearl Jam got their friends in Mudhoney, Soundgarden, Mad Season, and Nirvana's Krist Novoselic together to take over radio airwaves with a nearly five-hour musical variety show (the pre-dawn of livestreams). It was that radio show where Foo Fighters debuted their first-ever song "Exhausted." The other event was Eddie joining the Minutemen's Mike Watt on his small club solo tour that spring along with Dave Grohl and Hovercraft (featuring Eddie's then-wife Beth Liebling), where everyone traveled in vans as a way to bring back the old-school days of being one with the people. As *Rolling Stone* said, "This tour is about doing things the old way, the 'real' way, before punk hit the shopping malls." For Pearl Jam's 1995 tour, Eddie continued to travel from date to date in the same manner, often going live from the van after the show to talk directly to fans.

There was a real sense of getting back to the roots as Pearl Jam continued to struggle with fame in the mid-'90s, with many members embarking on side projects.

"There was a point where we sort of disbanded for six months, didn't really talk to one another, didn't really know where each other was at and went off to live life and refuel. It gave us a lot of energy creatively to get away from the bubble," Jeff told *Daily Record*. "Right around that time everybody started doing side projects, started working on their own music, and that's been really important and satisfying individually."

Stone formed the beloved alt rock/psych band Brad with hometown friends, the late, great Shawn Smith, Jeremy Toback, and Regan Hagar (formerly in Malfunkshun); they released their first album *Shame* in 1993 on Epic and would complete five more albums, including 2023's *In The Moment That You're Born*, a posthumous tribute to Shawn. By 2014, Stone had also formed

Painted Shield with Mason Jennings, old Pearl Jam chum Matt Chamberlain, and Brittany Davis, but the group didn't release their self-titled debut until 2021 as the COVID-19 pandemic finally opened up a window of time. Stone was also the first member of Pearl Jam to break off into solo work with his 2001 album *Bayleaf*. Early on, he had his own record label, too, called Loosegroove, again teaming up with Regan Hagar in the effort. It was established in 1994 as an imprint of Sony but became its own independent mission by 1996 and famously released the debut album by Queens of the Stone Age. Loosegroove shuttered in 2000, but Stone and Regan revived it in 2020.

Jeff also entered into a slew of side projects beginning in the '90s, starting with Three Fish, where he joined forces with Richard Stuverud of

Stone Gossard (second from right) with band Brad circa 2002.

Jeff Ament's side project RNDM performs at the Bottle Rock Napa Valley Festival in Napa, California on May 11, 2013.

the Fastbacks and Robbi Robb of Tribe After Tribe, who had opened for Pearl Jam in the era. Three Fish released their self-titled debut in 1996 and followed it up with *The Quiet Table* in 1999. Richard Stuverud would also team up with Jeff again in two more projects: Tres Mts, also featuring dUg Pinnick of King's X (to date, they've released one album in 2012) and RNDM where they were joined by singer-songwriter Joseph Arthur (to date, they have two albums). During the COVID-19 pandemic, Jeff joined Fitz and the Tantrums drummer John Wicks in the group Deaf Charlie, releasing *Catastrophic Metamorphic* in 2023; the duo played Eddie's Ohana Festival that October. Like other Pearl Jam members, Jeff went solo in 2008 with the self-released *Tone* and has issued three additional albums under his name.

Mike had perhaps the most famous side project with Mad Season, established in 1994. The lineup offered a who's who of the Seattle scene, also including Alice In Chain's Layne Staley and Screaming Trees' Barrett Martin as well as musician John Baker Saunders, who Mike met while in rehab during the *Vitalogy* era. "They like the fact I'm getting experience doing something else," Mike told *Guitar World* about his Pearl Jam brethren's thoughts on the project. "For a long time, I kind of went along with everybody else's ideas. I've never been a very assertive person. They're excited about me finally being clean and gaining confidence as a player . . . and they like the music, too." Columbia Records released Mad Season's debut *Above* in 1995 but the supergroup was short-lived, as John and Layne died from drug overdoses in 1999 and 2002, respectively. Several live editions and reissues of Mad Season's works have come along in the

QUICK ESCAPE 143

Mike's partner in Mad Season, Layne Staley, during an Alice In Chains concert on November 19, 1990.

years since, including a deluxe edition of *Above* in 2013 featuring Screaming Trees' Mark Lanegan on some new vocal tracks. Mike also had a few other side projects, including The Rockfords with his former Shadow bandmates plus vocalist Carrie Akre. There was also Walking Papers and Levee Walkers, both with Barrett Martin and Guns N' Roses bassist Duff McKagan and featuring a range of vocalists like Jeff Angell and guest star Jaz Coleman of Killing Joke.

With Matt Cameron serving double duty in Soundgarden and Pearl Jam for many years, finding time for anything else was a feat. Yet he was part of two jazz-focused groups, the Tone Dogs and Harrybu McCage in the '90s and aughts, as well as a pair of more psych rock-leaning projects, Hater and Wellwater Conspiracy (both alongside Soundgarden's Ben Shepherd). In 2020, Matt, the late Taylor Hawkins, Red Kross's Steven McDonald, and the Melvins' Buzz Osborne also announced their group Nighttime Boogie Association and released a pair of singles. A year later, in 2021, Matt teamed up with Soundgarden's Kim Thayil and Nirvana's Krist Novoselic plus former Hater collaborator Jon "Bubba" Dupree and vocalists Jillian Raye and Jennifer Johnson in the supergroup 3rd Secret. Matt's incredible drumming talent has been called upon by a number of groups over the years, from the Prodigy to Smashing Pumpkins and Black Sabbath's Tony Iommi. In 2013, Matt was part of the album *Drumgasm* featuring fellow skinspeople Janet Weiss from Sleater-Kinney and Zach Hill of Death Grips. Matt also

My Pearl Jam Moment

OHANA FESTIVAL, DOHENY STATE BEACH, DANA POINT, CA, MULTIPLE YEARS

Several artists have curated their own one-off, single-day, or multi-day music festivals and events. Tyler, The Creator's Camp Flog Gnaw Carnival. Perry Farrell's Lollapalooza. Travis Scott's AstroWorld. And Foo Fighters' Cal Jam immediately come to mind.

But there's something special about Pearl Jam frontman Eddie Vedder's Ohana Festival. A lot of it has to do with the location: It's stunning. Situated just steps from the Pacific Ocean at Doheny State Beach in Dana Point, California, Ohana offers panoramic views of the same waves Eddie first learned to surf on.

Eddie and current Pearl Jam manager Mark Smith partnered with Live Nation to bring Ohana to life in 2016, and it's still going strong. It has featured epic and eclectic lineups that match the vibe of the location, including sets from the likes of Stevie Nicks, Lana Del Rey, Band of Horses, Foo Fighters, Sting, Eric Church, My Morning Jacket, Pretenders, X, Red Hot Chili Peppers, Jack White, The Strokes, Pink, and so many more.

And Eddie doesn't just slap his name on the fest to drag out Pearl Jam for the evening or headline solo with all his famous musician friends (though he and/or Pearl Jam headline at least one evening each year).

He personally curates the lineups and pops out during sets throughout the day. He joined X for "The New World" and "(What's So Funny 'Bout) Peace, Love and Understanding" with Elvis Costello in 2016 and "Stop Draggin' My Heart Around" with Stevie Nicks in 2022.

The festival also leans heavily into ocean and beach conservation as well as sustainability. The Cove section of the fest includes the Storytellers Stage where global and local environmental leaders speak, and there are dedicated areas set up for art galleries that raise money for a variety of causes as well as a gathering of nonprofit organizations. Again, hand-selected by Eddie & Co.

During a special Ohana Luau benefit show, which raised funds for The San Onofre Parks Foundation ahead of the very first iteration of Ohana in 2016, Eddie put on an intimate performance for about five hundred guests where he shared, "My very first time surfing was at Doheny State Beach," adding that he has a scar from where his surfboard had smashed into his sternum. But getting a little banged up hasn't scared him away from surfing at Doheny Beach. The festival years all blend together now as I've covered eight of them, but one comes to mind. A couple of years ago, early on in the festival day, management was looking for Eddie backstage.

"Have you seen Eddie?" They asked, sort of frantic, as they quick-walked from trailer to trailer.

I didn't rat him out, but I did see Eddie. He was wearing a wetsuit, carrying a surfboard and heading to the water.

—*Submitted by Southern California music journalist Kelli Skye Fadroski*

SET LIST SPOTLIGHT

The First Show Broadcast by Monkeywrench Radio
July 11, 1995, Soldier Field, Chicago, IL

1. Release
2. Go
3. Last Exit
4. Spin The Black Circle
5. Tremor Christ
6. Corduroy
7. Whipping
8. I Got Id
9. Dissident
10. Even Flow
11. Sick Of Pussies (Bad Radio cover)
12. Deep
13. Jeremy
14. Glorified G
15. Daughter
16. Animal
17. Habit
18. Lukin
19. Not For You (followed by "Little Wing" tease)
20. Elderly Woman Behind The Counter In A Small Town
21. Immortality
22. Alive
23. Porch

— ENCORE —

24. Everyday People (Sly & the Family Stone cover)
25. Let My Love Open The Door (Pete Townshend cover)
26. Better Man
27. Rearviewmirror
28. Black
29. Blood

— ENCORE 2 —

30. Yellow Ledbetter

HIDDEN PEARL

Right before Pearl Jam played Soldier Field, the Grateful Dead did so two days earlier on July 9 (which would sadly be their last show, as Jerry Garcia died the next month). "I want to thank the Grateful Dead for letting us use their stage," Eddie told the crowd as Pearl Jam launched into a three-hour set. "We think it's only right that we play as long as they do." *Consequence of Sound* has ranked it Pearl Jam's greatest show ever.

released the solo album *Cavedweller* in 2017, followed by *Gory Scorch Cretins* in 2023.

Eddie, of course, went the Hollywood route, contributing to a number of film soundtracks, starting with *Dead Man Walking* in 1995 and famously offering up a whole album's worth of songs for the 2007 flick *Into The Wild*. The latter led to Golden Globe wins and Grammy nominations and Eddie's first solo tour in 2008. Two more solo albums would come with 2011's *Ukulele Songs* and 2022's *Earthling*; his *Earthling* backing band features Red Hot Chili Peppers' Chad Smith, former Jane's Addiction bassist Chris Chaney, plus Glen Hansard, Josh Klinghoffer, and Andrew Watt (also Pearl Jam's latest producer).

One of the special parts about the *Earthling* record is that Eddie was able to include the voice of his biological father on the album. Edward Louis Severson Jr. was actually a musician in his time, and by a stroke of luck, Eddie was able to come into possession of some of his dad's recordings. "About 10 years ago, the Chicago Cubs, some of their old-timers get together and play baseball for about a week," Eddie told *MOJO* recounting the story. "And I would go down there every other year and hang." One of the players, Carmen Fanzone, was also a trumpeter who had played with Edward. "He later brought me some photos of them in little basement studios. Then a couple of years after that, he brought me five songs of my dad singing on a disc." Eddie shared in the article that he stowed the disc in his suitcase for about three months while on tour. "Finally, I got the guts, and after a couple of bottles of wine, I played it one night in Argentina. . . . It was incredible—like he left a message for me."

Matt Cameron performing with Soundgarden at Red Rocks Amphitheatre in Denver, Colorado on July 18, 2011.

"Push Me, PULL ME"

Something magical happened that night at Soldier Field on July 11, 1995. Maybe it was the energy that Grateful Dead left behind that seeped into Pearl Jam by osmosis. Maybe it was the thrill of successfully broadcasting a radio show on their own terms that changed the power dynamic. Maybe it was just being in his old stomping grounds of Chicago that put Eddie in a good mood. Or maybe it was even the city's infamous '95 heat wave that made the band delirious.

Whatever it was, that Soldier Field show—their longest set at that point—was a game changer. Wanting to capitalize on the good vibes, Pearl Jam booked a room at Chicago Recording Company the very next day and started putting down the pieces of what would become their fourth album, 1996's *No Code*. The band had some song ideas percolating from their sporadic tour breaks in '95 they wanted to bring to the table, inspired by spending all that time with Neil Young and tuning in to his winding, jammy, classic rock petri dish.

No Code was also Jack Irons's first crack at a full album with Pearl Jam, having only been a small part of *Vitalogy*, and he wasted no time making great impressions. "Jack was like a session pro, a session-drumming assassin. Everybody was on their best musical behavior around him," producer Brendan O'Brien has said. Jack's funky, worldly percussion, which came from working with acts like Red Hot Chili Peppers as well as his love of jazz and the avant garde, became highly influential. "No one plays like him," Eddie told *Drum Magazine*. "There's some kind of wild card, the way he hears things and the way he plays things that's completely his own."

Jack's drum circle wall on "In My Tree" is a true anchor of *No Code* and a total departure from the straightforward, radio-friendly rock beat that most had come to expect of Pearl Jam. "Who You Are" is another one that has Jack's signature, a polyrhythmic beat he told *SPIN* was "inspired by a Max Roach drum solo I heard at a drum shop when I was a little kid." On top of it, Eddie brought in some Eastern-inspired influences to the number, taken directly from his sessions on the *Dead Man Walking* soundtrack, where he worked with Pakistani songwriter and Qawwali singer Nusrat Fateh Ali Khan.

ABOVE:
Jack Irons captured in a photo shoot in London on April 25, 1992.

OPPOSITE:
Eddie Vedder and Stone Gossard perform at a show in Miami, Florida in 1995.

PUSH ME, PULL ME 149

In total, Jack had four writing credits on *No Code*, also including "Red Mosquito" and "I'm Open." But, in addition to helping steer the band's wild sounds, Jack took on another incredibly important role: that of peacemaker. Just like Jack found Pearl Jam their singer back in 1990, he was pivotal in helping the band find each other again in 1995–96. "Jack's personality, maturity, and generosity have really helped us communicate with each other," Stone shared in *SPIN*.

The fact that individual band members could still trust each other's instincts (and that of the new guy) was a testament to putting the music first—and what they netted on *No Code* was a mixed bag of greatness. While there was more straightforward rock material on "Hail, Hail," "Habit," "Red Mosquito," and the punk-adjacent "Lukin" (gravely detailing Eddie's then-stalker problem), there was also the folky, harmonica-heavy "Smile," the mystic spoken word of "I'm Open," and the plucky rhythm of quiet track "Sometimes." On the latter, Eddie curiously exaggerates his enunciation of lyrics, which some suggest was a clapback to everyone saying they couldn't understand a word of the nonsensical mumbling on "Yellow Ledbetter," a song that was getting a lot of attention at the time.

Much of the material for *No Code* emerged out of studio jam sessions that were fit in around the band's increasingly marathon-like shows, a good portion of which continued to be broadcast for Monkeywrench Radio in the fall of 1995.

> **At a gig on September 13, Pearl Jam Concert Chronology noted that "Eddie announces that taping Pearl Jam shows is permitted," thereby ushering in a litany of sanctioned bootlegs in the years to come.**

Pearl Jam heroes the Ramones famously opened several dates that fall, too, and a live collaboration of "Sonic Reducer" with Joey Ramone became part of the double 7-inch single Pearl Jam distributed to Ten Club members that December.

Still, when *No Code* was released August 27, 1996, fans were incredibly confused by what they heard, especially as the first single was the world music travelogue "Who You Are." Where were the stadium dives of "Alive," the guitar riffs of "Corduroy"? *SPIN* noted the single "garnered little enthusiasm at radio and set the table for *No Code*'s subpar commercial performance," leading to the band's "first popular backlash of its career." Reviews were favorable, though, with many pundits loving the art rock detour. Pearl Jam was finally credited for an original sound rather than any suggestion they were pilfering off the Seattle trend, which, by 1996, was winding down anyway as a host of "post-grunge" acts were muddying the waters. *Rolling Stone*'s David Fricke praised *No Code* for offering "the kind of impulsive, quixotic, provocative ruckus that has become rare in a modern-rock mainstream" and *Q* magazine applauded the album's "unexpected and fascinating details."

Many loved the design, at least: an intricate labyrinth with 150-plus images taken from Polaroids, all locked together. There was a Magic Eye component too—zooming in on the full spread revealed the album's overarching motif, an eyeball wrapped in a triangle. The photo composite idea was steered by Jeff and the Ames Bros and was inspired by similar art direction by Bowie and The Talking Heads.

Like *Vs.* and *Vitalogy*, *No Code* hit No. 1 on the *Billboard 200* and stayed there for two weeks, but it only spent twenty-four weeks total tracking on the chart. The album still went platinum but just for one million units sold, unlike the 5x for *Vitalogy* and 7x for *Vs*. It was fine by Eddie. "It's great! We can be a little more normal now," he told *SPIN*.

Anyway, you couldn't put a price on the purpose of *No Code*. The album was about "gaining perspective," said Eddie, particularly as band members were all entering their existential thirties while also mining the band's growing pains. In hindsight, it's a record that many fans have grown to love too, like *Consequence of Sound*'s Ryan Bray. He believes the album was "essentially a test of fans' loyalty. . . . They weren't being dicks in veering their sound away from grunge toward art rock experimentalism; they did it because they had to follow their own course, regardless of whether or not I and others were ready to follow along with them."

By the time *No Code* wrapped, the band had turned a new leaf, and when it was time to make its follow-up, 1998's *Yield*, Jeff even admitted that, for the first time in years, it was "super fun." The album title was a double/triple/maybe even quadruple entendre, signifying the fact that the band was finally yielding to each other, yielding to the heaviness of outside pressures, yielding to fan's demands for more accessibility (both within the music and ability to see them live), and yes, yielding to their fight with Ticketmaster.

"We're not the same people we were five years ago," Eddie told the *Philadelphia Inquirer* in February 1998 as the band was starting to do more wide-ranging interviews beyond the rock bibles *SPIN* and *Rolling Stone*. "I'm a little more positive about the whole trip now. We've had time to count some blessings. I'm in a tremendous position, being in a band and making music. I'd be an idiot not to enjoy the opportunity."

Band members took inventory in the very noticeable shift in Eddie's demeanor. "I used to be afraid of him and not want to confront him on things," Mike shared with *Guitar World*, conceding, Eddie "seems very, very centered now, as opposed to two or three albums ago."

It wasn't just Eddie, though. Everyone in the band seemed to be in that same balanced space, and it calibrated the scales when it came to working together again on *Yield*. "Everyone got to be part of this album in a new kind of way, which was a nice evolution," Stone said. "Everyone learned a lot from that process, everyone kind of letting go and thinking you gotta kind of trust the band and let it do what it's naturally gonna do."

The intent for *Yield* was to lighten the mood, especially on the experimental drifting, and get back to more straightforward rock—even if it meant being part of the mainstream again. True to Eddie's words, this was definitely not the same band as five years ago.

Evolution was the definitive theme of the album, and "Do The Evolution" became its theme song. For the first time since *Ten,* Eddie was not the overlord in control. He, frankly, was exhausted from being the one to man the ship the past two records and finally asked for help. On *Yield,* the ethos changed from just "do your parts" to "we're in this together." Other members wrote lyrics, with Jeff penning the narrative for "Pilate" and "Low Light," and Stone on "No Way" and "All Those Yesterdays." Jack, too, contributed lyrics for the song that came to be known as "The Color Red."

The band was so united in their mission for the album, they nearly excluded all outside forces, including producer Brendan O'Brien, at least at first. As he shared in the *Pearl Jam Twenty* book, he got a call from the guys saying basically his services wouldn't be needed until maybe the mixing stage.

Pearl Jam performs at the Voters For Choice benefit concert in Washington, DC on January 14, 1995.

PUSH ME, PULL ME 153

"And I said, 'What?' Listen! I helped you on this last record. I went through all of that with you guys to get to *this*. And now you're telling me you want to make a more commercial-sounding record without my help? You're out of your mind!" He took a flight to Seattle and talked the guys off that ledge.

Yield was released February 3, 1998 and procured two of the band's biggest career hits to date: "Given To Fly," with its crescendo-building crest, peaked at No. 21 on the *Billboard Hot 100* chart and stayed in varying positions for sixteen weeks. The more pensive "Wishlist" topped out at No. 47 and remained on the chart for twenty weeks. Other standouts include the riff-led explosion on "Brain Of J" and the power pop/rock combo behind "In Hiding." *Entertainment Weekly* said *Yield* "veers between fiery garage rock and rootsy, acoustic-based ruminations," adding, "Perhaps mindful of their position as the last alt-rock ambassadors with any degree of clout, they've come up with their most cohesive album since their 1991 debut, *Ten*."

There was a definite positivity swirling about *Yield*, and with it, the band started loosening its grip on some of the previous stubborn-headed demands. First, they warmed up to videos again. Pearl Jam debuted their first music video in six years with a piece for "Do The Evolution," a comic book-style animation done by masters of the form, Todd McFarlane (who worked on *Spawn* and Korn's "Freak On a Leash" video) and Kevin Altieri (known for *Batman: The Animated Series*). "Basically we tried to make a good stoner video," the band joked in promotional materials. The video was nominated for a Grammy in the category of Best Music Video, Short Form, but lost out to Madonna's "Ray Of Light." *Yield* went platinum and was also nominated for Grammys in the categories of Best Recording Package (another nod to Jeff and the Ames Bros' design, which they'd brought out again to great effect) and Best Hard Rock Performance for "Do The Evolution."

The band's newfound video blessings went so far as to allow full access for the docu-style *Single Video Theory* VHS and DVD, a precursor to Cameron Crowe's *Pearl Jam Twenty* film. Cameron was an executive producer on this early one, too, along with manager Kelly Curtis, while direction came from "Jeremy" music video scion Mark Pellington. The forty-five-minute piece gave an incredibly rare look at Pearl Jam's creative process from inside their hallowed rehearsal room, captured during a three-day session in Seattle as they prepped *Yield* and prepared to open a few dates for the Rolling Stones.

In the first minutes of the film, Eddie pulls up in his tiny European car. Jeff bikes to the spot. And the rest of the guys stroll in, all clocking in on a punch card. The message was clear—they were there to work. And by giving audiences a bird's eye view into the process, it was a kind of olive branch after disenfranchising many with *No Code*. In interviews and raw performance footage, the band comes off as uplifted and committed. Jeff called the sessions "intense," noting how much he sweat during them. Jack is seen taking ice baths to soothe his playing hands.

"It feels like now . . . we sound like a band again," Stone said in the video.

"We probably have to change our name," joked Jeff, conceding, "We made it through the storm, we're sitting back in a room together as friends with all of these experiences behind us."

That included leaving behind the Ticketmaster saga. Having no dog left in the fight and finding it increasingly hard to do the one thing they loved—play live—Pearl Jam crawled back into Ticketmaster's good graces, using their services for a 1998 tour. In a press release, Pearl Jam said the move was to "better accommodate concertgoers" who had struggled for years to get access to Pearl Jam shows at smaller, independent venues, while larger outdoor parks felt "too impersonal" and came with their own set of headaches. "We'll work with them where we have to," Eddie told *Chicago Tribune,* adding, "We're not touring to make a point, we're touring to share our music with whoever wants to hear it."

Manager Kelly Curtis added in the *Philadelphia Inquirer* feature in 1998, "The pressure is finally off them. They can go be a rock band, be pure about music. They're more concerned with playing now than fighting the system."

The refueled road show started in Hawai'i and Australia in early 1998, before Pearl Jam descended upon America again. Though, this time, they did so without Jack, who took a medical leave. In an interview with *Pearl Jam Twenty*, Jack said he struggled to cope with his bipolar medical condition while on Hawaiian and Australian dates and had suffered manic episodes.

> **Jack requested to sit out the North American tour, and in a pinch, Pearl Jam asked good friend Matt Cameron to fill in temporarily. Matt agreed and learned more than eighty songs in two weeks.**

The lauded drummer was fresh off a break from Soundgarden, who had hit pause in 1997, but he wasn't necessarily looking for another full-time rock gig; in the anniversary book, Matt said he assumed it was going to be like the demos in 1990 when he was just a utility man filling in a small gap. Of course, 1998 began a long twenty-seven-year (and counting) partnership, the longest tenure of any drummer in Pearl Jam's history. His introduction began with a stop at the *Late Show with David Letterman* on May 1 where the band played "Wishlist." It was also a special show for the host, by now good friends with Pearl Jam, who had booked the band for his milestone 1,000th episode.

The TV appearance came two years after an awkward encounter. In the mid-'90s when "Black" was climbing the charts and Pearl Jam was still in their blackout period, night after night, David Letterman would hum a bit of the *Ten* song and joke about getting Eddie on the show, often looking at the camera directly to try and appeal to the Pearl Jam frontman. Eddie told Howard Stern he was getting a little "freaked out" by the trolling and decided to call the show bookers. "Can I just come by and stop this? Is there anything I can do to stop this?" he recalled asking. In May 1996, it happened. While Eddie was in town to see the Ramones play Coney Island High, he headed over to the Ed Sullivan Theater where Letterman taped. Eddie slipped in the side door, sang a few lines, and then bounced. Though Eddie was visibly annoyed at the time, the moment developed into a lifelong friendship. In 2017, not only did Dave induct Pearl Jam into the Rock & Roll Hall of Fame, as previously mentioned, but Eddie did the honors for Dave when he was awarded the Mark Twain Prize for American Humor at the Kennedy Center in Washington, DC that November.

OPPOSITE: Eddie Vedder sitting on the shoulders of NBA star Dennis Rodman during Pearl Jam's Lollapalooza set in Chicago, Illinois on August 5, 2007.

A few days after the Letterman appearance on May 1, 1998, Pearl Jam was back in Seattle, with an unannounced gig at local watering hole Moe's (billing themselves as Harvey Dent and the Caped Crusaders), where Matt got his first take at a full Pearl Jam headline show. His entrance into the mix garnered great live reviews for the band in this era. In Raleigh, North Carolina, a reviewer said Matt's "hammer of the gods pounding nudged Pearl Jam close to Led Zeppelin territory." You gotta believe Stone was pinching himself reading that.

In June, Pearl Jam returned to venues of yore like Chicago's United Center and Dallas' Reunion Arena, where basketball star and friend Dennis Rodman showed up wasted for a version of "Hail, Hail" and then didn't take the hint to leave the stage (Eddie even sat in his lap for a song).

The run also included the band's first dates at Madison Square Garden, and Iggy Pop, Cheap Trick, and Mudhoney opened some dates during the East Coast and Midwest portion of the tour in the fall.

> **It felt like the glory days for Pearl Jam again, so much so that the band took the occasion to release their first live album *Live on Two Legs* on November 24, 1998, compiling takes from various dates on the summer and fall tour.**

There's "Given To Fly," "Do The Evolution," and "Off He Goes" at The Forum in Los Angeles, "MFC" from Alpine Valley Music Theatre in Wisconsin, and "Corduroy" from the United Center in Chicago. *Live on Two Legs* was a huge success, another album certified platinum. And it

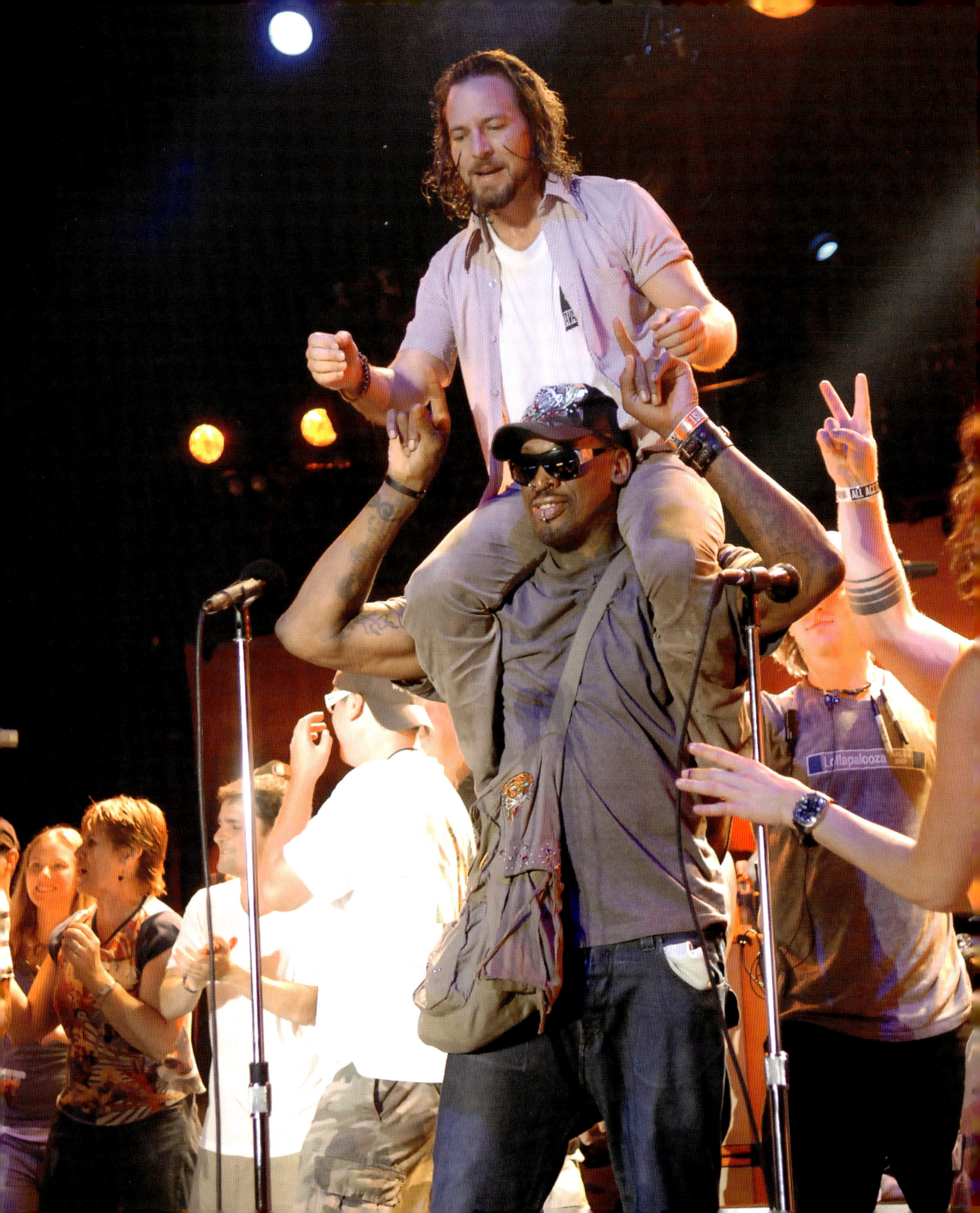
Lollapalooza

proved that, regardless of sluggish studio album sales, Pearl Jam fans' enthusiasm would never abate for the band's live experiences—or the desire to relive them. Heeding the call, Pearl Jam released additional live editions in the years ahead, including *Live At Benaroya Hall* (released in 2004, from a date in Seattle in 2003); *Live In NYC* (released in 2006, from Pearl Jam's 1992 New Year's Eve show in New York); *Live at Easy Street* (released in 2006, from a surprise live appearance at the Seattle record store in 2005); *Live at the Gorge 05/06* (released in 2007, from dual performances at the famous Washington amphitheater in 2005 and 2006); *Live At Third Man Records* (released in 2016 from a stop at Jack White's shop); *Let's Play Two* (released in 2017, encompassing Pearl Jam's shows at Wrigley Field in 2016); and *Give Way* (released in 2023, taken from Pearl Jam's show in Melbourne in March 1998, a show that was broadcast on Australia's Triple J Radio).

Pearl Jam also released a few live recordings digitally, such as *Live at Lollapalooza 2007* and *9.11.2011 Toronto Canada*, as well as a series of eleven vault recordings issued via Monkeywrench Records. With Pearl Jam shows becoming so memorable—and often sold-out—there was a huge demand for bootleg copies, and Pearl Jam soon took matters into their own hands to help out their dedicated fans.

My Pearl Jam Moment

KEYARENA, SEATTLE, WA, 2000

In 1999, I celebrated my fiftieth birthday with a big party. Before my guests arrived, I loaded the CD player up with Pearl Jam discs. PJ was my favorite band at the time, and I felt that the youthful energy of their music would get the evening off to a good start.

But my mid-life friends did not share my taste in music. I overheard someone ask, "What is it that we are we listening to here?" He sounded annoyed. Another guest replied, "I dunno, but it is her birthday, so . . ."

No one understood what I heard in this music "at my age." It began to be a bit of a joke. Before long, and to this day, I've become known as the World's Oldest Pearl Jam Fan.

In November of the following year, Pearl Jam closed out their world tour with two shows here in Seattle. I decided to treat myself to a ticket for one of them. I went alone, for obvious reasons.

The night of the concert, I headed to KeyArena expecting the audience to be people in their teens and twenties. I wondered if people would think I was an "elderly woman from behind the counter in a small town." Instead, I was surprised to see that there were a lot of parents, mostly dads, with their pre-teen and teenaged kids. Some of those dads were not much younger than I was.

When I think of rock concerts, the idea of a family show is not what comes to mind. But that is what it felt like. And it is why this particular concert is among my favorite musical memories.

When the music started, we stood in the stands, swaying back and forth, singing along to classics like "Even Flow" and "Better Man." I felt a connection, not just with the band we all loved, but with each other. I don't know if I was the Oldest Pearl Jam Fan there, but it didn't matter. For a couple of hours, we were all just one big family.

—*Submitted by Marie McKinsey*

"I Am MINE"

If anyone knows what it feels like to be a fan, it's Pearl Jam. Eddie and the Who. Stone and Led Zeppelin. Mike and KISS. Jeff and the Ramones. Matt and Pink Floyd. Each of them knows firsthand what it means to pledge allegiance to your favorite artist, to be the first one at the record store when an album drops, to wait in marathon lines for limited-edition merch, to pour over every interview, to wear out your favorite band T-shirt. To meet your idols. They did it day in and day out in Seattle when their punk idols like Black Flag and Fugazi would come to town. Mike recalled meeting Ace Frehley in 1985. In interviews in 1991 and 1992, Eddie namedropped Pete Townshend numerous times, bidding the universe for a chance meeting. "Give him a call Pete, please get it over with," Stone joked.

It's never really been about just the five members of the band. And even when it felt like "five against one" during the hysteria era, Pearl Jam always knew that, in the background, it was five plus millions. Over the past thirty-five years, the band has had fans' backs just as much as fans have had theirs. It's why they went to bat with Ticketmaster to keep tickets equitable and out of the grubby hands of scalpers. It's why they went to hell and back trying to find a way to stage their own rogue shows at ski clubs and became inexperienced show bookers and producers. It's why

OPPOSITE:
Eddie Vedder performs at "An Evening Celebrating the Who with Pete Townshend" in Rosemont, Illinois on May 14, 2015.

BELOW:
Eddie Vedder with Johnny Ramone at the 17th annual Rock & Roll Hall of Fame induction ceremony on March 18, 2002.

they still put on shows pushing two hours even as the members push into their sixties. It's why they did one better on fans' recorded bootlegs (usually a faux pas where most bands are concerned) and released their own, in an effort to offer fans better recordings. And it's why, in 1990, they established the Ten Club.

"Our fan base is very important to us. They are everything," Mike told *Daily Record*. "It keeps us alive as a band. . . . [When] people go and see hundreds of shows, it just blows me away."

The Ten Club came out of the ashes of the Mother Love Bone Earth Affair, "a fan organization started by Pearl Jam . . . as a way for the band to give back to their fans and create a community around Pearl Jam's music," the band explains on their official website.

Although total membership has never been disclosed, *Inc.* magazine reported in 2013 that there were 200,000 active members. As of publication, the official Facebook group has 103,500 members. One could say it's so popular because the perks are so good and full of Pearl Jam–sanctioned staples: bootlegs, video content, a forum to find like-minded fans, Ten Club radio access, and exclusive merch. Plus, of course, the best tickets to Pearl Jam shows.

Eddie Vedder poses with fans backstage at the Rock For Choice concert in Los Angeles, California on January 23, 1993.

A hearty crowd waits for Pearl Jam at the Hard Rock Calling Festival in Hyde Park, London on June 25, 2010.

Since the early '90s, Pearl Jam has consistently parceled off substantial blocks of tickets for fan club members, with access to the best seats assigned by tenure in the Ten Club. It's a mission the band takes very seriously—after all, who would they rather see in the front row, someone losing their marbles at a Mike McCready solo or a disinterested influencer on their phone missing the message as Eddie pleads "this is not for you"?

"We learned a lot about the importance of looking after fans and our members when it came to ticketing," Ten Club manager Tim Bierman told *Inc.*, and that attention paid off. "The band now packs arenas for two, sometimes three, nights in a row, thanks to thousands of intensely dedicated fans who call themselves the Jamily and travel hundreds of miles to sing along with every word," wrote *Entertainment Weekly*.

Over time, in addition to novel ticketing structures, Ten Club members have had access to a surplus of special memorabilia and mementos including members-only basketballs, an exclusive magazine *Deep* (now out of print), as well as, at one time, the Ten Club Single subscription series that offered a series of 7-inch one-offs that couldn't be heard elsewhere (whether a B-side, cover, live version, or collaboration). Pearl Jam discontinued the series in 2019 (likely with the surging costs of producing vinyl coming into play).

The Single subscription series netted some big gets over the years; the very first edition in 1991 offered the holiday jingle "Let Me Sleep (Christmas Time)," and in 1998 came "Last Kiss," a cover of Wayne Cochran and the C.C. Riders '60s surf rock song. The song became so popular it actually was picked up by radio and hit No. 2 on the *Billboard Hot 100* chart the following summer. It's still the band's best and longest-charting track to date.

"After we sold a bazillion records on *Ten,* we had a bit of power, so we decided to exert that power. What would a music fan want? We approached things from that standpoint," Jeff shared with the *Daily Record* about how the band designed the Ten Club, citing examples they personally admired. "The way that Pink Floyd put out packages using Hipgnosis artwork, Led Zeppelin used real special packaging. It was mystical and super creative and a lot of times it was totally off the wall. I like to think that we used that little bit of power to make stuff that looked cooler."

In 2006, Pearl Jam manager Kelly Curtis spoke to *Entertainment Weekly* about how the band were also "studying the Grateful Dead model." As Kelly said, "We just went and hung out in their offices and looked at how they did things. It was so grassroots and so great."

In no short order, the Ten Club has become one of the biggest fan club models in modern rock music, a concept that *Billboard* says goes back to the 1960s when "Beatles fans who sent a few bucks to the band . . . received through the mail exclusive Christmas records, locks of George Harrison's hair and shreds of John Lennon's clothing." While fan clubs still exist, many have dissipated and most others (like the BTS Army) are now part of the digital dichotomy where social media has largely become the new order. Pearl Jam has changed with the times, too, with fewer physical mail packages and more online assets.

A one-time Ten Club member, Matt Young even went on to a pretty high-ranking role in the music biz, now president of Warner Music Artist Services where he imparts what he learned in the Ten Club environment to help more bands connect with fans. He told *Billboard* that, nowadays, a "'fan club' feels ancient—[like when] paper mailers would come to your house once every three months when you were a kid and you'd get stickers and maybe a T-shirt and it was the only way you'd hear from the artist because it was so mysterious. A fan club today is any and all of the ways to build community around an artist. It's the concept of behind-the-scenes access—wanting to be close to the music and connect with like-minded fans."

At the core of the Ten Club, says *Guitar Tracks,* is "a loyal, rabid, some might say obsessive fanbase that is legendary in the music industry," explaining just what makes it so special.

SET LIST SPOTLIGHT

The One Curated by Superfan Brian Farias

June 27, 2012, Ziggo Dome, Amsterdam, the Netherlands

1. Wash
2. Last Exit
3. Animal
4. State Of Love And Trust
5. Severed Hand
6. Corduroy
7. I Got Id
8. Daughter
9. Nothing As It Seems
10. Got Some
11. Dissident
12. Once
13. Glorified G
14. Deep
15. The Fixer
16. Bugs
17. Better Man

— ENCORE —

18. Release
19. Hail, Hail
20. Alone
21. Footsteps
22. Rearviewmirror

— ENCORE 2 —

23. Crown Of Thorns (Mother Love Bone cover)
24. Sonic Reducer (Dead Boys cover)
25. Alive
26. Baba O'Riley (The Who cover)
27. Yellow Ledbetter

HIDDEN PEARL

Brian said he created forty to fifty drafts of the set list before deciding on the final version, which many fans have hailed as one of the greatest Pearl Jam sets of all time. At the end of the show, Brian was invited to the stage to take a bow with the band.

My Pearl Jam Moment

DARK MATTER TOUR, MULTIPLE DATES, 2024

I have been in love with Pearl Jam since 1991. And it was in 2016 when social media was thriving, when I found the Pearl Jam groups. This has forever changed my life in the best way. Pearl Jam is synonymous with the word *community*.

In 2011, I was diagnosed with breast cancer. It reappeared in 2018 and has been so stubborn in 2024. The Pearl Jam community has been a lifeline for me. They are a big source of love and encouragement. I am very thankful that I was able to see Pearl Jam in 2024. The statement "buy the damn concert tickets" rings so true for me.

I was able to get Ten Club tickets for the Missoula show on August 24. I had started chemo and radiation at the end of March. I had a scan in August that showed the chemo did not work and I had progression. I would be starting a new chemo round on August 30. I wanted to go to the Missoula concert because Jeff Ament is from Montana and my birthday is August 24. I saw old friends and met a lot of new friends. "Hard To Imagine" was amazing to hear live; it is a rarity. "Just Breathe" is a favorite song of mine, as it reminds me of my mother, who passed in 2010. Seeing Lukas Nelson and Eddie sing it as a duet was so special.

I'd also had lawn tickets to the Indianapolis show that was canceled in 2023. Once again, I was able to get pavilion seats from someone in the Pearl Jam community. This show was on August 26, 2024, and my next chemo was scheduled for August 30. The Pearl Jam community had started a campaign for me to get a shout out from the band. I will never forget Eddie saying, "She is battling, battling with courage. And courage is the cornerstone of hope!" He asked the crowd to give me their good energy. I turned around and I saw the whole crowd cheering for me. That is forever ingrained in my memory and my heart.

It was a fluke that I was able to attend the Boston shows on September 15 and 17, 2024. Again, I had my next chemo scheduled for a couple days after the shows, on September 20. I combined visiting my sisters and seeing Pearl Jam. Boston was so special to me because I got to take each sister to a show, and now my sisters finally understand that Pearl Jam is synonymous with community.

To me, Pearl Jam is music, community, love, support, and friendships. Music heals!

—*Submitted by Pearl Jam fan Michele Menke aka Triple M*

In 2012, Ten Club member Brian Farias had the ultimate thank you from Pearl Jam for attending more than one hundred shows: He got to personally curate the band's set list for a night in Amsterdam.

"[Ten Club] members enjoy all sorts of perks . . . and consider it a cardinal sin to sell an extra ticket for more than face value," added *Guitar Tracks*. "Fans snatch up show posters in a frenzy, which they often get professionally framed, and they buy, sell, and trade these posters among themselves. They dissect set lists on the fan club's forum and get together at shows, which are more like family reunions. Sometimes fan club members even marry each other. Many have separate bank accounts set aside to support their touring habit, and some have time off for Pearl Jam shows written into their contracts at work. They amass scores of concert recordings . . . and set up fundraisers to support the band's charitable causes. The result is a remarkably close connection between one of the most beloved bands on the rock scene and their most passionate fans." Or, as *Inc.* so wisely summarized, "Invest in your superfans and they'll invest in you."

Eddie Vedder opens his arms out to the crowd during a Dark Matter Tour stop in Los Angeles, California on May 22, 2024.

I AM MINE 167

"State Of LOVE And TRUST"

After nearly a decade of consistent returns, nonstop touring, musical experimentation, industry shakeups, and near-breakups, Pearl Jam rightfully took a year off from the road in 1999.

Instead, the band focused on staying productive in the studio, cobbling together their sixth album *Binaural*. It was named for the untraditional recording technique Pearl Jam used on the album, again trying to expand their wings and do something a bit left of center, while also pushing back against the advent of technology in the new millennium that was forcing digital methods on analog believers.

Seattle Post-Intelligencer explained the binaural process as a double-mic setup that's "normally used in acoustic laboratory environments for testing and studying the nuances of human hearing," adding that the contraption resembles "a plastic human head with microphones where the ears would be."

As Eddie told CNN in a 2000 interview, the purpose is "not just to record the instruments but to record the air around the instruments . . . you really feel the space of the room." He added that doing so taps into "something missed from modern recordings done on Pro Tools or a computer."

To accomplish the textured sound, Pearl Jam opted to go with another producer for *Binaural,* leaving Brendan O'Brien for the first time in about eight years. "It was time for that. There was no weirdness," Brendan told *SPIN*, though it wouldn't be long until they found their way to him again.

Instead, the band tapped Tchad Blake, who was an expert in the technique and had also worked on albums for Tom Waits, U2, and Sheryl Crow, among others (he's also a member of the Los Lobos side project Latin Playboys). The other "new" person in the mix was Matt Cameron; *Binaural* was the first time he was officially part of Pearl Jam's writing and recording sessions (save for the *Stone Gossard Demos 91*).

The lofty atmospherics from the binaural process can be heard on opener "Breakerfall" and within the outlaw acoustics of the dark crooner "Of The Girl," where you can almost see the reverb come off the strings of the guitar. The first single, "Nothing As It Seems," was the inaugural song slated for the technique, and, through it, the song takes on a neo-psychedelic spin heavily influenced by Pink Floyd; it's one of Mike's finest shredding moments.

The softer, more uptempo "Light Years" was the second and final single. It's one of the lighter-sounding moments on the album (as is Eddie's ukulele on "Soon Forget"). While *Binaural* dealt with messages of love and life, it was also mired in the heavy themes hanging over the year 2000. The world was

OPPOSITE:
Mike McCready performing live circa 1998.

STATE OF LOVE AND TRUST

getting over Y2K, technology was expanding at a rapid rate (Pearl Jam tepidly launched their first fan website at this time), and Napster was becoming a real threat, as was the idea of a new Bush in the White House. And then Columbine happened, bringing back the haunting mood of "Jeremy" all over again.

"While we were working on the album, the whole Columbine High School tragedy happened and it started reflecting some of that stuff, too. So it just kind of has a weird mishmash of influences," Stone told *Seattle Post-Intelligencer* about how it all parlayed into *Binaural*. Some inner band turmoil was also coming to the surface again—Mike had gone back to rehab for a growing addiction to pain pills and was dealing with his Crohn's condition, and Eddie was suffering from a horrible case of writer's block (at the end of the album, you can hear his frustration as it closes with a hidden snippet of him just typing nonsense on a typewriter).

Binaural turned out to be a sleeper of an album for Pearl Jam, though the song "Grievance" was nominated for a Grammy. Some have said it was "lightyears ahead of its time" (*TV Obsessive*) while *Rolling Stone* had an odd review that lumped it in with the works of Matchbox Twenty. The album did track at No. 2 on the *Billboard* charts a few weeks after it was released on May 16, 2000 (wedged just behind Britney Spears). Still, it was the band's first album not to go platinum. Stone told *SPIN* that, even for him, *Binaural* is "a little bit of a black sheep in my mind. People like it, but it doesn't necessarily carry them. We can make a better record than that."

Yet, something else happened around the time of *Binaural* that Pearl Jam ultimately would become better known for: their acceptance and encouragement of bootlegs. The medium has long been the bane of many recording artists. "Bob Dylan hates them," said a 1986 story in *The Washington Post*. "Bruce Springsteen despises them," the article adds, with The Boss's manager calling the recordings "out and out theft." Upon discovering one of the first known publicly distributed bootlegs in 1969, a composite of unreleased Bob Dylan songs called *Great White Wonder,* CBS Records shared in a statement, "we consider the release of this record an abuse of the integrity of a great artist."

Yet, there were bands that not only supported the idea of bootleg copies, they also provided the space to make them—bands like the Grateful Dead, who allowed bootleggers space near the mixing board to get the best audio take. As drummer Mickey Hart told *Ultimate Classic Rock*, "We had the choice of either taking their machines away from them, putting them somewhere and giving them a ticket to reclaim them afterwards, because they were getting in the way of the other audience members. . . . It became a real hassle. . . . We decided we didn't want to be cops, and so we said, 'Ah, let them come in, let them tape.'" The magazine reported that the result was that "2,000 of the band's estimated 2,300 concerts have been preserved by tapers."

Pearl Jam adopted the same position as the Dead as early as 1995 (around the time of that pivotal Soldier Field show in Chicago) when the band "began allowing fans to bring hand-held, Walkman-style audio recorders to their shows," said ABC News.

> **A statement on the band's website at the time shared, "The spirit of the taping policy is for each person to have a personal memory of the show."**

But Pearl Jam, like the Who and Frank Zappa, soon decided to beat bootleggers at their own game and release "official" versions.

"It's impossible, in practical effect, to enforce rules against bootlegging," Frank Zappa's lawyer Owen Sloane told *The Seattle Times* in 2007. Bands are "telling the fans, 'Here, you can have it official.' Who wouldn't rather have an official bootleg than an illegitimate one?"

That was Pearl Jam's stance. Eddie recalled in *The Believer* that he used to make his own bootlegs as a kid, the first time being when he saw the Who in 1980. "I'd sneak [a Walkman] into shows for just my own personal kind of thing. I never made copies or anything. . . . I was just so into being able to relive [it]. So much energy comes out of concerts sometimes . . . and that energy, no matter how great the show is, it dissipates within two weeks or a month. And that was my way of being able to put myself back there into a great space."

As Mike told *Daily Record,* "We've always liked bootlegs as a band, but we would see our own bootlegs out there, we'd collect them, and they would be inferior quality. So we decided let's just put our own out and charge a little bit less for them and make 'em sound as good as they possibly can."

Eddie also told *USA Today,* "A lot of people out there buy bootlegs, and it's risky, because you can spend a lot of money and get very poor quality. I used to buy them online for 35 bucks and get lousy sound. At least there's some consistency here. If you're going to hear our mistakes, you might as well hear them clearly."

Pearl Jam started the effort in 2000 with seventy-two official bootlegs pulled from dates on the global *Binaural* tour. They were released in three phases: the Europe Bootlegs in September 2000; the North America Leg 1 Bootlegs in February 2001; and the North America Leg 2 Bootlegs in March 2001. Pearl Jam's website at the time fully advertised the sale: "There's no need to fork over those hard-earned bucks for some low-quality, high-priced bootlegger bootlegs."

A police van on the grounds of the Roskilde music festival just days after nine people died during Pearl Jam's set on June 30, 2000.

The band's soundman, Brett Eliason, was in charge of doing all the mixing, and it was quite a valiant effort. As he told SPIN, "They gave me two weeks to mix 25 shows. In man-hours, it took me 15 hours a show. My assistant stayed here at the house and we just went, 'Tag, you're it.' One slept while the other worked." The effort was worth it, though, Brett said. "We had 14 records in the Top 200! Nobody's ever done that."

In fact, with the official bootleg releases in 2000–2001, Pearl Jam broke the record for the number of albums to debut simultaneously on the *Billboard 200*. Given the success and demand, the band has continued the practice over time, morphing into digital versions and partnerships with Verizon and their own Pearl Jam Radio channel on SiriusXM. In 2008, it was estimated that Pearl Jam had sold 3.5 million copies of bootlegs up to that point.

Scott Heisel, a music editor with *Alternative Press,* told *The Seattle Times* that Pearl Jam's bootleg genius came at just the right time: "The market for CDs is in the toilet, but at the same time the concert and the touring industry and the club circuit are booming. There are bands selling out theaters and clubs every single night. Obviously, there's a market for this. It can only grow." And as *Forbes* journalist Jim Ryan also shared, "I think the success of the bootlegs so shortly after Roskilde really was the beginning of a bigger and bigger focus on the incredible live reputation they've developed since."

Of course, the 2000 *Binaural* Tour in Europe would also have a lasting legacy for a far more unfortunate reason: the events at Roskilde on June 30, 2000. It's estimated that around fifty thousand people were in attendance for Pearl Jam's set at the Danish festival that day, one that was incredibly rainy and muddy. As the band played "Daughter," twelve songs in, a rush of fans surged to the front to get closer to the stage. In the process, many lost their footing in the soaked ground and nine young men were killed while twenty-eight sustained injuries from the stampede.

It's considered one of the worst mass casualty events at a concert in rock history.

In the analysis afterward, many focused on the breakdown of communication between Roskilde security and Pearl Jam's team. Pearl Jam was investigated early on as Danish investigators alleged the band was in part responsible, citing a history of rowdy crowds. The band vehemently refuted that claim and said in the weeks following, "It is our belief that if we had been informed of a potential problem at the moment that it was first identified by the festival security, we could have stopped the show earlier and lives could have been saved." Ultimately, both the band and the festival were cleared of any wrongdoing.

Pearl Jam issued a heartfelt statement shortly after the event, sharing, "This is so painful. . . . I think we are waiting for someone to wake us and say it was just a horrible nightmare. . . . And there are absolutely no words to express our anguish in regard to the parents and loved ones of these precious lives that were lost. We have not yet been told what actually occurred, but it seemed random and sickeningly quick . . . it doesn't make sense. When you agree to play a festival of this size and reputation, it is impossible to imagine such a heart-wrenching scenario. Our lives will never be the same, but we know that is nothing compared to the grief of the families and friends of those involved. It is so tragic . . . there are no words." They signed it, "Devastated, Pearl Jam."

With every anniversary that has gone by, Pearl Jam has reflected on the events of June 30, 2000 with remembrances and their own tributes. In 2003, Stone traveled back to Denmark to meet with the families of those who lost their lives that day. On the twentieth anniversary in 2020, a letter appeared on Pearl Jam's website that read, in part, "Nothing has been the same since. An unexpected moment intervened that forever changed all involved. . . . 20 years later our band has 11 more kids, all of them precious, and another 20 years between us . . . Our understanding of gravity and the loss felt by the parents of those boys has grown exponentially magnified as we imagine our own children dying in circumstances like Roskilde 2000. It is unthinkable, yet there it is. Our worst nightmare."

For six years after Roskilde, Pearl Jam abstained from playing any festivals, not until Reading and Leeds in 2006. Two songs also manifested as the band's direct response to the tragic events—"I Am Mine" and "Love Boat Captain"—both appearing on the band's next album, 2002's *Riot Act*.

The band even wondered for a time if they should go on. "There was at least one person in the band, I remember, that thought maybe we should never play again," Eddie shared in his Audible Original *I Am Mine* in 2021. He remembered the day starting on such a high, with Chris Cornell and his then-wife Susan Silver calling the band overseas to share the news that their daughter Lily had been born. And then everything turned dark. Jeff shared in the

SET LIST SPOTLIGHT

The Tenth Anniversary Show
October 22, 2000, MGM Grand, Las Vegas, NV

1. Interstellar Overdrive (Pink Floyd cover)
2. Corduroy
3. Breakerfall
4. Grievance
5. Last Exit
6. Animal
7. Dissident
8. Nothing As It Seems
9. Given To Fly
10. Wishlist
11. Untitled
12. MFC
13. Even Flow
14. Jeremy
15. Insignificance
16. Better Man
17. Lukin
18. Rearviewmirror

– ENCORE –

19. Do The Evolution
20. Once
21. Crown Of Thorns (Mother Love Bone cover)
22. Black
23. Can't Help Falling In Love (Elvis Presley cover)
24. Elderly Woman Behind The Counter In A Small Town
25. Mankind
26. Last Kiss (Wayne Cochran cover)
27. Porch

– ENCORE 2 –

28. Baba O'Riley (The Who cover)
29. Yellow Ledbetter

HIDDEN PEARL

The band gave several speeches that night, according to fans in attendance. Eddie thanked various Pearl Jam personnel like Kelly Curtis and Michael Goldstone as well as individual members of the band, and, before the band dove into "Crown Of Thorns" for the first time, he ended with a toast to Stone and Jeff's "seventeen-year musical relationship."

Pearl Jam Twenty documentary, "From that point on we rethought everything . . . the last time I felt like that was when Andy Wood died and I didn't know if I wanted to play music anymore."

Pearl Jam was at a crossroads, with the moment going on to define the band by what happened before Roskilde and what happened after. Another wise elder who understood what they were going through stepped in to help Pearl Jam reconcile with the event and find a way forward. This time, it was Pete Townshend. The Who had experienced a similar tragic event, when eleven fans were trampled and died in Cincinnati in 1970. Pete was able to relate to what the band was going through and pushed them to persevere. "Ultimately, Pearl Jam was able to go on with the summer shows and forge ahead as a band, thanks in part to a well-timed call from an understanding legend," *SPIN* reported.

After taking a month off, Pearl Jam returned on August 3, 2000 with a show at the Virginia Beach Amphitheatre. As *Rolling Stone* reported, "When it was time for 'Daughter,' which Pearl Jam never got to finish at Roskilde, Vedder made another plea: 'The last time we asked the crowd to do something, it was a completely different set of circumstances. But it would be nice to try again . . . Start singing, and sing loud, because you're still alive.'" The magazine continued, "The crowd obeyed, chanting 'It's OK!' with full hearts and lungs. And as the band played, a large butterfly swooped over Vedder's head, in and out of the overhead lights, like a sign of blessing, a mark of Pearl Jam's own walk through tears and toward the sunshine."

By October, Pearl Jam decided it was time to lock down the past and look toward the future. The band marked their tenth anniversary with a show at the MGM Grand Arena in Las Vegas, where they played Mother Love Bone's "Crown Of Thorns" for the first time in a beautiful display of full-circle acceptance. The recording was also featured as the band's fan club 7-inch that Christmas. "It was the first time I properly reflected on what we'd gone through and what a journey it's been," Jeff told *SPIN*. "And that moment was reflected in a purely positive way, feeling blessed, happy to still be playing music."

Pearl Jam performs at the Roskilde festival near Copenhagen, Denmark on June 30, 2000.

My Pearl Jam Moment

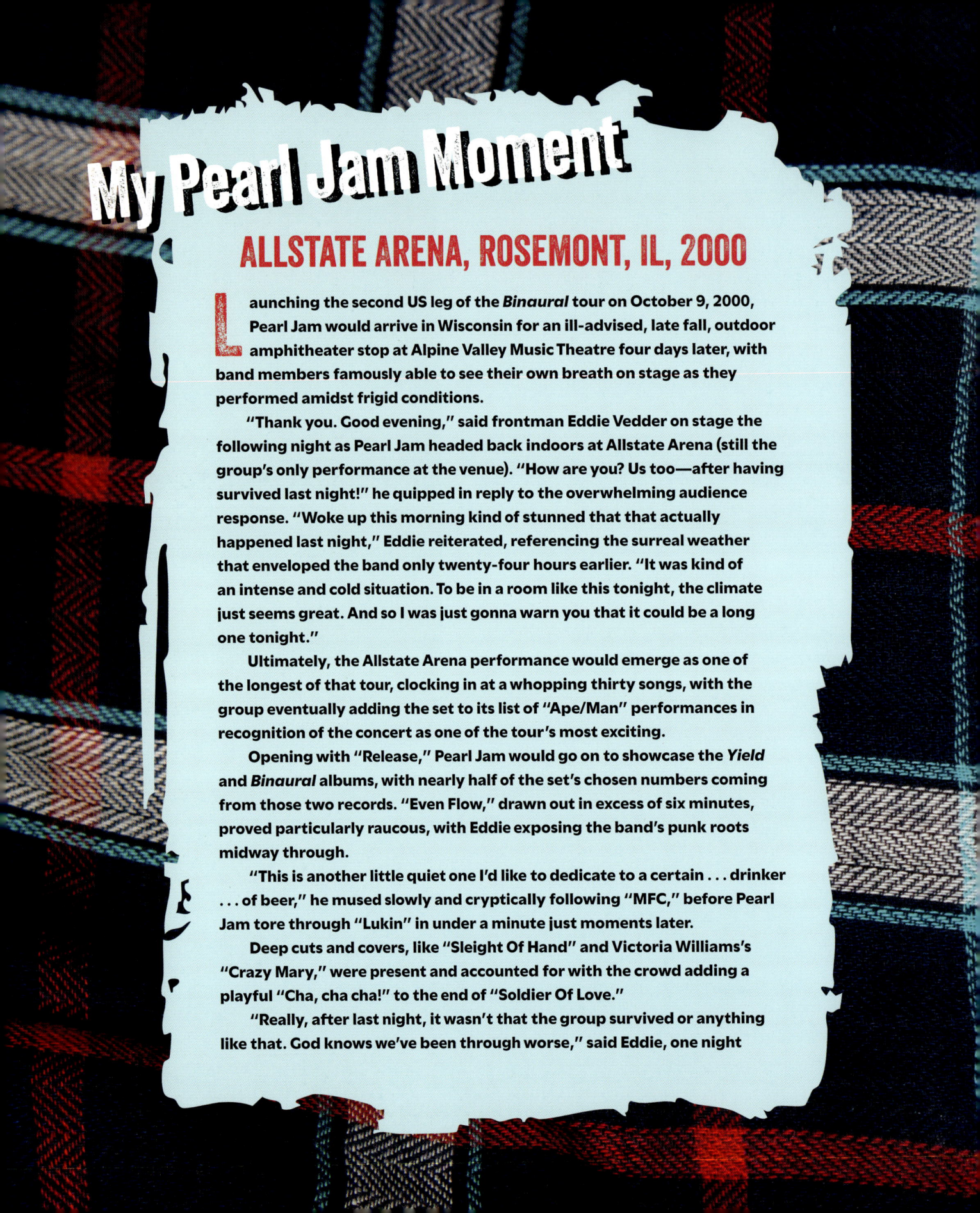

ALLSTATE ARENA, ROSEMONT, IL, 2000

Launching the second US leg of the *Binaural* tour on October 9, 2000, Pearl Jam would arrive in Wisconsin for an ill-advised, late fall, outdoor amphitheater stop at Alpine Valley Music Theatre four days later, with band members famously able to see their own breath on stage as they performed amidst frigid conditions.

"Thank you. Good evening," said frontman Eddie Vedder on stage the following night as Pearl Jam headed back indoors at Allstate Arena (still the group's only performance at the venue). "How are you? Us too—after having survived last night!" he quipped in reply to the overwhelming audience response. "Woke up this morning kind of stunned that that actually happened last night," Eddie reiterated, referencing the surreal weather that enveloped the band only twenty-four hours earlier. "It was kind of an intense and cold situation. To be in a room like this tonight, the climate just seems great. And so I was just gonna warn you that it could be a long one tonight."

Ultimately, the Allstate Arena performance would emerge as one of the longest of that tour, clocking in at a whopping thirty songs, with the group eventually adding the set to its list of "Ape/Man" performances in recognition of the concert as one of the tour's most exciting.

Opening with "Release," Pearl Jam would go on to showcase the *Yield* and *Binaural* albums, with nearly half of the set's chosen numbers coming from those two records. "Even Flow," drawn out in excess of six minutes, proved particularly raucous, with Eddie exposing the band's punk roots midway through.

"This is another little quiet one I'd like to dedicate to a certain . . . drinker . . . of beer," he mused slowly and cryptically following "MFC," before Pearl Jam tore through "Lukin" in under a minute just moments later.

Deep cuts and covers, like "Sleight Of Hand" and Victoria Williams's "Crazy Mary," were present and accounted for with the crowd adding a playful "Cha, cha cha!" to the end of "Soldier Of Love."

"Really, after last night, it wasn't that the group survived or anything like that. God knows we've been through worse," said Eddie, one night removed from the frigid Wisconsin weather and having had less than four months to attempt to process the Roskilde tragedy. "But the fact that I think there were as many thousand people as it was degrees out, which I think was like 26 degrees and 26,000 people that dealt with it," he explained. "And that was just so impressive this morning. And we're just gonna keep playing," Eddie said, returning to the stage for the group's first encore.

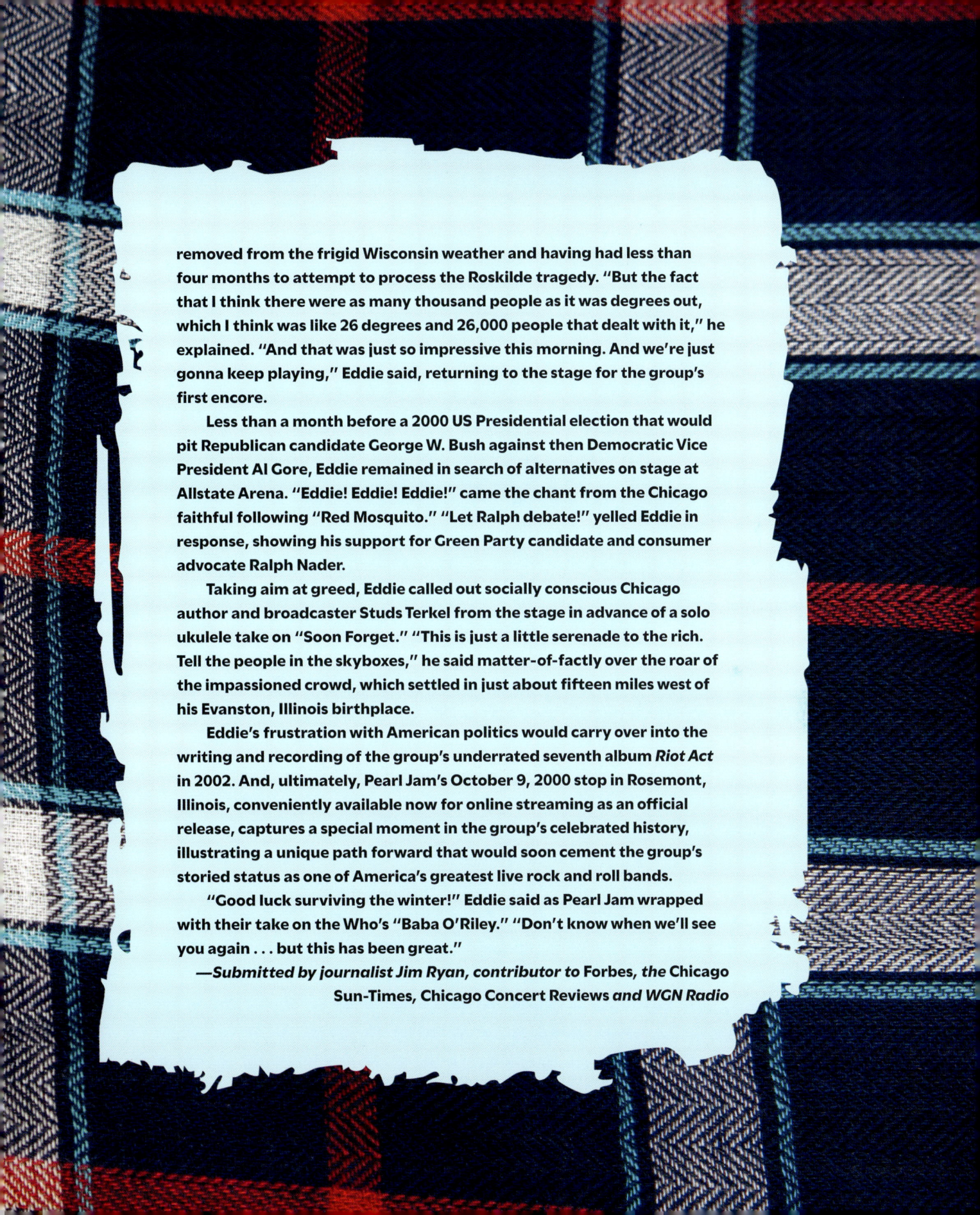

Less than a month before a 2000 US Presidential election that would pit Republican candidate George W. Bush against then Democratic Vice President Al Gore, Eddie remained in search of alternatives on stage at Allstate Arena. "Eddie! Eddie! Eddie!" came the chant from the Chicago faithful following "Red Mosquito." "Let Ralph debate!" yelled Eddie in response, showing his support for Green Party candidate and consumer advocate Ralph Nader.

Taking aim at greed, Eddie called out socially conscious Chicago author and broadcaster Studs Terkel from the stage in advance of a solo ukulele take on "Soon Forget." "This is just a little serenade to the rich. Tell the people in the skyboxes," he said matter-of-factly over the roar of the impassioned crowd, which settled in just about fifteen miles west of his Evanston, Illinois birthplace.

Eddie's frustration with American politics would carry over into the writing and recording of the group's underrated seventh album *Riot Act* in 2002. And, ultimately, Pearl Jam's October 9, 2000 stop in Rosemont, Illinois, conveniently available now for online streaming as an official release, captures a special moment in the group's celebrated history, illustrating a unique path forward that would soon cement the group's storied status as one of America's greatest live rock and roll bands.

"Good luck surviving the winter!" Eddie said as Pearl Jam wrapped with their take on the Who's "Baba O'Riley." "Don't know when we'll see you again . . . but this has been great."

—Submitted by journalist Jim Ryan, contributor to Forbes, the Chicago Sun-Times, Chicago Concert Reviews and WGN Radio

ENCORE
(2001-Present)

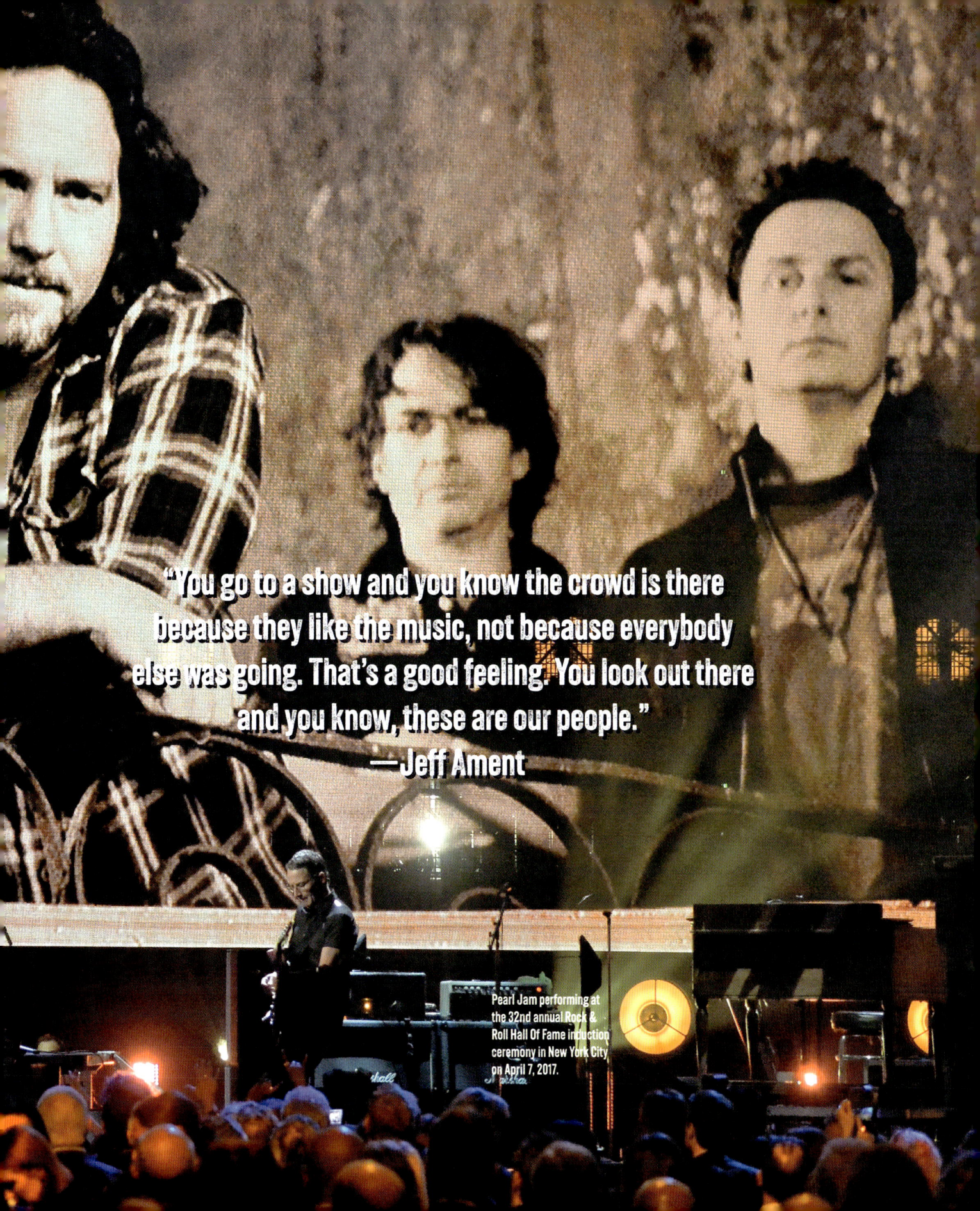

"You go to a show and you know the crowd is there because they like the music, not because everybody else was going. That's a good feeling. You look out there and you know, these are our people."
—Jeff Ament

Pearl Jam performing at the 32nd annual Rock & Roll Hall Of Fame induction ceremony in New York City on April 7, 2017.

TOUR DATES: 2001-Present

2001
October 20 and October 21: Mountain View, CA @ Shoreline Amphitheatre **(Bridge School Benefit)**
October 22: Seattle, WA @ Key Arena **(Groundwork Benefit Show)**

2002
September 23: Chicago, IL @ House of Blues
December 5 and December 6: Seattle, WA @ The Showbox
December 8 and December 9: Seattle, WA @ Key Arena

2003
February 8 and February 9: Brisbane, Australia @ Brisbane Entertainment Centre
February 11, February 13, and February 14: Haymarket, Australia @ Sydney Entertainment Centre
February 16: Adelaide, Australia @ Adelaide Entertainment Centre
February 18, February 19, and February 20: Melbourne, Australia @ Rod Laver Arena
February 23: Perth, Australia @ Burswood Dome
February 28: Sendai, Japan @ Isumity 21/Sun Plaza
March 1: Yokohama, Japan @ Pacifico Yokohama
March 3: Chiyoda-ku, Japan @ Budokan
March 4: Osaka, Japan @ Kosei Nenkin Kaikan
March 6: Nagoya, Japan @ Nagoy-ashi Kokaido
April 1: Denver, CO @ Pepsi Center
April 3: Oklahoma City, OK @ Ford Center
April 5: San Antonio, TX @ Verizon Wireless Amphitheatre San Antonio
April 6: The Woodlands, TX @ Cynthia Woods Mitchell Pavilion
April 8: New Orleans, TX @ UNO Lakefront Arena
April 9: Birmingham, AL @ Oak Mountain Amphitheatre
April 11: West Palm Beach, FL @ Sound Advice Amphitheatre
April 12: Orlando, FL @ House Of Blues Orlando
April 13: Tampa, FL @ St. Pete Times Forum
April 15: Raleigh, NC @ Alltel Pavilion Walnut Creek
April 16: Charlotte, NC @ Verizon Wireless Amphitheatre Charlotte
April 18: Nashville, TN @ AmSouth Amphitheatre
April 19: Atlanta, GA @ Hi Fi Buys Amphitheatre
April 21: Lexington, KY @ Rupp Arena
April 22: St. Louis, MO @ Savvis Center
April 23: Champaign, IL @ Assembly Hall
April 25: Cleveland, OH @ Gund Arena
April 26: Pittsburgh, PA @ Mellon Arena
April 28: Philadelphia, PA @ Wachovia Spectrum Arena
April 29: Albany, NY @ Pepsi Arena
April 30: East Garden City, NY @ Nassau Coliseum
May 2: Buffalo, NY @ HSBC Arena
May 3: State College, PA @ Bryce-Jordan Center
May 28: Missoula, MT @ Adams Field House
May 30: Vancouver, BC, Canada @ General Motors Place
June 1, October 25 and October 26 **(Bridge School Benefit)**: Mountain View, CA @ Shoreline Amphitheatre
June 2 and June 3: Irvine, CA @ Verizon Wireless Amphitheatre Irvine
June 5: San Diego, CA @ San Diego Sports Arena
June 6: Las Vegas, NV @ MGM Grand
June 7: Phoenix, AZ @ Cricket Pavilion
June 9: Dallas, TX @ Smirnoff Music Centre
June 10: Little Rock, AR @ Alltel Arena
June 12: Bonner Springs, KS @ Verizon Wireless Amphitheatre Kansas
June 13: Council Bluffs, IA @ Mid-America Center
June 15: Fargo, ND @ Fargo Dome
June 16: Woodbury, MN @ Xcel Energy Center
June 18: Chicago, IL @ United Center
June 21: East Troy, WI @ Alpine Valley Music Theatre
June 22: Noblesville, IN @ Verizon Wireless Amphitheatre Indiana
June 24: Columbus, OH @ Germain Amphitheatre
June 25 and June 26: Clarkston, MI @ DTE Energy Music Theatre
June 28: Toronto, ON, Canada @ Molson Amphitheatre
June 29: Montreal, QC, Canada @ Bell Center
July 1: Bristow, VA @ Nissan Pavilion at Stone Ridge
July 2, July 3, and July 11: Mansfield, MA @ Tweeter Center
July 5 and July 6: Camden, NJ @ Tweeter Center at the Waterfront
July 8 and July 9: New York, NY @ Madison Square Garden
July 12: Hershey, PA @ Hersheypark Stadium
July 14: Holmdel, NJ @ PNC Bank Arts Center
July 17, July 18, and July 19: Mexico City, Mexico @ Palacio De Los Deportes
October 22: Seattle, WA @ Benaroya Hall
October 28: Santa Barbara, CA @ Santa Barbara County Bowl

2004
September 24: Seattle, WA @ The Showbox
September 28 and September 29: Boston, MA @ Fleet Center
October 1: Reading, PA @ Sovereign Center
October 2: Toledo, OH @ Sports Arena
October 3: Grand Rapids, MI @ Delta Plex
October 5: St. Louis, MO @ Fox Theatre
October 6: Asheville, NC @ Civic Center Asheville
October 8: Kissimmee, FL @ Silver Spurs Arena
October 11: Washington, DC @ MCI Center **(Vote For Change Benefit)**

2005
March 18: Seattle, WA @ Paramount Theater **(Concert for the Northwest School)**
April 29: Seattle, WA @ Easy Street Records
August 29: Missoula, MT @ Adams Field House **(Concert for Jon Tester for Senate)**
September 1: George, WA @ Gorge Amphitheatre
September 2: Vancouver, BC, Canada @ General Motors Place
September 4: Calgary, AB, Canada @ Scotiabank Saddledome
September 5: Edmonton, AB, Canada @ Rexall Place
September 7: Saskatoon, SK, Canada @ Credit Union Center
September 8: Winnipeg, MB, Canada @ MTS Center
September 9: Thunder Bay, ON, Canada @ Fort William Garden
September 11: Kitchener, ON, Canada @ Kitchener Memorial Auditorium
September 12: London, ON, Canada @ John Labatt Centre
September 13: Hamilton, ON, Canada @ Copps Coliseum
September 15: Montreal, QC, Canada @ Bell Center
September 16: Ottawa, ON, Canada @ Scotiabank Place
September 19: Toronto, ON, Canada @ Air Canada Centre
September 20: Quebec City, QC, Canada @ Colisee Pepsi Arena
September 22: Halifax, NS, Canada @ Metro Centre
September 24 and September 25: St. Johns, NL, Canada @ Mile One Stadium
September 28: Pittsburgh, PA @ PNC Park
September 30 and October 1: Atlantic City, NJ @ Borgata Events Center
October 3: Philadelphia, PA @ Wachovia Center

October 5: Chicago, IL @ House of Blues **(Hurricane Katrina Benefit)**
November 22 and November 23: Santiago, Chile @ Estádio San Carlos de Apoquindo
November 25 and November 26: Buenos Aires, Argentina @ Ferrocarril Oeste Stadium
November 28: Porto Allegre, Brazil @ Gigantinho Gymnasium
November 30: Curitiba, Brazil @ Pedreira Paulo Leminsky
December 2 and December 3: Sao Paulo, Brazil @ Pacaembu
December 4: Rio de Janeiro, Brazil @ Apoteose
December 7: Monterrey, Mexico @ Auditorio Coca Cola
December 9 and December 10: Mexico City, Mexico @ Palacio De Los Deportes

2006
April 20: London, England @ Astoria
May 4: New York, NY @ Ed Sullivan Theatre **(Exclusive show for Ten Club members)**
May 5: New York, NY @ Irving Plaza
May 6 and May 10: Toronto, ON, Canada @ Air Canada Centre
May 12: Albany, NY @ Pepsi Arena
May 13: Hartford, CT @ New England Dodge Music Arena
May 16 and May 17: Chicago, IL @ United Center
May 19: Grand Rapids, MI @ Van Andel Arena
May 20: Cleveland, OH @ Quicken Loans Arena
May 22: Auburn Hills, MI @ Palace of Auburn Hills
May 24 and May 25: Boston, MA @ TD Garden
May 27 and May 28: Camden, NJ @ Tweeter Center at the Waterfront
May 30: Washington, DC @ Verizon Center
June 1 and June 3: East Rutherford, NJ @ Continental Arena
June 23: Pittsburgh, PA @ Mellon Arena
June 24: Cincinnati, OH @ US Bank Arena
June 26 and June 27: St. Paul, MN @ Xcel Energy Center
June 29 and June 30: Milwaukee, WI @ **Summerfest**
July 2 and July 3: Denver, CO @ Pepsi Center
July 6: Las Vegas, NV @ MGM Grand
July 7: San Diego, CA @ Viejas Arena
July 9 and July 10: Inglewood, CA @ The L.A. Forum
July 12: Los Angeles, CA @ Henry Fonda Theater
July 13: Santa Barbara, CA @ Santa Barbara County Bowl
July 15, July 16, and July 18: San Francisco, CA @ Bill Graham Civic Auditorium
July 20: Portland, OR @ Arlene Schnitzer Concert Hall
July 22 and July 23: George, WA @ Gorge Amphitheatre
August 23: Dublin, Ireland @ The Point
August 25: Leeds, England @ **Leeds Festival**
August 27: Reading, England @ **Reading Festival**
August 29: Arnhem, Netherlands @ Gelredome
August 30: Antwerp, Belgium @ Sportpaleis

September 1: Barcelona, Spain @ Pavello Olimpic de Badalona
September 2: Vitoria-Gasteiz, Spain @ **Azkena Rock Festival**
September 4 and September 5: Lisbon, Portugal @ Pavilhao Atlantico
September 7: Madrid, Spain @ Palacio de Deportes
September 9: Marseille, France @ Le Dome de Marseille
September 11: Paris, France @ Bercy
September 13: Bern, Switzerland @ Bern Arena
September 14: Bologna, Italy @ PalaMalaguti
September 16: Verona, Italy @ Arena di Verona
September 17: Assago, Italy @ Forum Milan
September 19: Turin, Italy @ Palaisozaki
September 20: Pistoia, Italy @ Duomo Square
September 22: Prague, Czech Republic @ Sazka Arena
September 23: Berlin, Germany @ Wuhlheide
September 25: Wien, Austria @ Stadthalle
September 26: Zagreb, Croatia @ Dom Sportova
September 30: Athens, Greece @ OAKA Sports Hall
October 21 and October 22: Mountain View, CA @ Shoreline Amphitheatre **(Bridge School Benefit)**
November 7 and November 8: Sydney, Australia @ Acer Arena
November 10 and November 11: Brisbane, Australia @ Brisbane Entertainment Centre
November 13, November 14, and November 16: Melbourne, Australia @ Rod Laver Arena
November 18: Sydney, Australia @ Acer Arena
November 19: Newcastle, Australia @ Newcastle Entertainment Centre
November 21 and November 22: Adelaide, Australia @ Adelaide Entertainment Centre
November 25: Floreat, Australia @ Subiaco Oval
November 30: Waimea, HI @ Waimea Falls Audubon Center **(Surprise show for the Surfrider Foundation)**
December 2: Honolulu, HI @ Blaisedell Center
December 9: Honolulu, HI @ Aloha Stadium

2007
June 8: Lisbon, Portugal @ Passeio Marítimo Algés **(Optimus Alive Festival)**
June 9: Madrid, Spain @ **Festimad**
June 12: Munich, Germany @ Olympiahalle
June 13: Katowice, Poland @ Stadion Slaski
June 16: Vienna, Austria @ **Nova Rock Festival**
June 18: Wembley, England @ Wembley Arena
June 21: Düsseldorf, Germany @ ISS Dome
June 23: Neuhausen ob Eck, Germany @ **Southside Festival**
June 24: Scheeßel, Germany @ **Hurricane Festival**
June 26: Copenhagen, Denmark @ Forum Copenhagen
June 28: Nijmegen, Netherlands @ Goffertpark
June 29: Werchter, Belgium @ **Werchter Festival**
August 2: Chicago, IL @ Vic Theatre
August 5: Chicago, IL @ **Lollapalooza**

2008
June 11: West Palm Beach, FL @ Cruzan Amphitheatre
June 12: Tampa, FL @ St. Pete Times Forum
June 14: Manchester, TN @ **Bonnaroo**
June 16: Columbia, SC @ Colonial Center
June 17: Virginia Beach, VA @ Verizon Amphitheatre
June 19 and June 20: Camden, NJ @ Susquehanna Bank Center
June 22: Washington, DC @ Verizon Center
June 24 and June 25: New York, NY @ Madison Square Garden
June 27: Manchester, CT @ Dodge Music Center
June 28 and June 30: Mansfield, MA @ Tweeter Center
July 1: New York, NY @ Beacon Theater **(Benefit for the Robin Hood Foundation)**

2009
August 8: Calgary, Alberta, Canada @ Canada Olympic Park
August 11: London, England @ Shepherd's Bush Empire
August 13: Rotterdam, Netherlands @ Sportspaleis Ahoy
August 15: Berlin, Germany @ Wuhlheide
August 17: Manchester, England @ Manchester Evening News Arena
August 18: London, England @ O2 Arena
August 21: Toronto, ON, Canada @ Molson Amphitheatre
August 23 and August 24: Chicago, IL @ United Center
August 28: San Francisco, CA @ **Outside Lands Festival**
September 21 and September 22: Seattle, WA @ Key Arena
September 25: Vancouver, BC, Canada @ GM Place
September 26: Ridgefield, WA @ Clark County Amphitheater
September 28: Salt Lake City, UT @ E Center
September 30, October 1, October 6, and October 7: Los Angeles, CA @ Gibson Amphitheater
October 3 and October 4: Austin, TX @ **Austin City Limits**
October 9: San Diego, CA @ Viejas Arena
October 27, October 28, October 30, and October 31: Philadelphia, PA @ Wachovia Spectrum Arena
November 14: Perth, Australia @ Members Equity Stadium
November 17: Adelaide, Australia @ Adelaide Oval
November 20: Docklands, Australia @ Etihad Stadium
November 22: Sydney, Australia @ Sydney Football Stadium
November 25: Brisbane, Australia @ QSAC Stadium
November 27: Auckland, Australia @ Mt Smart Stadium
November 29: Christchurch, New Zealand @ AMI Stadium

2010

May 1: New Orleans, LA @ **New Orleans Jazz and Heritage Festival**
May 3: Kansas City, MO @ Sprint Center
May 4: St. Louis, MO @ Scottrade Center
May 6: Columbus, OH @ Nationwide Arena
May 7: Noblesville, IN @ Verizon Wireless Amphitheatre Indiana
May 9: Cleveland, OH @ Quicken Loans Arena
May 10: Buffalo, NY @ HSBC Arena
May 13: Bristow, VA @ Jiffy Lube Live
May 15: Hartford, CT @ XL Arena
May 17: Boston, MA @ TD Garden
May 18: Newark, NJ @ The Prudential Center
May 20 and May 21: New York, NY @ Madison Square Garden
June 22: Dublin, Ireland @ The O2
June 23: Belfast, Ireland @ Odyssey Arena
June 25: London, England @ Hyde Park
June 27: Nijmegen, Netherlands @ Goffertpark
June 30: Berlin, Germany @ Wuhlheide
July 1: Gdynia, Poland @ **Open'er Festival**
July 3: Arras, France @ **Main Square Festival**
July 4: Werchter, Belgium @ **Werchter Festival**
July 6: Venice, Italy @ **Jammin' Festival**
July 9: Bilbao, Spain @ **BBK Live Festival**
July 11: Oeiras, Portugal @ **Optimus Alive!**
October 23 and October 24: Mountain View, CA @ Shoreline Amphitheatre **(Bridge School Benefit)**

2011

September 3 and September 4: East Troy, WI @ Alpine Valley Music Theatre **(PJ20 Weekend)**
September 7: Montreal, QC, Canada @ Bell Center
September 11 and September 12: Toronto, ON, Canada @ Air Canada Centre
September 14: Ottawa, ON, Canada @ Scotiabank Place
September 15: Hamilton, ON, Canada @ Copps Coliseum
September 17: Winnipeg, MB, Canada @ MTS Center
September 19: Saskatoon, SK, Canada @ Credit Union Center
September 21: Calgary, AB, Canada @ Scotiabank Saddledome
September 23: Edmonton, AB, Canada @ Rexall Place
September 25: Vancouver, BC, Canada @ Pacific Coliseum
November 3 and November 4: Sao Paulo, Brazil @ Morumbi
November 6: Rio de Janeiro, Brazil @ Apoteose
November 9: Curitiba, Brazil @ Estádio Parana do Clube
November 11: Porto Alegre, Brazil @ Zequinha
November 13: Buenos Aires, Argentina @ Estádio Unico La Plata
November 16: Santiago, Chile @ Estádio Monumental
November 18: Lima, Peru @ Estádio San Marcos
November 20: San Jose, Costa Rica @ Estádio Nacional
November 24: Mexico City, Mexico @ Foro Sol

2012

June 20 and June 21: Manchester, England @ M.E.N. Arena
June 23: Newport, England @ Isle of Wight
June 26 and June 27: Amsterdam, Netherlands @ Ziggo Dome
June 29: Werchter, Belgium @ **Werchter Festival**
June 30: Arras, France @ **Main Square Festival**
July 2: Prague, Czech Republic @ O2 Arena
July 4 and July 5: Berlin, Germany @ O2 World
July 7: Stockholm, Sweden @ Ericsson Globe
July 9: Oslo, Norway @ Oslo Spektrum
July 10: Copenhagen, Denmark @ Forum
September 2: Philadelphia, PA @ **Made In America Festival**
September 21: Pensacola, FL @ **De Luna Festival**
September 22: Atlanta, GA @ **Music Midtown Festival**
September 30: Missoula, MT @ Adams Center

2013

March 31: Sao Paolo, Brazil @ **Lollapalooza Brazil**
April 3: Buenos Aires, Argentina @ **El Festival Mas Grande**
April 6: Santiago, Chile @ **Lollapalooza Chile**
July 16: London, ON, Canada @ Budweiser Gardens
July 19: Chicago, IL @ Wrigley Field
October 11: Pittsburgh, PA @ Consol Energy Center
October 12: Buffalo, NY @ First Niagara Center
October 15 and October 16: Worcester, MA @ DCU Center
October 18 and October 19: Brooklyn, NY @ Barclays Center
October 21 and October 22: Philadelphia, PA @ Wells Fargo Arena
October 25: Hartford, CT @ XL Center
October 27: Baltimore, MD @ 1st Mariner Arena
October 29: Charlottesville, VA @ John Paul Jones Arena
October 30: Charlotte, NC @ Time Warner Cable Arena
November 1: New Orleans, LA @ **Voodoo Festival**
November 15: Dallas, TX @ American Airlines Center
November 16: Oklahoma City, OK @ Chesapeake Energy Arena
November 19: Phoenix, AZ @ Jobing.com Arena
November 21: San Diego, CA @ Viejas Arena
November 23 and November 24: Los Angeles, CA @ LA Sports Arena
November 26: Oakland, CA @ Oracle Arena
November 29: Portland, OR @ Rose Garden
November 30: Spokane, WA @ Spokane Arena
December 2: Calgary, AB, Canada @ Scotiabank Saddledome
December 4: Vancouver, BC, Canada @ Rogers Arena
December 6: Seattle, WA @ KeyArena

2014

January 17: Auckland, New Zealand @ **Big Day Out Western Springs Stadium**
January 19: Gold Coast, Australia @ **Big Day Out Metricon Stadium**
January 24: Melbourne, Australia @ **Big Day Out Flemington Racecourse**
January 26: Sydney, Australia @ **Big Day Out Sydney Fairgrounds**
January 31: Adelaide, Australia @ **Big Day Out Bonython Park**
February 2: Perth, Australia @ **Big Day Out Arena Joondalup**
June 16 and June 17: Amsterdam, Netherlands @ Ziggo Dome
June 20: Milano, Italy @ San Siro Stadium
June 22: Trieste, Italy @ Nereo Rocco Stadium
June 25: Vienna, Austria @ Stadhalle
June 26: Berlin, Germany @ Wulheide
June 28: Stockholm, Sweden @ Friends Arena
June 29: Oslo, Norway @ Telenor Arena
July 3: Gdynia, Poland @ **Open'er Festival**
July 5: Werchter, Belgium @ **Rock Werchter Festival**
July 8: Leeds, England @ First Direct Arena
July 11: Bletchley, England @ Milton Keynes Bowl
October 1: Cincinnati, OH @ US Bank Arena
October 3: St. Louis, MO @ Scottrade Center
October 5 and October 12: Austin, TX @ **Austin City Limits**
October 8: Tulsa, OK @ BOK Center
October 9: Lincoln, NE @ Pinnacle Bank Arena
October 14: Memphis, TN @ Fedex Forum
October 16: Detroit, MI @ Joe Louis Arena
October 17: Moline, IL @ iWireless Center
October 19: Woodbury, MN @ Xcel Energy Center
October 20: Milwaukee, WI @ Bradley Center
October 22: Denver, CO @ Pepsi Center
October 25 and October 26: Mountain View, CA @ Shoreline Amphitheatre **(Bridge School Benefit)**

2015

September 26: New York, NY @ **Global Citizen Festival**
November 4: Santiago, Chile @ Estádio Nacional
November 7: Buenos Aires, Argentina @ Estádio Unico Ciudad La Plata
November 11: Porto Alegre, Brazil @ Arena do Grêmio
November 14: Sao Paulo, Brazil @ Estádio Do Morumbi
November 17: Brasília, Brazil @ Estádio Nacional Mané Garrincha
November 20: Belo Horizonte, Brazil @ Estádio Mineirão
November 22: Rio de Janeiro, Brazil @ Estádio Maracanã
November 25: Bogotá, Colombia @ Parque Simon Bolivar
November 28: Mexico City, Mexico @ Foro Sol

2016

April 8: Fort Lauderdale, FL @ BB&T Center
April 9: Miami, FL @ American Airlines Arena
April 11: Tampa, FL @ Amalie Arena
April 13: Jacksonville, FL @ Jacksonville Veterans Arena
April 16: Greenville, SC @ Bon Secours Wellness Arena
April 18: Hampton, VA @ Hampton Arena
April 21: Columbia, SC @ Colonial Life Arena
April 23: New Orleans, LA @ **New Orleans Jazz and Heritage Festival**
April 26: Lexington, KY @ Rupp Arena
April 28 and April 29: Philadelphia, PA @ Wells Fargo Center
May 1 and May 2: New York, NY @ Madison Square Garden
May 5: Quebec City, QC, Canada @ Centre Videotron
May 8: Ottawa, ON, Canada @ Canadian Tire Centre
May 10 and May 12: Toronto, ON, Canada @ Air Canada Center
June 11: Manchester, TN @ **Bonnaroo**
July 9: Telluride, CO @ Town Park **(Ride Festival)**
July 17: Pemberton, BC, Canada @ **Pemberton Music Festival**
August 5 and August 7: Boston, MA @ Fenway Park
August 20 and August 22: Chicago, IL @ Wrigley Field

2017

No shows other than the Rock & Roll Hall of Fame Ceremony

2018

March 13: Santiago, Chile @ Movistar Arena
March 16: Santiago, Chile @ **Lollapalooza Chile**
March 21: Rio de Janeiro, Brazil @ Maracanã Stadium
March 24: Sao Paolo, Brazil @ **Lollapalooza Brazil**
June 12 and June 13: Amsterdam, Netherlands @ Ziggo Dome
June 15: Landgraaf, Netherlands @ **Pinkpop Festival**
June 18 and July 17: London, England @ O2 Arena
June 22: Milan, Italy @ Area Expo **(I-Days Festival)**
June 24: Padova, Italy @ Stadio Euganeo
June 26: Rome, Italy @ Stadio Olimpico
July 1: Prague, Czech Republic @ O2 Arena
July 3: Kraków, Poland @ Tauron Arena Kraków
July 5: Berlin, Germany @ Waldbühne
July 7: Werchter, Belgium @ **Rock Werchter Festival**
July 10: Barcelona, Spain @ Palau St. Jordi
July 12: Madrid, Spain @ **Mad Cool Festival**
July 14: Lisbon, Portugal @ **NOS Alive Festival**
August 8 and August 10: Seattle, WA @ Safeco Field
August 13: Missoula, MT @ Washington-Grizzly Stadium
August 18 and August 20: Chicago, IL @ Wrigley Field

September 2 and September 4: Boston, MA @ Fenway Park

2019

No shows; dates were canceled due to illness

2020

No shows due to the COVID-19 pandemic

2021

September 18: Asbury Park, NJ @ **Sea.Hear.Now Festival**
September 26 **(Ohana Festival)**, October 1 and October 2 **(Ohana Festival Encore)**: Dana Point, CA @ Doheny State Beach

2022

May 3: San Diego, CA @ Viejas Arena
May 6 and May 7: Los Angeles, CA @ The Forum
May 9: Glendale, AZ @ Gila River Arena
May 12 and May 13: Oakland, CA @ Oakland Arena
May 16: Fresno, CA @ Save Mart Arena
June 18: Landgraaf, Netherlands @ **Pinkpop Festival**
June 21: Berlin, Germany @ Waldbühne
June 23: Zürich, Switzerland @ Hallenstadion
June 25: Imola, Italy @ Autodromo Internazionale Enzo e Dino Ferrari
June 28: Frankfurt, Germany @ Festhalle
June 30: Werchter, Belgium @ **Rock Werchter Festival**
July 3: Stockholm, Sweden @ **Lollapalooza Stockholm**
July 5: Copenhagen, Denmark @ Royal Arena
July 8 and July 9: London, England @ Hyde Park
July 12: Budapest, Hungary @ Budapest Arena
July 14: Kraków, Poland @ Tauron Arena
July 17: Paris, France @ **Lollapalooza Paris**
July 25: Amsterdam, Netherlands @ Ziggo Dome
September 1: Quebec City, QC, Canada @ Videotron Centre
September 3: Ottawa, ON, Canada @ Canadian Tire Centre
September 6: Hamilton, ON, Canada @ FirstOntario Centre
September 8: Toronto, ON, Canada @ Scotiabank Arena
September 10: New York, NY @ Apollo Theater
September 11: New York, NY @ Madison Square Garden
September 14: Camden, NJ @ Freedom Mortgage Pavilion
September 16: Nashville, TN @ Bridgestone Arena
September 17: Louisville, KY @ Kentucky Expo Center **(Bourbon & Beyond)**
September 18: St. Louis, MO @ Enterprise Center
September 20: Oklahoma City, OK @ Paycom Center
September 22: Denver, CO @ Ball Arena

2023

August 31 and September 2: St. Paul, MN @ Xcel Energy Center
September 5 and September 7: Chicago, IL @ United Center
September 13 and September 15: Fort Worth, TX @ Dickies Arena
September 18 and September 19: Austin, TX @ Moody Center

2024

May 4 and May 6: Vancouver, BC, Canada @ Rogers Arena
May 10: Portland, OR @ Moda Center
May 13: Sacramento, CA @ Golden 1 Center
May 16 and May 18: Las Vegas, NV @ MGM Grand Garden Arena
May 21 and May 22: Los Angeles, CA @ Kia Forum
May 25: Napa Valley, CA @ **Bottlerock Festival**
May 28 and May 30: Seattle, WA @ Climate Pledge Arena
June 22: Dublin, Ireland @ Marlay Park
June 25: Manchester, England @ Co-Op Live
July 6 and July 8: Barcelona, Spain @ Palau Sant Jordi
July 11: Madrid, Spain @ Iberdrola Music
July 12: Lisbon, Portugal @ Passeio Marítimo de Algés **(Lisbon Live Festival)**
August 22: Missoula, MT @ Washington - Grizzly Stadium
August 26: Indianapolis, IN @ Ruoff Music Center
August 29 and August 31: Chicago, IL @ Wrigley Field
September 3 and September 4: New York, NY @ Madison Square Garden
September 7 and September 9: Philadelphia, PA @ Wells Fargo Center
September 12: Baltimore, MD @ CFG Bank Arena
September 15 and September 17: Boston, MA @ Fenway Park
September 27 and September 29: Dana Point, CA @ Doheny State Beach **(Ohana Festival)**
November 8 and November 10: Auckland, New Zealand @ Go Media Stadium Mt Smart
November 13: Gold Coast, Australia @ People First Stadium
November 16 and November 18: Melbourne, Australia @ Marvel Stadium
November 21 and November 23: Sydney, Australia @ ENGIE Stadium

2025

April 24 and April 26: Hollywood, FL @ Hard Rock Live
April 29 and May 1: Atlanta, GA @ State Farm Arena
May 3: New Orleans, LA @ Fair Grounds Race Course **(New Orleans Jazz & Heritage Festival)**
May 6 and May 8: Nashville, TN @ Bridgestone Arena
May 11 and May 13: Raleigh, NC @ Lenovo Center
May 16 and May 18: Pittsburgh, PA @ PPG Paints Arena

"Bu$hleaguer"

Since the birth of Pearl Jam in 1990, the band's story has followed a traditional three-act structure nearly to the letter. In filmmaker or screenwriter speak, it's a trifecta of events known as the setup, the confrontation, and the resolution.

In Pearl Jam's case, this manifested in their establishment in the Seattle scene, then grappling with the unending chain of tense events that came with fame. But Pearl Jam's third act, the era we come upon now, brings with it that sense of resolution, coupled with an air of calmness and perhaps greater purpose. In this era, Eddie has quieted his urge to risk life and death and put a stop to crazy stage hijinks. He even created his own festival, Ohana, that takes place along the oceanfront. How much more zen can it get?

If Pearl Jam's timeline can be divided, as band members have said, into before Roskilde and after, there is little question that the era after 2000 has resulted in a kind of rebirth. One where the band is still largely abstaining from the radio and media hamster wheel, though this time not out of spite or to backpedal on fame, but rather to put greater emphasis and energy into the immediacy of their music and direct unfiltered access to fans. In the process, they have continued to foster the live experience that has become their legacy.

Back at the dawn of the new millennium, there were hints of this renewed love of live, not only with the unprecedented unboxing of an eventual seventy-two-disc bootleg series but also with the release of *Touring Band 2000,* Pearl Jam's first concert DVD. Released in 2001, it

OPPOSITE:
Eddie Vedder dons a political T-shirt, circa 1992.

BELOW:
Pearl Jam prepare to take a bow at the end of their set during Ohana Festival in Dana Point, California on September 29, 2024.

spooled together footage from the explosive *Binaural* tour. As Jeff told *Billboard,* "I think we felt like we were playing better than we'd ever played. Two or three weeks into the European tour, we were just really excited about being a band. . . . We were feeling really good about what we were doing and how we were playing." He added that the band had been attempting to put together a live film for six or seven years, but that when it came to the footage, "We've just never been that excited about what we saw or what we heard."

Some of the shows on this run were remarkable fodder, too. Of the nineteen concerts and twenty-eight songs featured in *Touring Band 2000*, there was "Dissident" taken from the infamous frozen show at Alpine Valley Music Theatre in Wisconsin in October 2000. "That was one of the strangest shows I think we've ever played. We had little heaters on stage, so in between songs we could warm our hands up," Jeff told *Billboard*. "It really did feel like a Packers game or something." There's also "In My Tree" from Boston that August where a special "Matt Cam" was set up to capture detailed footage of Matt's prowess on the kit. In addition, five songs from the three-plus-hour tour finale in Seattle that November made the cut, which makes sense since it's regarded as one of the band's best shows ever (and the only date on the tour where they played "Alive" after the events at Roskilde). A review by ABC News said the musicians were "deeply feeling the bond between band and fan . . . both sides wanted something special to end the tour. Both sides got it." And there's a cut from Albuquerque on October 20 where a young fan, barely ten years old, joined Pearl Jam for a rendition of "Rockin' In The Free World." Pearl Jam end-capped the DVD with that number, just as they have done so many times in the course of their live career.

Pearl Jam was so satisfied with the work they did on the *Binaural* tour, they gave a new designation to some of the shows as "Ape/Man" sets, with distinct logos on the back of the bootlegs to set them apart as particularly primal or beyond human. "For each leg [one in Europe and two in North America], we sat down and picked six shows purely from memory that we felt were really exciting," Jeff explained.

The distinction aligned with Pearl Jam's commitment to treating their set lists with as much care as the show itself. With multiple albums under their belt, Pearl Jam had been experimenting with varying set lists for a few years, but it's in this era when the band really leveled up their curation to make each show a completely individual piece of art.

> **In a 2024 interview with *CBS Sunday Morning*, it was revealed that it's actually Eddie's beautiful calligraphy that adorns each handwritten set list, which the band often shares on social media after shows.**

It's a craft he learned to "pass the time" while on tour, said the news feature. "It keeps me focused and entertained," Eddie shared.

"It would be so much easier to play a similar set every night and yet we can't find it in ourselves to do that," Eddie famously shared in the *Pearl Jam Twenty* documentary, noting that sometimes final decisions on the song collection can be made just ten minutes before the band takes the stage.

Stone explained more about the very careful cherry-picking set list process in an interview with *Total Guitar* in 2012. "We have a 20-minute session backstage when we look at the set list and say, 'Let's do that one again' and we have a stereo system that has all the Pearl Jam songs on it so we'll play along with that" to rehearse them, he shared, adding it's a construct that has evolved over time. "When we first started out, I would have probably been one of those people that thought, 'Let's just go out and play the hits—why play anything other?' . . . As you get more songs, we consistently work them in. Even the ones that didn't work so well. It's given us so much more room because our fans now expect nothing less than to have something very different each night. . . . It's a good thing to be able to have that challenge."

One great example of the set list effort is Pearl Jam's monolithic forty-five-song set in Boston on July 11, 2003 that included a full acoustic set ahead of openers Sleater-Kinney.

> **It was the last of three nights in the East Coast city in which Pearl Jam attempted to play all eighty-plus original songs from the tour and twelve covers with no repeats.**

What was heard on some of the bootlegs and in person at these seminal gigs in the new millennium went beyond the music, however. Beginning on the *Binaural* tour and continuing through the present day, Eddie started taking a more vocal stance on political posturing. In the all-important 2000 election year, he put his support behind Green Party candidate Ralph Nader. As one of the show memories in this book recounts, Eddie declared "Let Ralph debate!" at an October 2000 show just outside Chicago; it was weeks before the actual vote would occur, as Republican candidate George W. Bush (soon to be the bane of Eddie's existence) and Democrat Al Gore dominated the race and left little room for others outside the two-party system.

In late September 2000, Eddie also played one of his first rallies for Ralph at KeyArena in Seattle. "I've never been to one of these," Eddie shared with the crowd, adding, "I think the reason why is I've never had anyone I could believe in before."

A report from ABC News noted that Mike, Jeff, Stone, and Matt were in the audience. "Four months ago, the singer donated a few thousand dollars of the group's money to Nader's campaign—without consulting the others first. Having reportedly expressed some reservations concerning Vedder's actions, they came out to the Arena to learn more about their investment," said the article. Eddie would continue his support for Ralph with appearances at similar events in Chicago and New York City (alongside Patti Smith) that October.

Of course, this was not the first or last time Pearl Jam used their platform to promote the democratic process. In the '90s, both Eddie and Chris Cornell participated in commercials for Rock the Vote; Pearl Jam has continued their association with the organization as well as voter registration nonprofit HeadCount over the years. There was also Drop in the Park in 1992, Pearl Jam's free concert staged in an effort to get young people registered to vote in that election year. During a Lollapalooza date a few months earlier, Eddie declared, "You'd all better vote to keep it a fuckin' free world." And in 1996, Pearl Jam aligned with Gloria Steinem for a show in North Carolina meant to be a "going away party" for conservative senator Jesse Helms.

In future years, Pearl Jam would endorse candidates on every scale, from presidential nominee John Kerry and former POTUS Barack Obama to Montana senator Jon Tester, Washington attorney general Bob Ferguson, and Portland, Oregon city councilman Jesse Cornett, among others. In 2024, the band invited Second Gentleman Doug Emhoff, husband of Vice President Kamala Harris, onto their SiriusXM channel for a discussion ahead of the 2024 election.

Yet back when George W. Bush won the presidency in 2000, it helped open up the floodgates for Pearl Jam's political punting amidst their ongoing activism. It's a theme that turned up on Pearl Jam's 2002 album, appropriately called *Riot Act,* with Jeff's choice of cover art depicting two skeletons wearing crowns as the world crumbles around them.

When Pearl Jam headed back to the studio in February 2002 to begin building *Riot Act,* they had plenty to write about. Between Bush's presidency, the tragic events of 9/11, and the remembrance of Roskilde, their worldview transferred into song material

Eddie Vedder with actors Tim Robbins and Susan Sarandon at a Ralph Nader rally in New York City on October 13, 2000.

SET LIST SPOTLIGHT

The Forty-Five-Song Boston Marathon
July 11, 2003, Tweeter Center, Boston, MA

ACOUSTIC SET
1. Long Road
2. Of The Girl
3. Sometimes
4. Off He Goes
5. All Those Yesterdays
6. Driftin'
7. Thin Air
8. Sleight Of Hand
9. Footsteps
10. All Or None
11. Parting Ways
12. Indifference

MAIN SET
13. Can't Keep
14. Breakerfall
15. Brain Of J.
16. Spin The Black Circle
17. Ghost
18. Green Disease
19. Tremor Christ
20. Given To Fly
21. Nothing As It Seems
22. Cropduster
23. Faithfull
24. Why Go
25. Wishlist
26. Leatherman
27. Nothingman
28. Better Man
29. 1/2 Full
30. Untitled
31. MFC
32. Blood

— ENCORE —
33. Breath
34. Habit
35. Down
36. Mankind
37. U
38. Black
39. Jeremy

— ENCORE 2 —
40. Arc
41. I Believe In Miracles (Ramones cover)
42. Know Your Rights (The Clash cover)
43. Fortunate Son (Creedence Clearwater Revival cover with Sleater-Kinney)
44. Rockin' In The Free World (Neil Young cover with Sleater-Kinney)

— ENCORE 3 —
45. Yellow Ledbetter

HIDDEN PEARL

In terms of the number of songs, this remains the longest Pearl Jam show to date, and the second-longest in terms of length, second only to the Philly show at Spectrum Center in October 2009, which topped three and a half hours.

that came loaded with a strong message. "You start feeling like, 'What do I have to say? What is my opinion?'" Eddie told *Billboard*. "Then I realized I did have an opinion. Not only did I have one, but I felt like it was formed by processing a lot of information."

That sentiment manifested on the first single, the chunky guitar-driven anthem "I Am Mine," with existential lyrics that champion taking a stand and contributing something meaningful to the greater good. Eddie wrote it in a Virginia hotel room before Pearl Jam played their first show after the Roskilde events. "It's kind of a positive affirmation of what to do with one's life. I'm born and I die, but in between that, I can do whatever I want or have an opinion about something . . . It meant a lot to me and still does when I hear it," Mike shared with *Billboard*. At a show in New Orleans in 2003, Eddie further emphasized the song meaning with the crowd: "This song is about what's inside you. You own it, and you have the freedom for it to come out. It's allowed to come out."

Other standouts from *Riot Act* include the haunting one-minute chant "Arc," believed to be an acronym for "All Roskilde's Children." It was performed just nine times on the band's 2003 tour in symbolic reverence to the nine that lost their lives at the festival. The spiritual "Love Boat Captain" also references Roskilde with the poignant lyric about losing "nine friends." The tone is helped by the heavenly organ melody from the newly initiated Boom Gaspar, a friend and fellow musician that Eddie met while surfing in Hawai'i and invited into the PJ fold. He wasn't the only new personnel on the album, though.

Pearl Jam worked with another new producer for *Riot Act*, this time Adam Kasper, who had helped engineer previous Pearl Jam albums and also worked with Matt on Soundgarden's *Down on the Upside* as well as Matt's side project Wellwater Conspiracy. Adam supported the band's mission to continue recording and tracking live together in the studio, in order to make a defiantly "anti–Pro Tools record," Matt said. As the drummer told *Seattle Weekly*, "We tore through it, tracked everything in about four weeks. You're really hearing it 'live,' the sound of a band playing together in a room—which you don't hear too much these days."

Elsewhere on the record there's the bluesy-psychedelic fusion of "1/2 Full," the slow and sweet "Can't Keep," the punkier "Save You," and the harrowing acoustic closer "All Or None." Pearl Jam also tracked a song in tribute to Alice In Chains singer Layne Staley, who passed away on April 5, 2002, exactly eight years to the day from when Kurt died, and left another ripple of heartbreak in the Seattle scene. "It was a real personal song Ed wrote the night we all found out [Layne] died. He stayed in there, didn't work on anything else, and worked this song up," Stone told *Billboard* in a track-by-track assessment of *Riot Act*. Though Pearl Jam didn't release it at the time, the song, called "4/20/02" (in reference to the actual date Layne's body was found), was

Memorabilia including Eddie's notorious George W. Bush mask at the Pearl Jam Museum during the 2011 PJ20 weekend in East Troy, Wisconsin.

featured on the band's *Lost Dogs* B-sides and rarities compilation album released in 2003.

Perhaps the most loaded song on *Riot Act*, though, was "Bu$hleaguer," a folk-inspired, spoken word satirical rant about the newly elected forty-third president. Biting as it was on record, the song would take on even greater angst when Pearl Jam toured in 2003, just as the US entered into the highly controversial Iraq war.

"Right after 9/11, there was this sense of unity that was deeply moving, but what bothered me was how quickly that became a blind patriotism," Eddie shared with *Philly.com* about what inspired the song's political bent. "I remember a few days after the attacks realizing that the progress being made on the environment and other issues was going to take a hit, and it seemed like even questioning that was anti-American. Well, it's not anti-American to be critical of the government. . . . We wanted to put some ideas out there that might help create an open and honest debate."

Like many of Pearl Jam's mid-career albums, fans have called *Riot Act* an "underrated" gem. *PopMatters* hailed the album as "a cohesive attack" where "not since *Vitalogy* has Eddie Vedder presented such a consistent thread in his lyrics." In their review, *NME* said, "'Riot Act' is the sound of a band entering a powerful middle-age. They still deserve your attention." The album, released November 12, 2002, was certified gold by the RIAA® for selling a half-million copies. It peaked at No. 5 on the *Billboard 200* chart and was Pearl Jam's first album not to enter the top two spots. That said, it fared incredibly well overseas, particularly in Australia, where it inked platinum status.

When Pearl Jam toured in 2003, the reception was a mixed bag, particularly as Pearl Jam's live shows became more politically charged and hit a nerve with those still feeling patriotic post-9/11.

BU$HLEAGUER

> **At the opening night of the North American leg in Denver on April 1, 2003, Eddie wore a face mask of George W. Bush before taking it off and piercing it through his microphone stand, an act many saw as "impaling" the sitting president.**

It led to scores of threatening emails. Media harped on the fact that "two dozen fans walked out," according to *Rolling Stone*. But Eddie fought back on that assertion in the magazine, saying thousands of other fans stayed; he called it a tour highlight. Eddie clarified he couldn't sing with the mask on and when he put it on the microphone stand, facing forward, it was meant to be emblematic of singing right at Bush himself.

"In rock & roll, I should be able to do whatever I want—run around with a sixteen-inch dildo on my head. This was a rubber mask, mock theater. You have to be allowed to do that," Eddie told *Rolling Stone,* adding, "A close friend of mine, who's hardcore right, said, 'It's too sensitive. You can't do it during time of war.' If you can't be critical of a president during time of war, doesn't that encourage him to be at war? . . . When it comes down to having an opportunity to speak from the stage, at least I feel like it's coming from a true place."

When boos followed the theatrics at a few more gigs on the 2003 tour, the band had the Clash's "Know Your Rights" in their back pocket, meant to back up Eddie's remarks on free speech and also pay a timely homage to one of their heroes, Joe Strummer, who had passed away in December 2002.

Eddie has continued being outspoken, critics be damned. In 2016, his face mask flex returned, this time in honor of Donald Trump at Pearl Jam's 2016 tour kickoff in Florida. Pearl Jam's 2018 digital track "Can't Deny Me" and the song "Wreckage," from their 2024 album *Dark Matter,* are also apparently about the forty-fifth/forty-seventh president. "There is a guy in the United States who is still saying he didn't lose an election, and people are reverberating and amplifying that message as if it is true," Eddie shared with UK outlet *Sunday Times* about "Wreckage," adding, "The song is saying, let's not be driven apart by one person, especially not a person without any worthy causes."

In response to some of the criticism that Pearl Jam has received for being outspoken, Eddie told *Magnet,* "How can you not be talking about this stuff? I'd be talking about it if I was a bartender. I'd be talking about it if I was a druggist. I'd be talking about it if I was the head of a corporation and how we'd deal with that. If there's any job you should be expressing yourself this kind of way, it would be that of a musician or a writer. When some of these bigger problems end, we can shut up and play. I look forward to the day and welcome it."

My Pearl Jam Moment

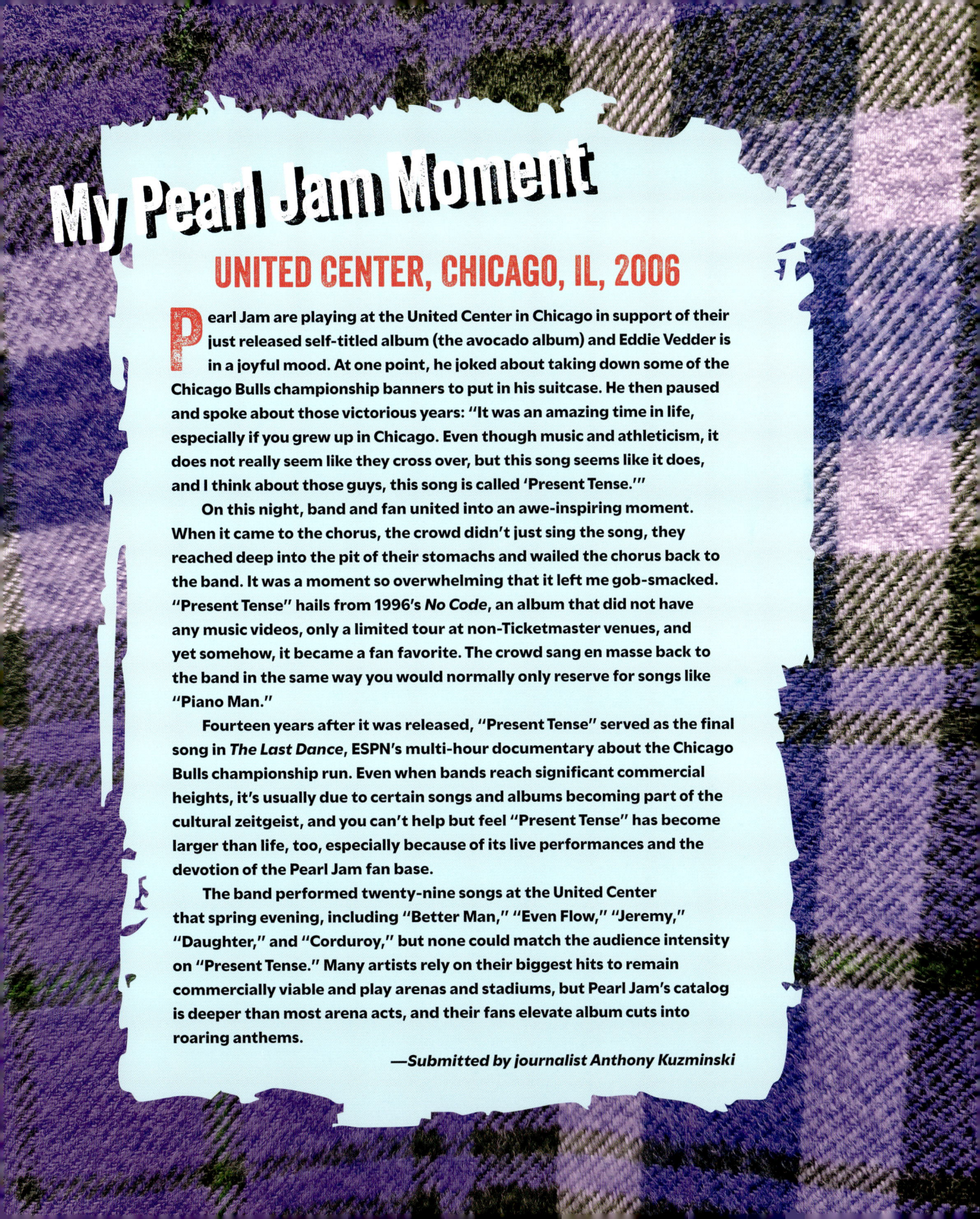

UNITED CENTER, CHICAGO, IL, 2006

Pearl Jam are playing at the United Center in Chicago in support of their just released self-titled album (the avocado album) and Eddie Vedder is in a joyful mood. At one point, he joked about taking down some of the Chicago Bulls championship banners to put in his suitcase. He then paused and spoke about those victorious years: "It was an amazing time in life, especially if you grew up in Chicago. Even though music and athleticism, it does not really seem like they cross over, but this song seems like it does, and I think about those guys, this song is called 'Present Tense.'"

On this night, band and fan united into an awe-inspiring moment. When it came to the chorus, the crowd didn't just sing the song, they reached deep into the pit of their stomachs and wailed the chorus back to the band. It was a moment so overwhelming that it left me gob-smacked. "Present Tense" hails from 1996's *No Code*, an album that did not have any music videos, only a limited tour at non-Ticketmaster venues, and yet somehow, it became a fan favorite. The crowd sang en masse back to the band in the same way you would normally only reserve for songs like "Piano Man."

Fourteen years after it was released, "Present Tense" served as the final song in *The Last Dance*, ESPN's multi-hour documentary about the Chicago Bulls championship run. Even when bands reach significant commercial heights, it's usually due to certain songs and albums becoming part of the cultural zeitgeist, and you can't help but feel "Present Tense" has become larger than life, too, especially because of its live performances and the devotion of the Pearl Jam fan base.

The band performed twenty-nine songs at the United Center that spring evening, including "Better Man," "Even Flow," "Jeremy," "Daughter," and "Corduroy," but none could match the audience intensity on "Present Tense." Many artists rely on their biggest hits to remain commercially viable and play arenas and stadiums, but Pearl Jam's catalog is deeper than most arena acts, and their fans elevate album cuts into roaring anthems.

—Submitted by journalist Anthony Kuzminski

"WHO You Are"

By the end of 2003, Pearl Jam was a free agent. After releasing the *Lost Dogs* collection of rarities and B-sides and finalizing the *Rearviewmirror Greatest Hits 1991–2003* collection, the band successfully completed a multi-album contract with Epic. And they intended to keep it that way for as long as possible. "We're not going to re-sign with a major, under current ways of thinking," Kelly Curtis told *SPIN* at the time.

It was an interesting turn since, just a couple of years prior, band members voiced a great appreciation for the way in which Epic and parent company Sony supported Pearl Jam's unheard of plan to put out seventy-two bootleg albums. "I think we were shocked that Sony even was at all into taking this on, which is . . . hats off to them for wanting to do it," Jeff told *Billboard* in 2001. "I thought initially they'd turn it down and we'd just put it out through the fan club . . . it felt good to just kind of fuck with the system a little bit, and do something a little bit differently."

Yet, by 2003, Pearl Jam was selling recordings from the *Riot Act* tour on the official band website and, having had a taste of the independent life, they enjoyed the model. "We're in this amazing position for the first time in 12 years," Jeff told the *Seattle Times* about being label-less. "We can do whatever we want. Even the feeling of being free is exciting."

The move also started to align them more with mom-and-pop record stores. In 2005, Pearl Jam released a recording taken from a surprise set at a favorite Seattle record store. *Live at Easy Street* was issued in an exclusive deal with the Coalition of Independent Music Stores, which *Billboard* said was "a move aimed to strengthen its ties with the independent retail community." That instinct would manifest again in 2019 when Pearl Jam was picked as the ambassador for Record Store Day. In a press release announcing the designation, Mike commented, "Independent record stores are hugely important to me, and have been ever since I was 12 years old." This independent streak would eventually lead to the development of their own label, Monkeywrench Records.

But, before that (perhaps a bit gun shy about fully going rogue), Pearl Jam got their feet wet with a one-record-only deal with J Records, a subsidiary of BMG owned at the time by music mogul Clive Davis. It was a curious partnership as the label was best known in the early 2000s as the brains behind Alicia Keys and had fellow R&B stars like Monica, D'Angelo and some *American Idol* alums on its roster. But it was also an organic connection with Matt Shay, a former lead on Stone's imprint Loosegroove Records who was now J Records's A&R rep and helped orchestrate the deal that was largely on Pearl Jam's terms. Matt was keenly aware of the band's concerns and needs, and went to bat for them in the contract, which stipulated closely aligning

OPPOSITE:
Eddie Vedder at one with the crowd during a benefit show for Hurricane Katrina survivors at House of Blues in Chicago, Illinois on October 5, 2005.

Pearl Jam fans play guitar, waiting at Tower Records in New York City for the band's self-titled album to be released on May 1, 2006.

with the distribution format of the Ten Club. "The key to the deal is that it gives the band freedom and control of its career," Matt told *Billboard*. "They have a big hand in approving everything we do as a partnership, and it's a true partnership."

The merger commenced with the 2004 release of *Live at Benaroya Hall,* which sold 168,000 units, a solid return that gave J Records executives confidence in the band. In turn, they "left Pearl Jam alone for more than a year" as they worked on their next LP, the defiant self-titled record, otherwise known as the avocado album.

Pearl Jam headed back into the studio in February 2005, working with producer Adam Kasper again. Recording took place at the band's go-to, Bad Animals' Studio X in Seattle, when they were home from various show appearances that year.

Among the show highlights were a benefit show for the Northwest School (Stone's alma mater) in March; the Live at Easy Street session in April; a benefit show for Montana senator Jon Tester in August; a date opening for the Rolling Stones in September; and a Hurricane Katrina benefit show with Robert Plant in Chicago that October.

> **Pearl Jam also toured South America for the first time in November.**

Recording sessions wrapped in February 2006 and *Pearl Jam,* the album, was released on May 2. It was one of the longest recording processes of the band's career—and, at that point, their longest gap between records, with *Pearl Jam* coming four years after *Riot Act*.

But the extra time paid off, with many hailing the album as a return to form that harkened back to the band's heartier alt rock roots. It also marked the band's return to the top of the *Billboard 200* chart, as the record debuted at No. 2.

Billboard declared, "Pearl Jam sounds more at home in its skin than ever" and *Rolling Stone* asserted that 2006 marked the band's "second coming." The article said of the self-titled album, "Pearl Jam are in the process of reclaiming their long-abandoned place at rock's forefront . . . [with] an album bristling with anti-Bush, punk-rock energy. It is, by universal acclaim, their best work since 1994's *Vitalogy*—and the first one in a long while to demand attention with unabashed anthems."

The band would be the first to agree. Mike shared with *Seattle Post-Intelligencer,* "I think it's a fresh new beginning for us with a new label, and there's a lot of energy surrounding that. . . . It harkens back to the energy of our second record, I believe."

Eddie's perspective, as he told *Rolling Stone,* was that "we've been handing in our work on time, and we've been getting A's and B's, but we haven't really raised our hand and spoken out in class. This record is us speaking out in class."

Eddie Vedder and Robert Plant perform together at a benefit show for Hurricane Katrina survivors in Chicago, Illinois on October 5, 2005.

If it sounds like a "Jeremy" move, well, it kind of was. Part of the appeal of *Pearl Jam* is the fact that, in addition to Stone and Mike's aggressive guitars and Matt and Jeff's straightforward rhythm section, Eddie returned to his storyteller writing style in the vein of "Alive" and "Elderly Woman Behind The Counter In A Small Town."

"Through telling stories, you may be able to transmit an emotion or a feeling or an observation of modern reality rather than editorializing, which we've seen plenty of these days," Eddie told *Billboard*.

Of course, the material on the album is still chock full of the deep opinions Pearl Jam had gathered in recent years, especially as the US was still under the fog of war and the Bush administration remained intact after the 2004 election. The lingering feelings were nowhere more apparent than on the guttural track "World Wide Suicide," written reactively to the country being in combat.

In an interview with friend Tim Robbins for *Hobo* magazine, Eddie shared, "It's like going to a bar and even if you don't smoke, you come home and you're just covered in the smoke from the club. You know you got this dirt, this residue on you, and that's what it feels like living in the United States these days. Just by living here, you come home with this residue of being at war. The psychic energy of being a country at war. So it kind of starts out dealing with that, like 'What is this on my skin? And can I wash it off? And is it in my lungs?'"

A download of "World Wide Suicide" was released for free on Pearl Jam's official website on March 6, 2006 and quickly made an impression on fans and radio. It climbed its way up the *Billboard Hot 100* chart to No. 41, and placed at No. 2 on the *Mainstream Rock Airplay* chart. "It's kind of blown up bigger than we had imagined," Mike told *Seattle Post-Intelligencer.* "I've had

Eddie Vedder speaking at the memorial ceremony for Johnny Ramone at Hollywood Forever Cemetery in Los Angeles, CA in September 2004.

people calling me from around the country saying, 'Hey, I've heard your song a hundred times on the radio.' I haven't heard that in years."

Pearl Jam also returned to being on camera in a pair of new music videos for "World Wide Suicide" and the riotous opener "Life Wasted." The latter is a quirky trip where visages of the band members are basically tortured by the elements—fire, dirt, bugs—in a kind of ashes to ashes symbolism. In reality, the song was inspired by the one and only Johnny Ramone, with whom Eddie had formed a friendship before the punk legend passed away in September 2004. Eddie told *Rolling Stone* that the funeral made him think on "what a gift this is, to be alive. . . . You've got a renewed appreciation for life. . . . But then things start getting back to normal and you start taking this living and

Pearl Jam performs at Lollapalooza in Chicago, Illinois on August 5, 2007.

WHO YOU ARE 199

breathing and eating thing for granted. I think that song is there to remind you, 'This is that feeling.'"

Other themes on the album are a direct response to "living in tumultuous, frightening times," Mike told *Seattle Post-Intelligencer,* whether worrying about the Iraq war, the destruction left behind by Hurricane Katrina, or "anything that smacks of totalitarianism," he added. On many songs, there's also the viewpoint of a parent worried about the world they are going to pass on to their kids.

At this point, Matt had started his family with wife April Acevez, with son Ray born in 1998 and daughter Josie shortly thereafter, and Eddie joined the parent club around this time when daughter Olivia (with second wife Jill McCormick) was born in 2004, followed by sister Harper. "All of a sudden, I saw the world as her world that they were [messing] with. That really pissed me off," Eddie has said in the past about becoming a dad. Olivia has even followed in her famous dad's footsteps, appearing in the 2021 song "My Father's Daughter" for the movie *Flag Day* and sometimes taking the stage with Eddie, as she has done at the Ohana Festival multiple times since 2021. (Matt's son Ray is also a recording artist, under the stage name Six Figure Retirement.) In addition, Stone has four daughters—Vivian, with first wife Liz Weber, and Marlowe, Faye, and Gwinn with current wife Vivien Wang. Mike McCready has three children—Kaya, Jackson, and Henry—with wife Ashley O'Connor. Jeff and his wife Pandora Andre-Beatty don't have any kids.

Besides themes related to navigating parenting, material on the self-titled album deals with refreshed takes on wage inequality, as heard on the classic rock burner "Unemployable," as well as addiction on the built-up crescendo of "Severed Hand." *Pearl Jam* also included two new lyric contributors: Mike McCready on "Inside Job," and Damien Echols on "Army Reserve." Damien was one of the maligned West Memphis Three teenagers who served time on Death Row after being wrongly accused of a triple murder. Damien's case was profiled in the HBO documentary series *Paradise Lost,* and it's known as one of the biggest miscarriages of justice in US history. Pearl Jam has long supported Damien by contributing legal fees, and Eddie even appeared at some of his court dates before Damien was released in 2011 under an Alford plea deal.

Pearl Jam the album was certified gold by the RIAA® and favorably reviewed. *Rolling Stone* called it the band's "best in ten [years]" and *Entertainment Weekly* noted, "They stand and deliver on this belatedly eponymous barnstormer, the seriously hopped-up effort fans have been pining for since *Vitalogy.*" Pearl Jam promoted it with appearances on *Saturday Night Live* in April and *The Late Show with David Letterman* and a taping of *VH1 Storytellers* in May.

The 2006 global tour that followed was notable for being both the first time Pearl Jam stepped foot on the European continent—and their first festival—since the events of Roskilde six years prior, with bookings at UK's Leeds and Reading events that August. "It seems like an era to trust that we're aware enough to get through those bigger shows. We have a heightened awareness of what needs to happen every night so people are as safe as they can possibly be," Stone told *Billboard*. During the show, Eddie harped on that fact, sharing with the crowd that abstaining from the festival circuit "was nothing to do with the fact we had no guts. We just needed your trust."

More festival appearances continued in 2007 with Pearl Jam's return to Lollapalooza (by this point, permanently stationed in Chicago) and at Bonnaroo in Tennessee in 2008. Lollapalooza was an interesting affair:

> **The night prior, August 2, Pearl Jam played a show for 1,300 lucky fans at Chicago's Vic Theatre, where they brought out a substantial collection of rarities including "Low Light," "Rats," and "In Hiding." SPIN has ranked it the band's No.1 live show.**

The next day, Pearl Jam headlined Lolla and found part of their set censored in the Lollapalooza livestream when Eddie made off-the-cuff comments about George W. Bush. Afterward, the band released a statement on its website that read, in part, "This, of course, troubles us as artists . . . what happened this weekend was a wake-up call, and it's about something much bigger than the censorship of a rock band."

If Pearl Jam was feeling any sort of nostalgia with a return to the sound, festivals, and events of yesteryear, it translated into their next album, 2009's *Backspacer*, in which they tapped '90s-era producer Brendan O'Brien for the first time since 1998's *Yield*. (Or, it could've been nostalgia for old-school typewriters, which inspired the album's name.)

When asked by *Paste* if there was any awkwardness in the sessions, Brendan said, "Not even a little bit. We worked together for quite a while before that, and I think for a while they just wanted to do things on their own. At this point, they were ready to be, for lack of a better word, 'produced' again. . . . I think I can speak for all of us in that we all had a great time doing it."

Brendan's take on *Backspacer* was that "it feels more like it wants to let people in. They've made records in the past that have been more introverted." In particular, he called out the song "The Fixer" as one of the band's best ever and said "'Just Breathe' will just break your heart when you hear it." Those two tracks naturally became singles, as did "Amongst The Waves."

Matt Cameron with the jazz ensemble, Harrybu McCage, performing at Bonnaroo in Manchester, Tennessee on June 15, 2008.

It was all packaged up in clever artwork, not from Jeff or the Ames Bros this time but from cartoon artist Tom Tomorrow, aka Dan Perkins, a friend of the band who was behind the comic strip *This Modern World*. As part of the promotional push for the album, an online scavenger hunt was created to find his complete collection of art panels; if fans did so, they received an exclusive demo recording of album track "Speed Of Sound."

Another change on *Backspacer* is that listening to the album instills an uplifting spirit. It's a quality that Eddie told *Billboard* "just came out" when making it; the fact that Barack Obama was newly elected added to the overall sense of relief, too. "I've tried, over the years, to be hopeful in the lyrics, and I think that's going to be easier now," Eddie shared with *Rolling Stone* at the time. "The new record feels good so far—really strong and up-tempo, stuff we can sink our teeth into."

Rather than belabor topics on this record, Pearl Jam got right to the point and, in the process, made their shortest record to date, at just over thirty-six minutes. There's the punky one-two punch of openers "Gonna See My Friend" and "Got Some," the happy dance of "The Fixer," and the whimsical "Johnny Guitar," with lyrics that paint a narrative behind an album cover of Johnny "Guitar" Watson. As the album continues, out comes the more demure "Speed Of Sound" and evocative love song "The End." But it's "Just Breathe" that is the most haunting and, like "The End," took cues from Eddie's tinkering with his beloved ukulele while he worked on his solo album, *Into the Wild*. "There was something about that little instrument that taught me more about melody than anything or anyone else," he told *Billboard*.

There was also a sense that the band members' individual pursuits in 2008 added to the elevation in their sound. These included reunions, like Stone and Jeff reteaming with former Green River members for a special twentieth anniversary of Sub Pop Records, and Mike finding his way back to Shadow for a benefit show; Matt dug further into his love of jazz with the trio Harrybu McCage; and both Jeff and Eddie were pursuing solo projects, the former releasing *Tone* and the latter taking his solo debut *Into the Wild* on tour.

> As Eddie told *Billboard* of his first solo tour, "As liberating as it was on some levels, it just made it really exciting to know that you're in a band."

He explained, "The thing about touring on your own, you have a smaller crew and it's a little less intense. . . . But knowing you can get back and do the other thing really is kind of having your cake and eating it too. . . . It was getting better at what you do so you can make the band better with your new ability to contribute in different ways."

When *Backspacer* was released September 20, 2009, it was the first studio album officially released on Pearl Jam's own indie label Monkeywrench Records (with distribution from Universal/Republic). So it came as a headscratcher to some when the band then secured a deal with corporate chain Target to carry it—and filmed a commercial for the big box store too.

"We've put a tremendous amount of thought into this, and done it in a way that we think will be good for everybody. If somebody doesn't understand that right now, I don't blame them. We've thought about it for months; they just heard about it and have only thought about it for five minutes," Eddie shared with *Billboard* about the controversial decision, also reaffirming that the album was serviced to indie stores too. "I can't think of anything we've ever done without putting it through our own personal moral barometer. Target has passed for us. The fans just have to trust us."

The decision did move the needle in terms of sales. *Backspacer* was certified platinum by the RIAA® and was Pearl Jam's first album to hit No. 1 on the *Billboard 200* chart since *No Code* in 1996 (even more impressive since it was on an independent label). It also netted Pearl Jam's first

My Pearl Jam Moment

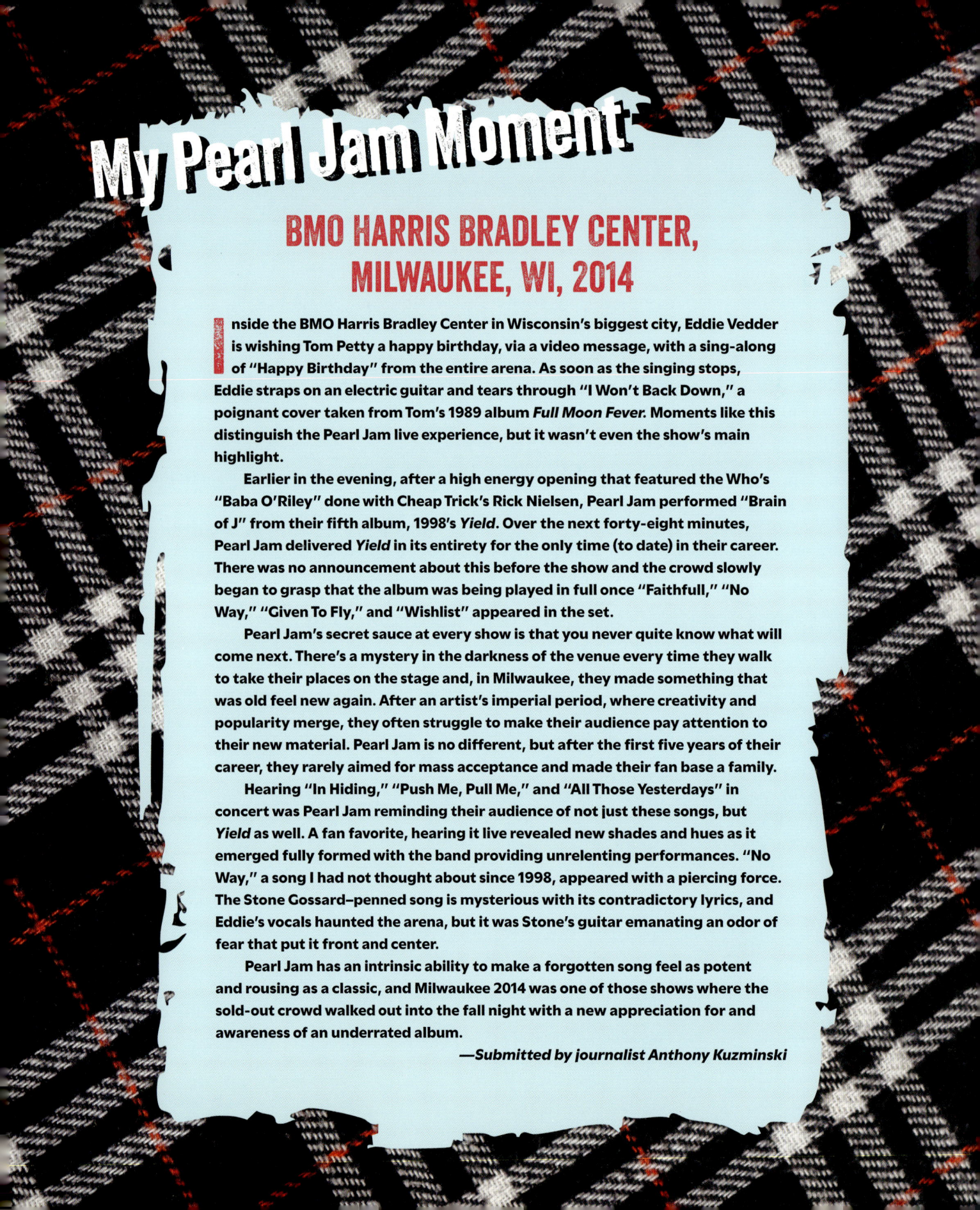

BMO HARRIS BRADLEY CENTER, MILWAUKEE, WI, 2014

Inside the BMO Harris Bradley Center in Wisconsin's biggest city, Eddie Vedder is wishing Tom Petty a happy birthday, via a video message, with a sing-along of "Happy Birthday" from the entire arena. As soon as the singing stops, Eddie straps on an electric guitar and tears through "I Won't Back Down," a poignant cover taken from Tom's 1989 album *Full Moon Fever*. Moments like this distinguish the Pearl Jam live experience, but it wasn't even the show's main highlight.

Earlier in the evening, after a high energy opening that featured the Who's "Baba O'Riley" done with Cheap Trick's Rick Nielsen, Pearl Jam performed "Brain of J" from their fifth album, 1998's *Yield*. Over the next forty-eight minutes, Pearl Jam delivered *Yield* in its entirety for the only time (to date) in their career. There was no announcement about this before the show and the crowd slowly began to grasp that the album was being played in full once "Faithfull," "No Way," "Given To Fly," and "Wishlist" appeared in the set.

Pearl Jam's secret sauce at every show is that you never quite know what will come next. There's a mystery in the darkness of the venue every time they walk to take their places on the stage and, in Milwaukee, they made something that was old feel new again. After an artist's imperial period, where creativity and popularity merge, they often struggle to make their audience pay attention to their new material. Pearl Jam is no different, but after the first five years of their career, they rarely aimed for mass acceptance and made their fan base a family.

Hearing "In Hiding," "Push Me, Pull Me," and "All Those Yesterdays" in concert was Pearl Jam reminding their audience of not just these songs, but *Yield* as well. A fan favorite, hearing it live revealed new shades and hues as it emerged fully formed with the band providing unrelenting performances. "No Way," a song I had not thought about since 1998, appeared with a piercing force. The Stone Gossard–penned song is mysterious with its contradictory lyrics, and Eddie's vocals haunted the arena, but it was Stone's guitar emanating an odor of fear that put it front and center.

Pearl Jam has an intrinsic ability to make a forgotten song feel as potent and rousing as a classic, and Milwaukee 2014 was one of those shows where the sold-out crowd walked out into the fall night with a new appreciation for and awareness of an underrated album.

—*Submitted by journalist Anthony Kuzminski*

Grammy nomination in ten years—for Best Rock Album. Reviews were favorable, too: *Billboard, Rolling Stone, All Music,* and *Q* magazine all featured *Backspacer* in their "best of" lists that year. *SPIN* said of the album's first three tracks, "The band hasn't put together a trifecta this energized and from-the-gut in a decade." And *The Guardian* equated the album to the band "rediscovering their mojo," adding, "the Seattle quartet have rarely sounded this energised."

It was a feeling that carried over into 2010, as Pearl Jam celebrated their milestone twentieth anniversary. After playing Austin City Limits, the final shows of Philly's Wachovia Spectrum Arena, and Eddie feting Bruce Springsteen at the Kennedy Center Honors at the end of 2009, even more special moments continued to fuel the band well into 2010, such as their fourth appearance on *Saturday Night Live,* their debut at the New Orleans Jazz & Heritage Festival, and a pair of shows at Madison Square Garden. They also launched their own SiriusXM channel that year, Pearl Jam's own kind of modern radio takeover that harkens back to those days in the van. Stone and Jeff also reteamed with their former Mother Love Bone bandmates for the first time in twenty years during a one-off show at Seattle's Showbox. And Soundgarden, with Matt in tow, staged their first show in thirteen years. Those historic, nostalgia-fueled moments came crashing into one of Pearl Jam's most memorable feats yet, staging the celebratory PJ20 weekend in 2011.

Pearl Jam onstage at the 41st annual New Orleans Jazz & Heritage Festival on May 1, 2010.

"Rearviewmirror"

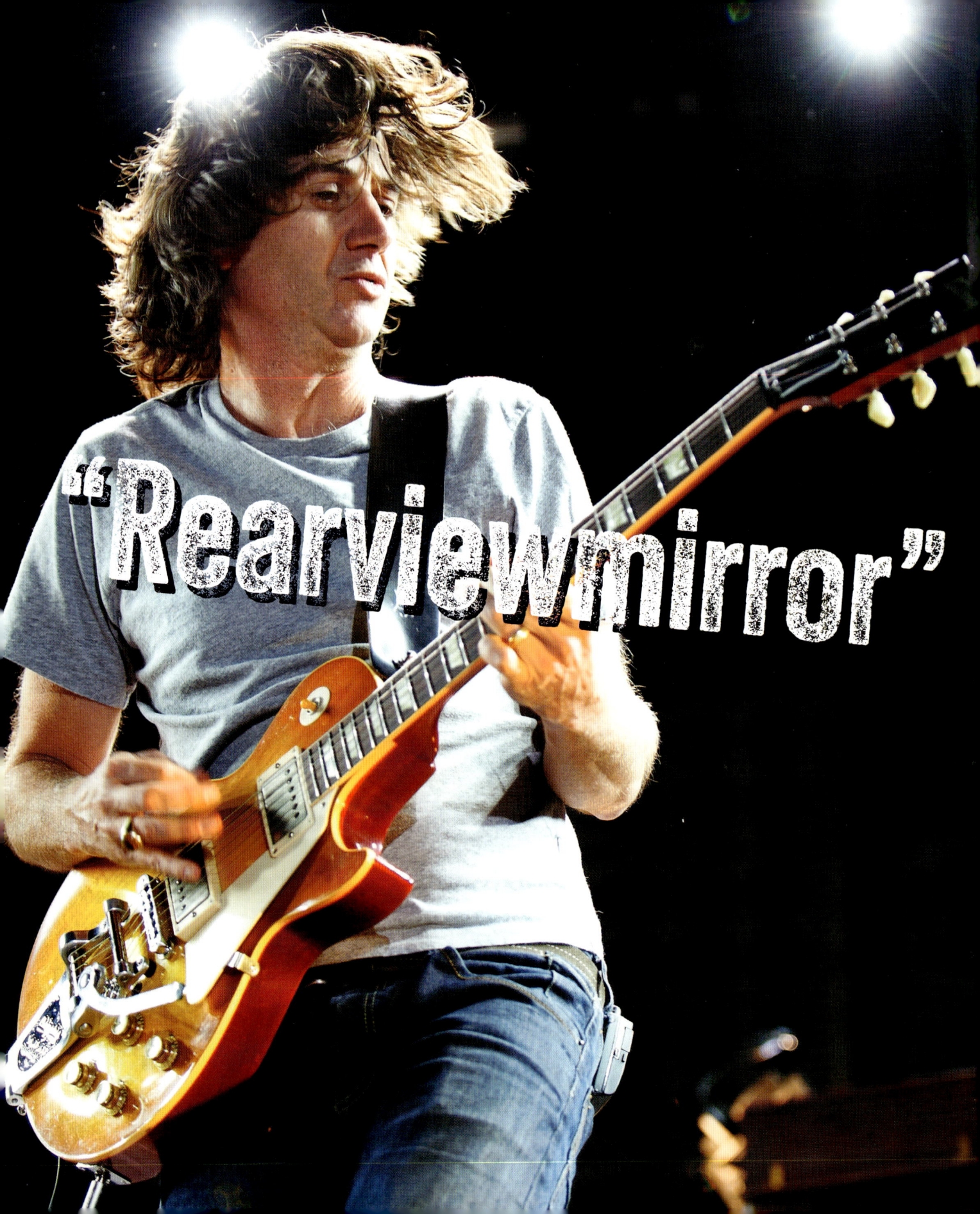

The traditional present for twentieth anniversaries is something platinum. But Pearl Jam had already received that gift—many times over—with their studio and live albums. So, when it came time to celebrate two decades of the long-enduring rock band, they took it up a notch with a smorgasbord of celebrations called Pearl Jam Twenty, including a film, a book, and a tour that featured a mini-festival.

Helming the documentary was Cameron Crowe, whose résumé speaks for itself (the story of *Almost Famous* is all his). There was no better person to make a movie about Pearl Jam.

Cameron, through his marriage to Heart's Nancy Wilson, moved to Seattle in the mid-'80s just as the Seattle sound was gelling. He befriended several of the main characters and then made the 1992 movie loosely based on them. "I liked the idea of working with actors I loved and having it be an ensemble, and just paying tribute to a city and a feeling," the filmmaker shared with *Rolling Stone* in 2017, upon the twenty-fifth anniversary of the cult classic film. "It was a chance to show what it's like when you have a city that you love, and a group of friends who have become your family."

Cameron returned to that idea and his found family with *Pearl Jam Twenty*. In the liner notes of the film's soundtrack, Cameron shared that the conversation around making a film had been percolating with Pearl Jam's manager Kelly Curtis for years: "At many a show, or on the occasion of a new Pearl Jam release, Kelly and I would casually have the same discussion—someday we had to do our PJ movie. Someday we're going to really tell the whole story. We'll use everything!"

They soft-launched the idea in 1998 with *Single Video Theory*. But there was still more to explore in the vast story of Pearl Jam, and the right time finally came as the band looked to mark the big 2-0. Cameron has said he was largely inspired by Martin Scorsese's Bob Dylan exposé *No Direction Home,* as well as Jeff Stein's *The Kids Are Alright,* a premier rock doc on the Who. "To any Who fan, that film caught the experience of being a fan of the band," Cameron said in the *PJ20* liner notes. "It gave their music a home on the big-screen, unfiltered and alive. That was our goal." (In homage, the DVD release of the Pearl Jam film offered an addendum called *The Kids Are Twenty,* with full performances of the songs featured in the flick.)

For *Pearl Jam Twenty,* Cameron and his crew filmed a series of intimate interviews with all the band members at their individual homes and scoured thirty thousand hours of archival footage, collected from various sources—the band, media, fans, and friends. One of the most interesting pieces, and the hardest to track down, according to Cameron, was video footage of Kurt Cobain doing a slow dance with Eddie in a tender moment backstage at the 1992 MTV VMAs. It was

OPPOSITE:
Stone Gossard onstage at the M.E.N. Arena in Manchester, United Kingdom on June 20, 2012.

"rumored to exist for a long time," Cameron told *Entertainment Weekly*. "People remembered cameras being around, but nobody knew if the footage actually existed anywhere." As it turns out, Hole guitarist Eric Erlandson owned it and "rightfully was laying low with it so as to not exploit it" before lending it for the film.

Seeing that moment again was "incredibly emotional," Eddie shared during a discussion at the film's premiere at the Toronto International Film Festival. As Eddie said, "You see Kurt looking over and [he puts his finger to his lips] and it's not saying, 'Don't tell anybody' or 'Keep the lid on this little private moment.' It was actually because on the stage above us, Eric Clapton was playing 'Tears In Heaven.' . . . He's smiling and you think, 'You just gotta pull through.'"

Another much-talked-about part of the film is footage of the disastrous *Singles* party hosted by MTV, when a very inebriated Pearl Jam, already growing disillusioned with media asks, showed up to perform as a favor to Cameron and basically destroyed the set.

"Over the years, we talked about everything. But we never talked about the *Singles* party," Cameron joked at the Toronto International Film Festival panel. In response, Stone said, "Actually, I think we owe you an apology. I figured you'd just say, 'Those guy are such assholes,' and never want to have anything to do with us again."

The band poses with the poster of the Pearl Jam Twenty *documentary during a press conference at the Toronto International Film Festival on September 10, 2011.*

208 PEARL JAM LIVE!

But it was quite the opposite. Cameron stayed in touch with the quintet, save that heavy period between 2002 and 2006 when Pearl Jam was still grappling with Roskilde, 9/11, and the Bush administration.

> **Upon attending a show at Los Angeles's Forum in July 2006, Cameron was drawn right back in, just like so many others when they see Pearl Jam live.**

"I really got knocked over by the fact that this group of fans that found them around the time of Ticketmaster had spawned into this whole other layer of PJ fandom. All these in-between songs that people who loved the band early and maybe took a break from them had missed were epic, and they were anthems. And the audience was right there for every one of them. That's when I turned to [Pearl Jam manager Kelly Curtis] and said, 'Holy crap.'"

In the end, Cameron said he wanted to tell the tale of "how Pearl Jam is the story of lightning striking twice," he told *Rolling Stone*. It's "the flipside of the classic rock tale where great promise ends in tragedy. This is where tragedy begins great promise."

Pearl Jam Twenty was officially released on September 10, 2011, spent a few weeks in theaters, and then aired on PBS's *American Masters* series on October 21 of that year. In addition to the DVD and soundtrack released shortly thereafter, there was also a commemorative book, written in collaboration with music journalists Jonathan Cohen and Mark Ian Wilkerson.

The celebrations continued with the incredibly special PJ20 weekend at Wisconsin's outdoor amphitheater Alpine Valley on September 3 and 4, 2011, which were the band's only US shows in that banner year. Those in attendance were treated to a once-in-a-lifetime concert experience featuring two massive Pearl Jam sets and an assembly of the band's extended musical family to open each day. Among them: the Strokes, Queens of the Stone Age, Mudhoney, John Doe, Joseph Arthur, Glen Hansard, Liam Finn, thenewno2 (the music project of George Harrison's son Dhani), and "special guests to be announced," which of course ended up being the much rumored-about Chris Cornell, resulting in a moving Temple of the Dog reunion on each night. The musicians also came together in a tribute to Mother Love Bone with a performance of "Stardog Champion."

Each of the day's earlier performers also guested on several tracks during Pearl Jam's sets (and the band of honor crashed their cohorts' performances throughout the weekend), drawing comparisons to the comradery behind the origin of the Seattle scene. Some notable examples included the Strokes' Julian Casablancas on "Not For You," Dhani Harrison on "State Of Love And Trust," and Queen of the Stone Age's Josh Homme on "In The Moonlight."

My Pearl Jam Moment

PJ20 WEEKEND, EAST TROY, WI, 2011

The first thing I noticed was all the flags. From Mexico to Japan, it was a United Nations of Pearl Jam fandom converging at Alpine Valley. *Is this what world peace looks like?* I remember wondering. At a Pearl Jam show, it comes pretty close. For two days that weekend in 2011, the outside world did not exist, nor did language barriers or cultural differences. All of us fans continually conversed and huddled together in some of the longest merch lines I've ever seen, and waited for our turn in the Pearl Jam museum.

It was my first time ever writing about Pearl Jam, on an assignment for *PopMatters*, though, by my estimates, I've done so about ten times since. They were all great shows, of course, including an incredible feat at Wrigley Field in 2013 when, Mother Nature be damned, Pearl Jam waited out the storm and played until 2 a.m. But I'll always remember my first.

By the time of their twentieth anniversary, Pearl Jam had pretty much dropped off my radar. In 1995, in my bedroom, I wore out my CDs of *Ten* and *Vs.* and *Vitalogy*, but then, for whatever reason, I stopped listening until that weekend.

When Pearl Jam played their epic sets that weekend—sixty-one songs in total—the emotions swept over me. I remember pulling the hooded part of my sweatshirt over my head, trying to hide the tears coming down my face as I scribbled notes into my notepad. But when I looked up, I saw others crying too. It was safe to feel here. And it was palpable.

I remember hearing that Chris Cornell was likely to be a guest during the weekend—and it's probably the first prayer I had uttered in fifteen years, begging the universe to make it true. Hearing "Say Hello 2 Heaven" was incredibly moving back then, as a beautiful tribute to Andy Wood, but my god has that moment lived in my head and taken on new meaning in the years since Chris died.

I was so glad this assignment had me get there early each day to capture and review the openers, too, especially Eddie joining Glen Hansard for "Falling Slowly" from *Once* and then taking on cowbell duty for Queens of the Stone Age's "Little Sister." But my one and only disappointment that weekend was trying to beat the crowd out and missing the epic finale of "Yellow Ledbetter" on the last night. I learned my lesson: At Pearl Jam shows, never go home early, and be ready for anything.

—*Submitted by Selena Fragassi, author of*
Pearl Jam Live! 35 Years of Legendary Music and Revolutionary Shows

SPIN ranked the weekend at No. 8 on its list of Pearl Jam's 10 Best Shows, and *Rolling Stone* called it "epic" and a "reward for fans."

The band, too, was caught up in the momentousness of it all, as Eddie shared at the Toronto International Film Festival: "We've been in grateful mode and appreciation mode for each other for quite some time. It's a galvanizing moment." But it was far from the end—more electrifying moments were soon coming for Pearl Jam.

Eddie Vedder and The Strokes's Julian Casablancas perform together during the PJ20 weekend at Alpine Valley Music Theatre in East Troy, Wisconsin on September 3, 2011.

SET LIST SPOTLIGHT

The Twentieth Anniversary Shows
September 3–4, 2011, Alpine Valley, East Troy, WI
NIGHT ONE

1. Release
2. Arms Aloft (Joe Strummer & the Mescaleros cover)
3. Do The Evolution
4. Got Some
5. In My Tree
6. Faithfull
7. Who You Are (with Glen Hansard)
8. Push Me, Pull Me
9. Setting Forth (Eddie Vedder song)
10. Not For You (with Julian Casablancas)
11. In The Moonlight (with Josh Homme)
12. Deep
13. Help Help
14. Breath
15. Education (with Liam Finn)
16. Once
17. State Of Love And Trust (with Dhani Harrison)
18. Better Man
19. Wasted Reprise
20. Life Wasted

– ENCORE –

21. Rearviewmirror

– ENCORE 2 –

22. Stardog Champion (Mother Love Bone cover, with Chris Cornell)
23. Say Hello 2 Heaven (Temple of the Dog cover, with Chris Cornell)
24. Reach Down (Temple of the Dog cover, with Chris Cornell)
25. Hunger Strike (Temple of the Dog cover, with Chris Cornell)
26. Love, Reign O'er Me (The Who cover)
27. Porch

– ENCORE 3 –

28. Kick Out The Jams (MC5 cover, with Mark Arm and Steve Turner)

NIGHT TWO

1. Wash
2. The Fixer
3. Severed Hand
4. All Night (with Glen Hansard)
5. Given To Fly
6. Pilate
7. Love Boat Captain
8. Habit (with Liam Finn)
9. Even Flow
10. Daughter
11. Leatherman
12. Red Mosquito (with Julian Casablancas)
13. Satan's Bed
14. Elderly Woman Behind The Counter In A Small Town (with Dhani Harrison)
15. Unthought Known
16. The New World (X cover, with John Doe)
17. Black
18. Jeremy

– ENCORE –

19. Improvisation
20. Just Breathe
21. Nothingman
22. No Way
23. Public Image (Public Image Ltd cover)
24. Smile (with Glen Hansard)
25. Spin The Black Circle

– ENCORE 2 –

26. Hunger Strike (Temple of the Dog cover, with Chris Cornell)
27. Call Me A Dog (Temple of the Dog cover, with Chris Cornell)
28. All Night Thing (Temple of the Dog cover, with Chris Cornell)
29. Reach Down (Temple of the Dog cover, with Chris Cornell)
30. Sonic Reducer (Dead Boys cover, with Mark Arm)

– ENCORE 3 –

31. Alive
32. Rockin' In The Free World (Neil Young cover, with all performers)
33. Yellow Ledbetter

HIDDEN PEARL

There were several songs noted on the set lists that were not played during the weekend, such as Mother Love Bone's "Chloe Dancer/Crown Of Thorns" and the Who's "The Real Me," as well as Pearl Jam songs "I Got Id," "Indifference," "All Those Yesterdays," "Down," and "Present Tense."

"Glorified G"

It may have just been an act of God, or maybe Pearl Jam summoned the best promotional plug even money can't buy. Either way, there was magic in the air when lightning struck Wrigley Field on July 19, 2013, just eight days after Pearl Jam announced their anticipated new album, *Lightning Bolt,* coming that October. In fact, the whole night was a mix of high-voltage emotions as the band played the historic ballpark for the first time in their career, satisfying a dream for lifelong Chicago Cubs fan Eddie Vedder. Though he had sung the "Seventh Inning Stretch" and thrown out countless first pitches at the Friendly Confines, Pearl Jam had yet to play the ballpark.

"It's kind of like I've been waiting a lifetime for this one," Eddie, who was raised in nearby Evanston, Illinois, shared with the forty-thousand-strong crowd at the sold-out show. "Not only is this the crown jewel of Chicago but the crown jewel of the whole planet Earth." Pearl Jam was able to get through seven songs—beginning the set with their favorite opener, "Release," and moving through mellow hits "Nothingman," "Low Light," and "Elderly Woman . . ." before Mother Nature had other plans.

"There's potential weather we might have to get through as a team," Eddie shared, alerting fans to take cover in the grandstands inside the ballpark and asking them to hang tight, promising the band would be back when it was safe to resume the show.

> "They're going to have to kick us off the stage tonight," he added as the rain delay set in. It took nearly three hours to get the all-clear, and when the show came back to life, Pearl Jam—with the blessing of the powers that be—ended up playing until 2 a.m. in a total display of showmanship.

There's all kind of accounts of the fan camaraderie that occurred that night—I personally remember it well. We were all huddled together in the concourse, in sweltering heat and humidity no less, as the sky lit up the night. Concession stands were running low on supplies, and bathroom lines were unreal, but still there was a palpable buzz in the air, as well as the idea that we were all in this together.

"At one point, we were keeping ourselves busy by checking off various tour shirts; I think we saw them all except for *Riot Act*," *Consequence of Sound* shared in their recap of the night. "These were dedicated fans: *No Code* supporters, Mookie Blaylock/Seattle Supersonics jersey owners, and one guy even had a faux bar shirt that read 'Welcome to Lukins.' The enthusiasm was a nice touch, and in a way, it was almost like the reverse-PCU rule, where those who DIDN'T wear a

OPPOSITE:
Jeff Ament during a Temple of The Dog show at The Forum in Los Angeles, California on November 14, 2016.

Frequent Pearl Jam photographer Danny Clinch posing next to his image of the band at Hard Rock Calling in London, England on June 25, 2010.

band shirt were The Uncool. . . . not only did the community make this a unique experience, but also acted as a crutch to lean on when the storm took things over."

For anyone wondering what the band was doing at this time, well, naturally they were on the phone with meteorologists. "Eddie [was] actually on the phone with the city weather guy talking about the cells coming through," Kelly Curtis shared with *Billboard*.

When Pearl Jam did come back to the stage, it was completely worth the wait—at least for those who kept their faith in the band's word and stuck around to see it all unfold in the pre-dawn. Eddie ripped into his unofficial Cubs theme song, "All The Way," accompanied by a guest appearance from baseball great (and his childhood hero) Ernie Banks. When the band rejoined him on the stage, they delivered twenty-five songs including an accordion-flanked rendition of "Bugs," covers of Van Halen, Pink Floyd, and Mother Love Bone, and three songs from *Lightning Bolt:* "Mind Your Manners," the title track, and "Future Days." The latter two were live debuts.

Pearl Jam made such an impression with their Wrigley Field debut, the band was invited back in 2016, 2018, and 2024. And, a few months after that incredible 2013 marathon, Fox Sports contracted the band to "soundtrack" the 2013 World Series. The network queued up forty-eight songs from the band's catalog, including all twelve tracks from *Lightning Bolt*. "The band loves baseball, so this one was a no-brainer," Kelly Curtis told *Billboard* about the licensing deal.

216 PEARL JAM LIVE!

And really what better way to promote a new album?

Maybe a mini-documentary by Danny Clinch. The photographer/filmographer, who has documented many moments in Pearl Jam's career, not only directed the music videos for *Lightning Bolt* singles "Mind Your Manners" and "Sirens" but also put together a nine-minute short film to give more context to the full album. It features pop culture and sports figures like moviemaker Judd Apatow, Sleater-Kinney's Carrie Brownstein, surfer Mark Richards, and former NFL star Steve Gleason interviewing the band, with commentary spliced between vignettes of rehearsal footage and more candid moments. They were some of the only interviews Pearl Jam did for this album promo cycle, finding another unique way around the media circus as they had done in years prior.

There's a moment in the mini-film where Eddie starts talking about some of the intensified feelings that surround the *Lightning Bolt* material: "If you're paying attention to what's going on . . . I feel like I can find something to be angry about pretty quick." If *Backspacer* was the calm, then *Lightning Bolt,* with its longer songs and more defiant and sometimes pessimistic sound, was definitely the storm brewing over the four years between albums. It reflects the band's percolating morosity and curiosity with the nature of getting older, particularly after reflecting on Pearl Jam's twentieth anniversary and its road ahead.

"The time has been one of reckoning with both the past and future," *Billboard* shared in a feature on the album, which again was steered by producer Brendan O'Brien and released on Monkeywrench Records.

In the article, Stone expanded on the idea, sharing, "As a band, we're all at an age now where there's a lot of reflection going on. [At] 40-something, almost 50-something, you're looking at life through your kids' eyes, through the filter of relationships that are 20 or 30 years long, through the filter of your parents getting older and the passing of friends and relatives—relationships and all that they encompass, the difficulties of them and the sacrifices you make in them and also the joy they bring you."

For Eddie, one flash of inspiration came from an injury he suffered in 2012 that resulted in nerve damage to his guitar-playing hand. After canceled solo tour dates and an intense round of rehab, it gave the frontman pause. "Not knowing how things are going to turn out—or if things are going to turn out, if you're going to heal—that's the hard part," he shared in *Billboard.* "When the magnifying glass of tragedy selects you, it changes you. It ends up making you so much more empathetic. So part of what the record is saying is, try to live an empathetic life. Don't wait for tragedy to hit you before you start understanding what other people are going through." You can hear him grappling with that existentialism on the acoustic

SET LIST SPOTLIGHT

The Rain Delay Victory
July 19, 2013, Wrigley Field, Chicago, IL

1. Release
2. Nothingman
3. Present Tense
4. Hold On
5. Low Light
6. Come Back
7. Elderly Woman Behind The Counter In A Small Town

INTERMISSION

8. All The Way (Eddie Vedder song with Ernie Banks)
9. All Night
10. Do The Evolution
11. Setting Forth (Eddie Vedder song)
12. Corduroy
13. Faithfull
14. Mind Your Manners
15. Lightning Bolt (live debut)
16. State Of Love And Trust
17. Wishlist
18. Even Flow
19. Leatherman
20. Eruption (Van Halen cover)
21. Bugs
22. Why Go
23. Unthought Known
24. Rearviewmirror

— ENCORE —

25. Future Days (live debut)
26. Mother (Pink Floyd cover)
27. Chloe Dancer/Crown Of Thorns (Mother Love Bone cover)
28. Porch
29. Wasted Reprise
30. Life Wasted
31. Black
32. Rockin' In The Free World (Neil Young cover)

HIDDEN PEARL

The original curfew for the show was 11 p.m. but the band successfully negotiated with officials to push it to 2 a.m. after the nearly three-hour weather delay. "If there was any way that we were going to get it done, whether it meant fines or whatever, we were going to take that on. At the end of the day, the city, and the Cubs, the promoter, fire department, everybody, they were on the same page in a great way. There was a little bit of yelling but no giant fines," Kelly Curtis told *Billboard*.

rocker "Swallowed Whole," the eerie piano-heavy "Pendulum" (with the expert playing of Boom Gaspar), and the gripping, cinematic ballad "Sirens."

> **"Sirens" is a high point for Mike, who wrote the music after being inspired by seeing Pink Floyd's Roger Waters in concert.**

The song "Future Days" was another one inspired by heavy events, namely the accidental death of the Frogs' Dennis Flemion in 2012. The band was one that Pearl Jam toured with in the early '90s and remained friends with over the years, and Dennis's passing gave credence to the fact that everyone was getting older, and that death seemed to be all around. Sadly, this would only continue in the years ahead. "It sounds so pedestrian and ridiculous, but death is everywhere," Eddie shared. "Maybe just because I read the paper every day. Maybe it's war, maybe it's the epidemic rates of suicide in veterans coming back. I just can't seem to get around it. . . . Songs end up being mantras that you end up playing for yourself as well."

Of course, there are thunderous moments on *Lightning Bolt* as well, like the breakneck pace heard on the Dead Kennedys–infused "Mind Your Manners" and the bluesy riffs of "Let The Records Play," a total stylistic disruptor for Pearl Jam. There's also the powerful aggression in "My Father's Son" that feels like it could have fit in with the best of Pearl Jam's '90s material, and of course it grapples with the same complicated family dynamics that served as a well of inspiration for Eddie back then. "Everybody's kind of playing out of their minds on this record," Eddie shared in the Danny Clinch mini-doc of the great musicality behind the album. *Lightning Bolt* also curiously features "Sleeping By Myself," which originally appeared on Eddie's 2011 solo album, *Ukulele Songs*, but it's given an overhaul on Pearl Jam's record via the inclusion of all of Pearl Jam's members lending their parts and serving as a reminder that the sum of the band has always been paramount to the individual band members.

Released October 15, 2013, *Lightning Bolt* was another No.1 hit on the *Billboard 200* chart and the single "Sirens" placed on the *Hot 100* chart at No. 76. *The A.V. Club* said, "The album still feels fresher and more relevant than the world at large might expect at this point—this classic-rock band still has at least a few classics left in it." *Popmatters* declared, the fact "that Pearl Jam can craft such a fine record at this stage in their storied career is astounding," adding that, with *Lightning Bolt,* the band was "rebounding after some divisive releases with one of the finest of their career." Jeff and collaborators Don Pendleton, Joe Spix, and Jerome Turner even took home a Grammy award for the Best Recording Package, honoring the artwork.

Pearl Jam toured the album heavily throughout 2013–2016 with stops at Voodoo Music + Arts Experience in New Orleans; a number of Big Day Out appearances across Australia during the festival's final year; the Global Citizen Festival in New York; North American tour dates with their old friends in Mudhoney; and a new round of shows in Europe and South America.

> **In 2016, there was a return to the gilded ballparks so dear to Pearl Jam, including two dates at Fenway Park and a pair at Wrigley Field, with the latter producing the *Let's Play Two* live album.**

There was also a stop at Bonnaroo, where Eddie took the occasion to pan Donald J. Trump before the 2016 election: "There's some candidate out there that's talking about building a giant wall . . . that would be disrespectful to millions of human beings. The United States of America was actually built on exactly the opposite idea. I was thinking about if there was an option, maybe we just build a wall around him."

Lightning Bolt was, remarkably, the only album Pearl Jam would put out in the 2010s, reversing course from their early days of churning out material every couple of years. In fact, the next album, *Gigaton,* wouldn't find its release until 2020. "It's good to wait until we feel like we do have something to say," Jeff shared in Danny Clinch's short documentary. In the dormancy, Pearl Jam members focused on solo projects, continued copious touring, and took some time to process the continual highs and lows that have eclipsed the course of their career. This time around, that contrast came into sharp profile in 2017 as Pearl Jam celebrated a big personal milestone while, soon after, mourning the grave loss of a close friend.

Pearl Jam onstage at Wells Fargo Center in Philadelphia, Pennsylvania on April 29, 2016.

My Pearl Jam Moment

TAURON ARENA, KRAKÓW, POLAND, 2018

I remember my cousin brought a cassette tape over to my house with the song "Daughter" on it, and from that first note Eddie Vedder hit with his powerful vocals, I was sucked in. I was in middle school in the mid-'90s when Pearl Jam quickly gained popularity, but as a pre-teen/teenager, I wasn't into going to shows; that happened much later.

I was never a huge fan of flying so going to Europe was something I never really thought I would make happen. However, when Pearl Jam announced a summer tour in Europe in 2018, a friend of mine encouraged me to buy a ticket to Poland, where I have ancestry I'd wanted to explore. I set an alarm to be awake to be able to buy a ticket when they went on sale at local Polish time, and did it!

It was a life-changing experience. When I arrived in Poland, I met some friends from Boston who were camping out at the arena. They introduced me to other friends who had also traveled from the States, and it felt like I was home and not multiple time zones away. The Pearl Jam show was unlike any other I had been to; the fans there aren't used to having them play in their cities as often as they do in the US. The merchandise flew off the shelves before I was able to get anything, but the experience superseded that feeling of disappointment. I had met someone in 2016 in New York City who I also met up with in Poland, and he introduced me to someone who upgraded my ticket for a closer General Admission spot than I originally purchased.

There were many emotions being so far away from home and on my first trip to Europe and exploring my ancestry ties. I remember crying during "Why Go," which was unusual for me because normally that song doesn't hit me like that, but the first time seeing my favorite band in a foreign country changed everything. It was also very interesting to see the active floor during "Better Man"—it seems like European fans enjoy that song, maybe even more so than their American counterparts. There was essentially a mosh pit happening while that song was being played, something I had not seen at a Pearl Jam show before. The set was pretty unique as well, as the band played thirty songs and included some rarities like "Green Disease" and the ultra-rare "Other Side."

After the show, I walked out with those friends who I had met the previous day camping out. I was explaining how I was somewhat bummed because I didn't get a T-shirt or anything show-specific to commemorate my experience. Their young son had gotten a few guitar picks from Mike McCready, and he proceeded to hand me one. That was another emotional moment for me and solidified why I love the community that has been built around the band.

I may not have realized it at the time, but that Pearl Jam show was probably one of my favorites. I stepped out of my comfort zone, saw a fantastic show, met some new friends, and got to spend time with older friends. This band has meant so much to me for more than half my life. It was great to have the thirtieth show be in a unique-to-me city and, since then, I have seen twenty-one more shows and hopefully more to come!

—*Submitted by photographer Matt Lambert (Trebmal Photo)*

"NOTHING As It Seems"

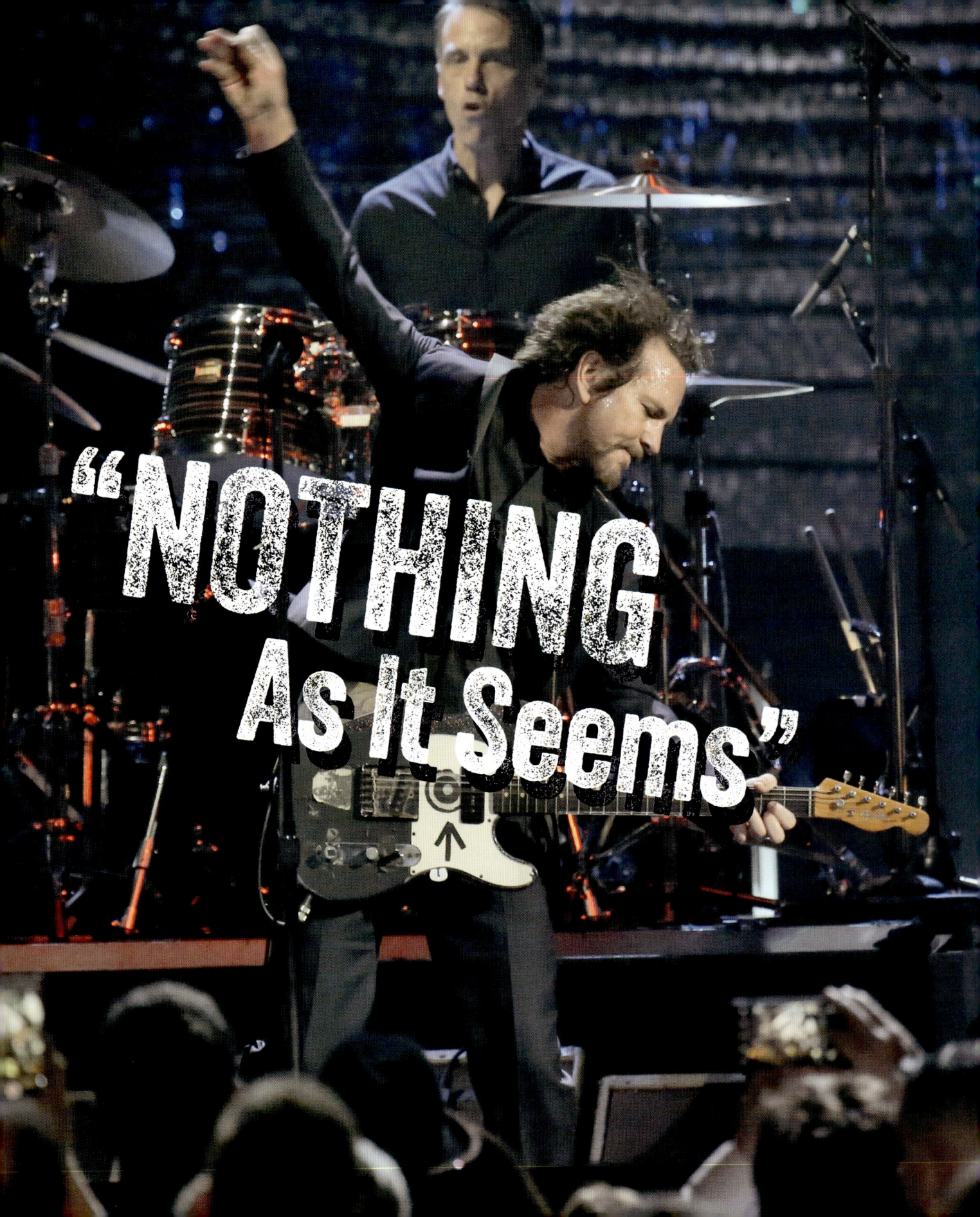

The year 2017 started off with incredible promise. On April 7, Pearl Jam was notably inducted into the Rock & Roll Hall of Fame. It was the band's very first year of eligibility (the window opens twenty-five years after a group's debut record), and the voting class of one thousand-plus historians, artists, and music industry insiders wasted no time in ushering Pearl Jam through. The Rock Hall's fan vote, established in 2012, no doubt helped Pearl Jam as well.

Pearl Jam's classmates included the late Tupac Shakur, Journey, Joan Baez, Electric Light Orchestra, Yes, and Nile Rodgers, most of whom were still alive and well and converged at the Barclays Center in Brooklyn for the induction ceremony. As mentioned, Pearl Jam was lovingly inducted by long-time friend David Letterman, replacing Neil Young who had to bow out due to illness.

Letterman offered a range of jokes, like jesting that he originally met the guys in 1988 as a member of Mother Love Bone.

> But he also took a serious tone when espousing the importance of live music and Pearl Jam's legacy as a "true, living cultural organism."

As the former late-night talk show host explained, the band was one that "would recognize injustice and stand up for it, whether it was human rights, whether it was the environment, whether it was poverty—they didn't let it wash over them, they would stand up and react."

When it came time to talk about Pearl Jam's music, Dave had plenty of praise there, too. "I used to have a television show, and they were on my show ten different times over the years, and every time they were there, they would blow the roof off the place." There was a heartfelt moment when Dave showed the audience a small acoustic guitar Eddie had gifted to his son Harry and read the letter Eddie addressed to the younger Letterman: "I'll make you a deal, if you learn even one song on this guitar, I'll get you a nicer, bigger one for your birthday. Maybe an electric one. You let me know." Dave, still touched by the gesture, shared, "Forgive me if I believe this personally is the most important reason they're in the Hall of Fame."

Pearl Jam ripped into three electric performances that night, forgetting they didn't have to prove themselves: they'd already won the award. And in addition to those rousing renditions of "Better Man," Neil Young's "Rockin' In The Free World," and "Alive" (with OG drummer Dave Krusen), band members gave their own acceptance speeches. They were a far cry from their "Thanks, I guess" comments at the Grammys twenty years prior.

OPPOSITE:
Pearl Jam's Eddie Vedder and Matt Cameron onstage at the 32nd Annual Rock & Roll Hall Of Fame induction ceremony in New York City on April 7, 2017.

Stone had a long list of behind-the-scenes people that he believed deserved credit beyond just the band members; he also thanked the "larger Pearl Jam community . . . whose belief in us carried us through the times where we didn't believe or we lost hope or we lost the plot or we lost each other." Dave Krusen, who came out from the shadows with a pair of drumsticks in his hand, shared just a few words and credited Pearl Jam with "saving my life." Matt thanked his parents "for letting me practice drums in their house" and his siblings for taking him to his first concert, David Bowie, in 1977. Among Mike's shout-outs were the Red Hot Chili Peppers "for taking us out in the beginning and treating us totally right," as well as the many bands that have inspired him over the years, including KISS, Cheap Trick, Queen, Bowie, Hendrix, the Stones, the Beatles, UFO, Kraftwerk, Ramones, Brandi Carlile, Sleater-Kinney, the Kills, Social Distortion, Muddy Waters, Sex Pistols, the Clash, "and my new favorite band Thunderpussy and also the Stereo Embers." Jeff reflected on the "pretty great fucking life" he has enjoyed in Pearl Jam, expounding that he was grateful for "making music and art, traveling the world supporting causes and programs together, making small differences, meeting great artists and creative minds all over the world," and dedicated the honor to "every small-town kid who has a dream."

Eddie, last to speak, did so in true Vedder fashion, beginning his speech by quoting the lyrics of "Do The Evolution," and talking about the effects of climate change. "We cannot be the generations that history looks back upon and wonders why didn't they do everything humanly possible to solve this biggest of crisis in our time. Anything can be attainable," he added, pointing to his beloved Chicago Cubs winning the World Series the year prior as proof. Eddie also apologized for making his bandmates "suffer" when he exhibited his crazy acrobatics early in their career, chalking them up to "the power of rock 'n' roll."

Wrapping up his remarks at the Rock & Roll Hall of Fame ceremony, Eddie said:

> "If it weren't for everybody out there that cared about our music, if it weren't for everybody out there who came to our shows and brought their energy . . . those were the things that really kept us together and we felt a responsibility to the music that was bigger than ourselves. It was you that galvanized us and forged a brotherhood and a family."

Yet just forty days later, the brotherhood would be rocked upon losing yet another member of their extended family. On May 18, 2017, it was announced that Chris Cornell had died by suicide, just hours after Soundgarden had played a show in Detroit the night before.

The news was devastating, shocking, and baffling to fans around the world who were left to grapple and process another huge and unexpected loss.

In an emotional essay for *Billboard,* former Jane's Addiction and Red Hot Chili Peppers guitarist Dave Navarro echoed that sentiment: "I just can't believe that all these people I came up with are gone: Scott [Weiland], Kurt [Cobain], Layne [Staley], now Chris. All my friends are dying. How is it possible?"

In the days that followed, many others posted remembrances of the iconic singer. Courtney Love shared, "Goodbye darling boy. Please say hi to all my loved ones. I cried for you today. Rip." And Heart's Nancy Wilson wrote, "No one is ever prepared to hear about a death in the family. And today Chris Cornell my brother from my Seattle music family is gone. I thought his voice would forever grace the world of music. Devastating."

Unsurprisingly, it was days before Pearl Jam could find any words to express how they felt. On May 20, the official band account posted a black-and-white photo of their friend hugging a dog on social media, simply accompanied by the word "Chris." How could they possibly sum up the life and death of a person who was so intimately a part of their tribe? Matt's bandmate, Eddie's friend and early mentor, Andy's one-time roommate, their guiding light in Temple of the Dog—Chris was part of their very fabric.

His passing weighed heavily on everyone in the band. On the one-year anniversary, Matt posted a solemn tribute that read, in part, "Can't believe

Soundgarden's Kim Thayil shows fans a shirt featuring a likeness of Chris Cornell before performing with Pearl Jam at Safeco Field in Seattle, Washington on August 10, 2018.

it's already been one year since I lost my musical soulmate and special friend Chris Cornell.... I will forever praise him for the decades of encouragement he gave me and for the fierce friendship we forged. I love you buddy." And in 2020, when Eddie appeared on *The Howard Stern Show* for the first time, he opened up about Chris's death, sharing, "I still haven't dealt with it." At the time of Chris Cornell's passing, Eddie was still grieving his half-brother, also named Chris, and the thought of two important figures vanished from his life was almost too much to bear. "It was a dark place. I just couldn't deal with the reality," he told Howard Stern. "I've had to be somewhat in denial."

Eddie was absent at Chris's private memorial in 2017 and a special tribute concert in January 2019, which bewildered many fans. But in the same way many of Pearl Jam's members have grieved at various points, Eddie also grieved by throwing himself into his music.

> During a solo tour in the summer of 2017, Eddie shared with the crowd, "So I haven't really been talking about some things . . . that's just how I'm dealing with it. I want to be there for the family, be there for the community, be there for my brothers in my band, certainly the brothers in his band. But these things will take time, but my friend is going to be gone forever. . . . He wasn't just a friend; he was someone I looked up to like my older brother."

The loss of Chris rippled through the Pearl Jam camp for a few years, in part contributing to the delay of their next studio album. In 2019, shortly after Jeff, Stone, and Matt participated in the January "I Am The Highway" tribute concert for Chris held in Los Angeles, Jeff spoke to *Rolling Stone,* admitting that Pearl Jam was in "a little bit of limbo." He added, "It'd be fun to record or even just to write a song together. I think when Chris passed—that's really been a tough one to wrap our heads around—and then there's just life stuff." At the time, Jeff was also busy leading the creative direction on a special box set simply called *Chris Cornell*. It was a process he had started while Chris was still alive and continued after he passed, winning a Grammy for Best Recording Package in 2020.

In an interview with *Rolling Stone,* Stone assured readers that Pearl Jam was "just going to keep plugging away [at the album] until we get one done." It came in the form of *Gigaton* in 2020, which, in total, took Pearl Jam three years to make. They laid some groundwork in 2017 and continued to chip at it during breaks from their tour in 2018.

That extensive run included new dates in South America, such as Lollapalooza Chile and Brazil, as well as Europe, including Pearl Jam's return to the Pinkpop Festival in the Netherlands

Pearl Jam performs at Fenway Park in Boston, Massachusetts on September 4, 2018.

(where, in 1992, Eddie notoriously scaled a camera crane and used it as a launchpad for one of his most ludicrous stage dives).

For years, Eddie believed a Pinkpop cameraman named Rob was mad at him, and perhaps wanting some penance in 2018, he tracked Rob down and discovered it was quite the opposite. "He told me a completely different story than what I've had in my head all these years," Eddie shared with the Pinkpop crowd those twenty-six years later. "What he was doing was, if I were to jump on that thing, he had to get other guys to hold the back, the ballast, otherwise I would've I jumped on and we just would've gone down. So . . . he's not yelling at me, he's yelling to get other guys to hold us up. So the whole time . . . we were working in tandem but we had no clue whatsoever!"

The 2018 tour also offered more dates at ballparks, including the Seattle Home Shows to raise money for the city's homeless population and another pair of dates at both Fenway and Wrigley Field.

By 2019, for the first time in the history of Pearl Jam, the band scheduled zero appearances in order to wrap up work on their new album. *Gigaton* marked yet another new roadmap for Pearl Jam in the progression of their album-making over the years. For the first time, it

NOTHING AS IT SEEMS

was a record "that we made by ourselves," Stone told *Vinyl Writer*. It was also the last record with long-time manager Kelly Curtis overseeing it; he retired in 2020, a long thirty years after becoming the band's right-hand man in 1990. Since then, Pearl Jam's long-time tour manager Mark "Smitty" Smith has stepped into the role.

Gigaton had some assistance from co-producer Josh Evans, an engineer who first worked with the band in 2006 on the avocado album and, later, joined them on tour as a guitar tech. But it was Pearl Jam leading the way on manifesting the material. "I think that *Gigaton* is a record that we really took on as a personal challenge to kind of see if we could do it ourselves," Stone added. "And it was a good growing experience also because everybody did something that they didn't expect to do or had songs that ended up on the record that represented a new plateau or something new for them."

That involved switching up instrumentation on several tracks in a welcome game of musical chairs. Stone took on bass for "Dance Of The Clairvoyants," Mike played keyboard parts on "Retrograde," Matt took on guitar for "Take The Long Way" and "Alright," and Jeff worked in some

Pearl Jam finally performs at Live At The Apollo Theater in New York City for SiriusXM's Small Stage Series on September 10, 2022.

kalimba percussion to "Alright" and "River Cross." Brendan O'Brien also participated, adding keyboards to "Quick Escape" and "Retrograde."

Over fifty-seven minutes, Pearl Jam's longest record to date, the music takes on an experimental tone. There's electronic, new wave influences on "Dance Of The Clairvoyants," a drone-y intro for "Who Ever Said," the cinematic calm of "Alright," and the use of a Victorian pump organ for incredible atmospherics on the devout "River Cross." There's also more straightforward cuts from the standard Pearl Jam playbook that take cues from classic rock and punk. Some of the standouts come through in the raw bite of "Superblood Wolfmoon," the buzzy staccato of "Quick Escape," and the heavily layered jam "Take The Long Way."

Some lyrics take on more of an abstract vibe to match the conceptual nature of the music. For example, many have assumed that the pensive "Comes Then Goes" is about Chris Cornell, although the band has never confirmed it. Though, there are more definitive name checks. On "Quick Escape," Eddie sings that he's trying to discover somewhere President Trump hadn't yet ruined. More thoughts on the government come alive on "River Cross." Talk of freedom and there still being a lot to do inundate "Seven O' Clock." The album cover itself is a pretty clear comment on climate change, with conservation photographer Paul Nicklen's capture of a majestic bluff and waterfalls overlayed with a graphic of a red heartbeat.

As the album launched in a pivotal election year, Pearl Jam continued their political canvassing outside the confines of the music, too. They launched the PJ Votes 2020 initiative, which urged fans to participate in the "Take Three Pledge: vote by mail, recruit three friends, and don't wait." In a press release announcing the effort, Eddie shared, "We believe America is at its best when every voice is heard. This is the most important election in our nation's history. Our democracy is at risk. Your vote is your voice, and it's time to use it. Join us by voting by mail—something our band has been doing for almost three decades, since we began touring in 1992. It's safe, it's easy, and it's secure."

Pearl Jam had big plans for rolling out *Gigaton,* some of which were able to happen (like setting up a hotline to hear songs "Dance Of The Clairvoyants" and "Superblood Wolfmoon") and others that were squashed due to the COVID-19 pandemic swiftly shutting down gatherings around the time the album was released via Monkeywrench on March 27, 2020. Among the canceled events was a Dolby surround sound listening experience for the album and a slew of tour dates, including a special show at the world-famous Apollo Theatre. In fact, Pearl Jam was one of the first major acts to cancel live shows early on in March of 2020, though they did release poster art for canceled dates as a consolation.

My Pearl Jam Moment

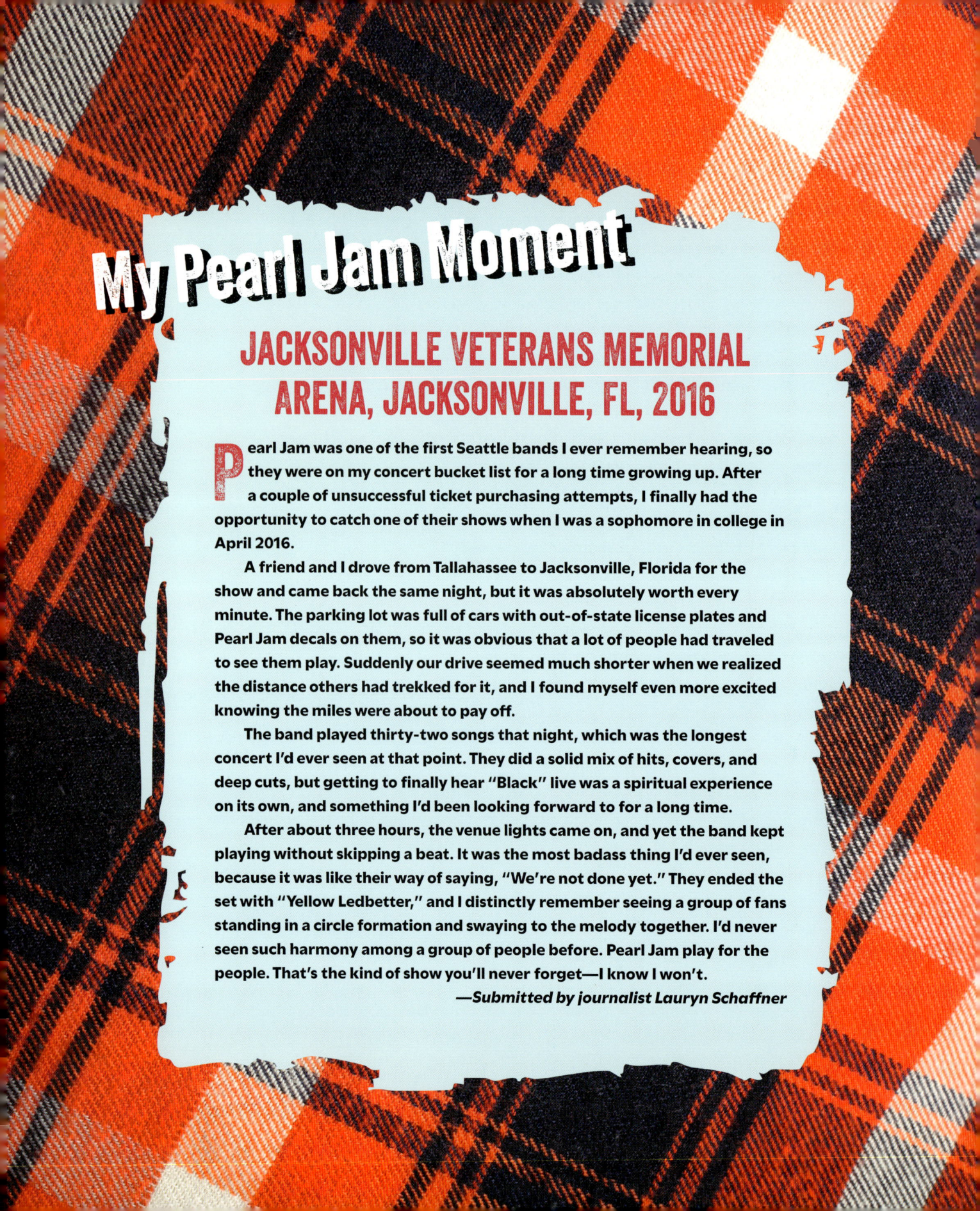

JACKSONVILLE VETERANS MEMORIAL ARENA, JACKSONVILLE, FL, 2016

Pearl Jam was one of the first Seattle bands I ever remember hearing, so they were on my concert bucket list for a long time growing up. After a couple of unsuccessful ticket purchasing attempts, I finally had the opportunity to catch one of their shows when I was a sophomore in college in April 2016.

A friend and I drove from Tallahassee to Jacksonville, Florida for the show and came back the same night, but it was absolutely worth every minute. The parking lot was full of cars with out-of-state license plates and Pearl Jam decals on them, so it was obvious that a lot of people had traveled to see them play. Suddenly our drive seemed much shorter when we realized the distance others had trekked for it, and I found myself even more excited knowing the miles were about to pay off.

The band played thirty-two songs that night, which was the longest concert I'd ever seen at that point. They did a solid mix of hits, covers, and deep cuts, but getting to finally hear "Black" live was a spiritual experience on its own, and something I'd been looking forward to for a long time.

After about three hours, the venue lights came on, and yet the band kept playing without skipping a beat. It was the most badass thing I'd ever seen, because it was like their way of saying, "We're not done yet." They ended the set with "Yellow Ledbetter," and I distinctly remember seeing a group of fans standing in a circle formation and swaying to the melody together. I'd never seen such harmony among a group of people before. Pearl Jam play for the people. That's the kind of show you'll never forget—I know I won't.

—*Submitted by journalist Lauryn Schaffner*

"We've worked hard with all our management and business associates to find other solutions or options, but the levels of risk to our audience and their communities is simply too high for our comfort level. Add to that we also have a unique group of passionate fans who travel far and wide," the band shared in a statement on their website.

Gigaton became its own kind of salve during lockdowns with many reviews praising its topical nature and engrossing soundtrack for what felt like the end times. A *Los Angeles Times* article headline declared *Gigaton* to be "hymns of the apocalypse" and said the "new album was made for this pandemic moment . . . Pearl Jam knows we're not feeling fine here at the end of the world, but they're hoping this helps." *USA Today* likewise opined, "Pearl Jam's *Gigaton* is the angry but hopeful album we need right now," adding the band's music "feels all the more reassuring in these uncertain times." As a result, *Gigaton* entered the *Billboard 200* chart at No. 5 and became a popular vinyl sale in 2020.

As the pandemic waged on and Pearl Jam, like so many others, was faced with the challenge of staying engaged while the world was stuck at home, they pivoted—and they took fans with them. What does a band who has built such a career and reputation on live shows do when everything is on pause? Release a swell of special offerings to tide fans over and give them hope when they need it most.

First among the lockdown releases, issued for the first time ever, was a vinyl edition of the *MTV Unplugged* session as well as a massive collection of five thousand-plus live songs from shows in 2000–2013 that were shared with streaming services (previously only available to Ten Club members). Pearl Jam also launched a new comprehensive Deep website allowing fans the chance to curate their own set lists and wade through a concert archive to look back on the good times. The band filmed a lockdown video of "Dance Of The Clairvoyants" for the *All In WA: A Concert For COVID-19 Relief,* and Eddie performed "River Cross" solo as part of the *One World: Together at Home* special for Global Citizen.

Pearl Jam's incredible offerings during the lockdown led to their latest personal-best record, taking the No. 1 spot in the Bandsintown list of the year's top streaming artists. Even when they couldn't perform live and in person, Pearl Jam—with the help of their passionate fan base—still kept their reputation and legacy intact. And when the world opened back up, it was once again Pearl Jam's oyster.

Jeff Ament captured in the All In WA: A Concert For COVID-19 Relief livestream filmed in Washington on June 24, 2020.

"FUTURE Days"

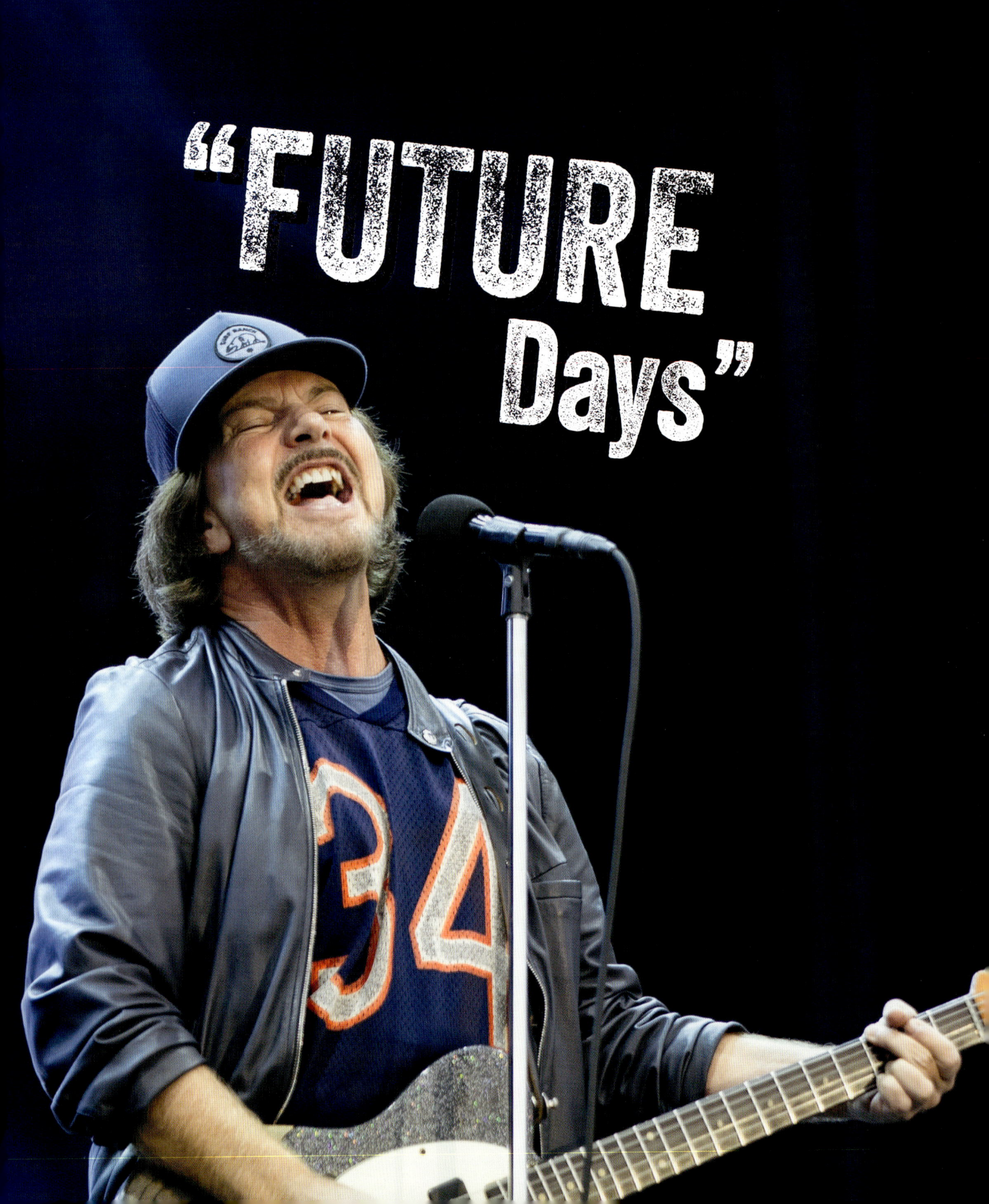

There are many theories as to why Eddie was seen, night after night, on the *Dark Matter* tour wearing a number-34 Walter Payton football jersey. Of course, he's a diehard Chicago sports fan; that wasn't new. Nor was wearing the jersey, which he'd done for at least a decade, after it was gifted to him by a late uncle. But why was it becoming his nightly uniform?

On Reddit, some theorized it was gloating about Donald Trump being convicted on thirty-four felony counts in his hush-money case, which seems like a fair take on Eddie, who once pettily joked about the president's manhood at a show in New York in 2016. But, would it be too innocent to believe that Eddie just wanted to celebrate thirty-four years of Pearl Jam's existence in 2024? Jarrett Payton, Walter's son who Eddie invited out to the PJ show at Wrigley Field that September, told local news station WGN that there's a bit of superstition behind it, too. "[He] will keep rocking the jersey because he doesn't want to jinx the good vibes they've had on stage along the way [on this tour]," Jarrett recalled Eddie telling him.

It makes sense when you think about it. After a tireless and dedicated thirty-four years and eleven albums in, Pearl Jam had one of their biggest career achievements in decades with their twelfth LP, *Dark Matter,* released on April 19. The title track was featured at No. 27 in *Consequence's* list of the Best 200 songs of 2024, as editors declared, "Welcome back, Pearl Jam," adding that the band "delivered one of their best albums of the millennium . . . proving the alternative icons can still make impactful music even as much of the industry moves away from similar sounds." SPIN also added the album to their best of 2024 list, writing, "*Dark Matter* is a bright light in the barren wilderness of 21st century rock'n'roll." Pearl Jam was soon nominated for three Grammy awards for the effort, including Best Rock Performance, Best Rock Album, and Best Rock Song—their first nominations in fourteen years.

"No hyperbole, I think this is our best work," Eddie said in an official press release announcing the album. The PR adds that *Dark Matter* "channels the shared spirit of a group of lifelong creative confidants and brothers in one room playing as if their very lives depended on it. All of the blood, sweat, tears, and energy of a storied career felt renewed and poured into this one body of work."

A prominent piece of the puzzle was producer Andrew Watt. It was the first time the band worked with the young, lauded producer who, in his short tenure, has manned the board for everyone from the Beatles' Paul McCartney to the Stones, Elton to Ozzy, Post Malone to Miley Cyrus, Iggy Pop to Justin Bieber.

It was a collaboration that was bigger than Pearl Jam itself, one that was born in the stars. Andrew's birthday just so happens to be October 20, 1990.

OPPOSITE:
Eddie Vedder wearing his trademark number-34 jersey on a *Dark Matter* tour stop in Dublin, Ireland on June 22, 2024.

FUTURE DAYS · 233

That's right, two days before Pearl Jam played their first show at the Off Ramp Café. "They've said to me they were probably writing 'Release' while my mom was giving birth to me," Andrew joked with *Rolling Stone*. "I don't want to get too biblical about it, but it's very, very strange."

> **Andrew, who had previously worked in bands like California Breed, had been a fan of Pearl Jam since he was a child, first seeing them live at Madison Square Garden in 2003 and attending shows at least forty times since.**

As Andrew explained to *Rolling Stone,* when he randomly found himself at the famed Shoreline Amphitheatre in California, where Pearl Jam has participated in so many Bridge School Benefit shows, Andrew took his shot. He left the receptionist a message for Eddie, along with a guitar to be given to the frontman at the next benefit gig. Sure enough, within a few months, Andrew had a voicemail from Eddie. As Andrew moved into the world of production, the two naturally had mutual friends and kept in touch. To the point where Eddie hired him to work on his 2022 solo album *Earthling* and asked him to join him on the road in his Earthlings backup band.

Andrew Watt performs with Pearl Jam during a Dark Matter tour stop at New York City's Madison Square Garden on September 4, 2024.

The experience was so great that Eddie couldn't wait to bring Andrew into the world of Pearl Jam, too. "It was based on the results I was feeling from this solo excursion," Eddie shared with Zane Lowe in a sweeping interview for Apple Music in 2024. "He's got a bit of a freight train energy about him."

The band said it was one of the most unusual but productive production sessions they've ever experienced. Andrew, coming at it from a fan's perspective, wore a different Pearl Jam T-shirt from his collection for each day in the studio (Rick Rubin's famous Shangri-La Studios in Los Angeles). "And he was kind of playing with the band," Stone told Zane Lowe about Andrew's direct involvement. "His enthusiasm and his understanding of the band, his love for the band, his ability to play any of our songs at any point and know the history . . . and then to be cheering us on, you'd laugh at it and think, this is kind of silly, but also it was infectious and you'd be caught up in his enthusiasm," Stone added. "That's why he's the perfect producer for us, we're so part of his childhood and he understands us so well, there's no color he's bringing to this band that sounds like . . . something different. He can fit in in a way that sounds right."

Andrew told *Rolling Stone* his motive was: "I just wanted them to be them. I didn't want to change them." In fact, his favorite thing about Pearl Jam has always been "watching them live," he added in *SPIN*. "They're one of very few bands that is even better live than they are on record. They sound bigger and better because there's no fancy trickery about them in the studio. My mission statement became, I'm going to put these five amazing guys together in a small space where they can all see

Pearl Jam in all their live glory during a concert in Berlin, Germany on June 21, 2022.

each other, and get them to play together and capture that energy of what happens on stage. Let's go for full takes. Let's go for solos that are a little too long."

The energy was contagious, and the band completed the album in just three weeks. Jeff told Zane Lowe the "hair was standing up on my neck" after sessions and, for the first time, Eddie was handing out lyric sheets, proud of his work.

"It's made by a fan for the fans, and I hope that they dig it," Andrew told *SPIN*. His wish came true. *Dark Matter* debuted on the *Billboard 200* chart at No. 5 (marking Pearl Jam's twelfth consecutive studio album in the Top 10) and both singles "Wreckage" and the title track made it to No. 1 on the *Mainstream Rock Airplay* chart; another track, "Waiting For Stevie," landed at No. 13 on the chart. That song—quite literally about a time in the studio when Eddie and Andrew were waiting for Stevie Wonder to show up to track parts on *Earthling*—was selected as Record Store Day's song of the year in 2024.

In total, the album takes on a similar thematic tone as previous records, conscious of the world and its pitfalls but trying to find hope while navigating it all. It's expressed over a familiar bedrock of anthemic shredders ("React, Respond"), crunchy alt rock ("Dark Matter"), slow burning folkies ("Wreckage"), punky quips ("Running"), and heartfelt ballads ("Setting Sun").

Many of the tracks came alive on tour, where Pearl Jam worked with visionary Rob Sheridan (another Seattlite, known for his conceptual work with Nine Inch Nails) to create textured, moody, abstract visuals, a total departure from Pearl Jam's normally bare-boned stages of years past.

Pearl Jam started touring again post-pandemic in 2021, beginning with a set at the ocean sustainability festival Sea.Hear.Now—and hasn't really stopped. In the past few years, they've attempted new Lollapalooza iterations in Stockholm, Sweden and in Paris; played "Hunger Strike" for the first time since Chris Cornell's untimely passing; returned to Wrigley Field and Fenway; soldiered through "near-death" illnesses; continued to deliver marathon sets as members enter their sixties; and announced their next run of shows for 2025. At thirty-five-years young, there's a sense that Pearl Jam is still just getting started. Through Andrew, the band has found revitalization. Through fans, they've sustained a lifeline. Through each other, they've maintained the brotherhood that has always made them so strong. And through their ideology, they've presented a humanism to music that is a rare gem—by sticking to causes closest to them, bucking trends, and bringing people together for so many years in a way that few other bands have been able to do for the long haul.

"I think at some point along the way we began feeling we wanted to give people something to believe in because we all had bands that gave that to us when we needed something to believe in," Eddie told *Los Angeles Times* in 2000. "The answers weren't always easy, but I think we found a way."

When it comes to what has made Pearl Jam survive for thirty-five years, even when the odds seemed stacked against them, band members have offered differing takes, though all return to the sense of community so deeply embedded in their identity.

"It's miraculous in some ways that we made it through it and then also it's just a testament to our friendship," Jeff told *CBS Sunday Morning* in 2024.

"There might have been a few speed bumps in the road, but we got through those by looking out for each other. In that way, we felt secure," Eddie told *MOJO*. "The goal is to keep making music. It's your passion, your special purpose. You lean on the relationships with the people who are still around."

"Pearl Jam has survived this long by luck and because over the years the five of us have confronted each other on issues," Mike told *Daily Record*. "The reason why we've lasted so long

Matt Cameron, Eddie Vedder, and Stone Gossard perform at Rogers Arena in Vancouver, British Columbia on May 4, 2024.

My Pearl Jam Moment

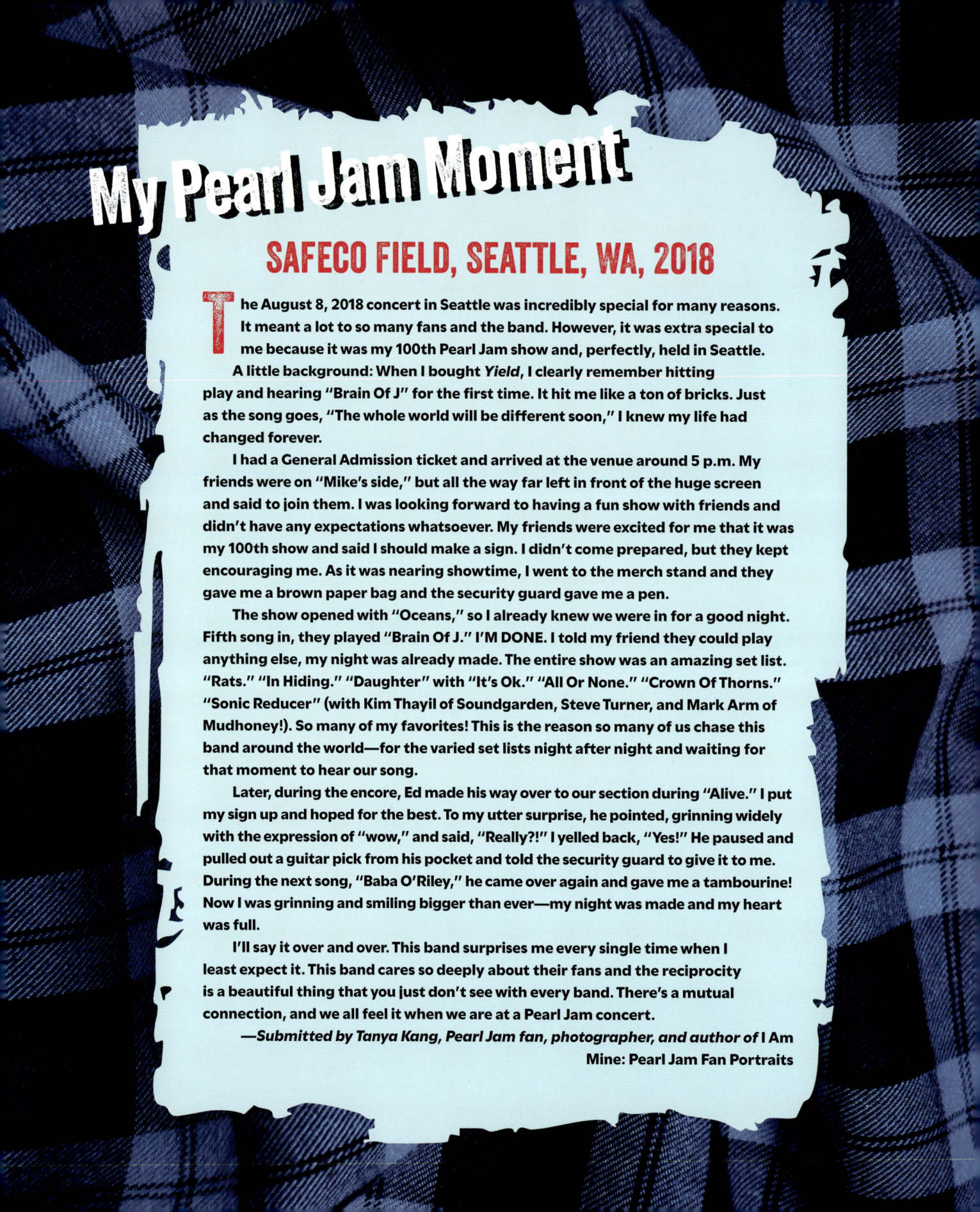

SAFECO FIELD, SEATTLE, WA, 2018

The August 8, 2018 concert in Seattle was incredibly special for many reasons. It meant a lot to so many fans and the band. However, it was extra special to me because it was my 100th Pearl Jam show and, perfectly, held in Seattle.

A little background: When I bought *Yield*, I clearly remember hitting play and hearing "Brain Of J" for the first time. It hit me like a ton of bricks. Just as the song goes, "The whole world will be different soon," I knew my life had changed forever.

I had a General Admission ticket and arrived at the venue around 5 p.m. My friends were on "Mike's side," but all the way far left in front of the huge screen and said to join them. I was looking forward to having a fun show with friends and didn't have any expectations whatsoever. My friends were excited for me that it was my 100th show and said I should make a sign. I didn't come prepared, but they kept encouraging me. As it was nearing showtime, I went to the merch stand and they gave me a brown paper bag and the security guard gave me a pen.

The show opened with "Oceans," so I already knew we were in for a good night. Fifth song in, they played "Brain Of J." I'M DONE. I told my friend they could play anything else, my night was already made. The entire show was an amazing set list. "Rats." "In Hiding." "Daughter" with "It's Ok." "All Or None." "Crown Of Thorns." "Sonic Reducer" (with Kim Thayil of Soundgarden, Steve Turner, and Mark Arm of Mudhoney!). So many of my favorites! This is the reason so many of us chase this band around the world—for the varied set lists night after night and waiting for that moment to hear our song.

Later, during the encore, Ed made his way over to our section during "Alive." I put my sign up and hoped for the best. To my utter surprise, he pointed, grinning widely with the expression of "wow," and said, "Really?!" I yelled back, "Yes!" He paused and pulled out a guitar pick from his pocket and told the security guard to give it to me. During the next song, "Baba O'Riley," he came over again and gave me a tambourine! Now I was grinning and smiling bigger than ever—my night was made and my heart was full.

I'll say it over and over. This band surprises me every single time when I least expect it. This band cares so deeply about their fans and the reciprocity is a beautiful thing that you just don't see with every band. There's a mutual connection, and we all feel it when we are at a Pearl Jam concert.

—*Submitted by Tanya Kang, Pearl Jam fan, photographer, and author of* I Am Mine: Pearl Jam Fan Portraits

is we write music, we get very intense, we go away from each other, do our own thing and then we get back together."

"You get so much more out of not breaking up. We have these relationships that nobody has to decide who they're going with. There's so much you get out of everybody keeping the focus on moving forward as opposed to dividing," Stone told *Billboard*. "[There's a] general appreciation for how special it all is. There's this gratitude where we all just can't believe that we get to do this and get to continue to do it. So it builds, it builds on itself."

And Matt, well, he's been the important glue the past twenty years, as Eddie shared in their Rock & Roll Hall of Fame speech: "Matt Cameron has really been the one that really kept us alive for this last fifteen, sixteen, seventeen years."

From an outsider's perspective, the late, great Seattle music journalist Charles R. Cross maybe said it best. "The remarkable thing about Pearl Jam is that they did not break up, and the music they create today still has meaning to them," he told *The Seattle Times*. "In the history of Seattle bands, that's a heck of an accomplishment."

(l-r) Josh Klinghoffer, Mike McCready, Jeff Ament, Eddie Vedder, Matt Cameron, Stone Gossard, and Boom Gaspar prepare to bow after taking over the Climate Pledge Arena in Seattle, Washington on May 28, 2024.

STUDIO ALBUM DISCOGRAPHY

This list encompasses studio albums released by Pearl Jam, and does not include live albums or bootlegs.

*Sales information provided by the Recording Industry Association of America®

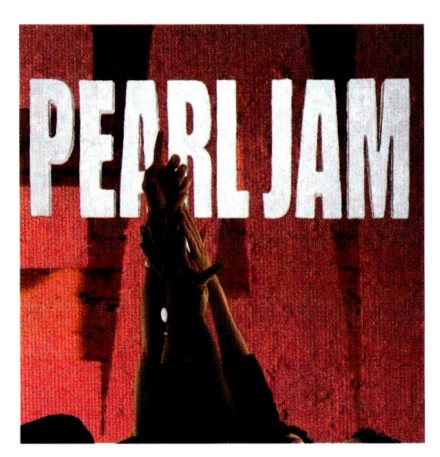

Ten

Original Release Date: August 27, 1991
Record Label: Epic
Singles:
"Alive" (July 7, 1991)
"Even Flow" (April 6, 1992)
"Jeremy" (August 17, 1992)
"Oceans" (December 7, 1992)
Producers: Rick Parashar & Pearl Jam
Sales: 13 million US

*In 2009, the album was reissued with remixes and remastering from Brendan O'Brien

Vs.

Original Release Date: October 19, 1993
Record Label: Epic
Singles:
"Go" (October 25, 1993)
"Daughter" (November 2, 1993)
"Animal" (April 4, 1994)
"Dissident" (May 16, 1994)
Producers: Brendan O'Brien & Pearl Jam
Sales: 7 million US

*In 2011, the album was reissued in honor of Pearl Jam's twentieth anniversary

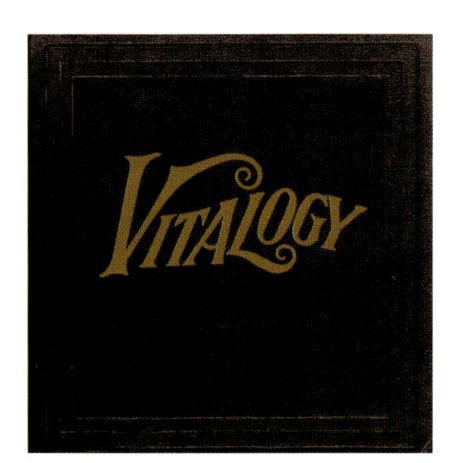

Vitalogy

Original Release Date: December 6, 1994 (first released on vinyl November 22, 1994)
Record Label: Epic
Singles:
"Spin The Black Circle" (November 8, 1994)
"Not For You" (February 13, 1995)
"Immortality" (June 6, 1995)
Producers: Brendan O'Brien & Pearl Jam
Sales: 5 million US

*In 2011, the album was reissued in honor of Pearl Jam's twentieth anniversary

240 PEARL JAM LIVE!

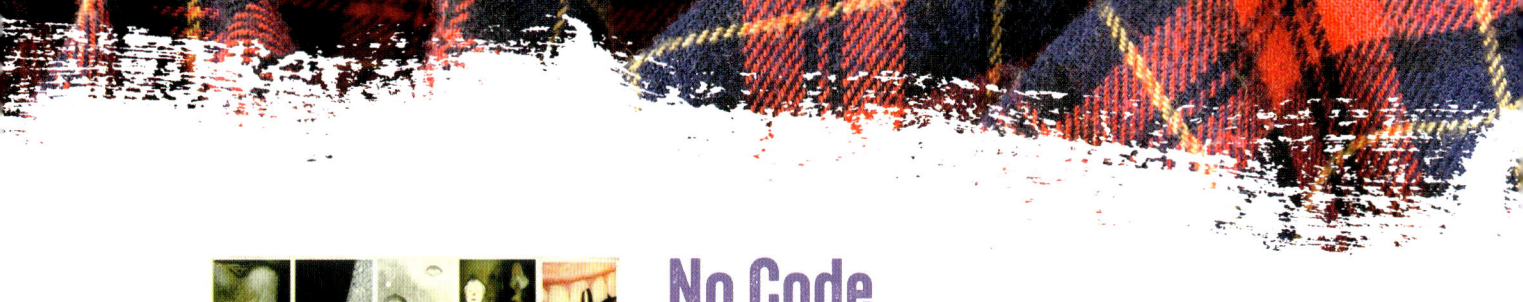

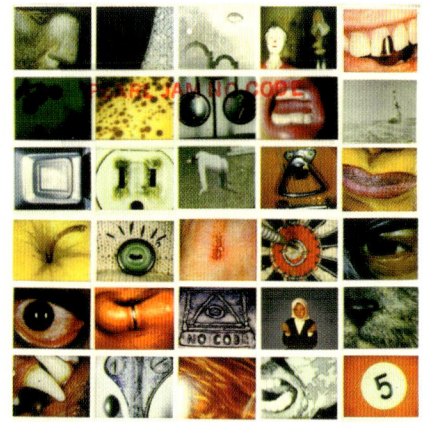

No Code

Original Release Date: August 27, 1996
Record Label: Epic
Singles:
"Who You Are" (July 30, 1996)
"Hail, Hail" (October 21, 1996)
"Off He Goes" (January 11, 1997)
Producers: Brendan O'Brien & Pearl Jam
Sales: 1 million US

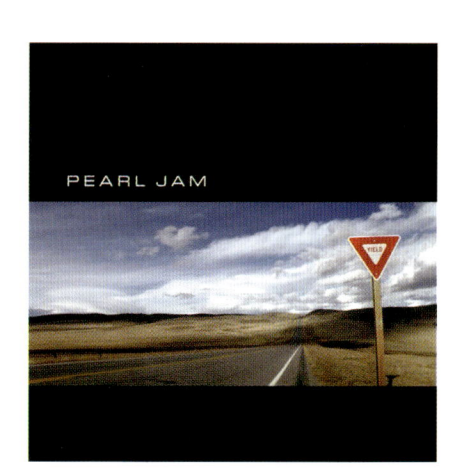

Yield

Original Release Date: February 3, 1998
Record Label: Epic
Singles:
"Given To Fly" (December 22, 1997)
"Wishlist" (May 5, 1998)
Producers: Brendan O'Brien & Pearl Jam
Sales: 1 million US

Binaural

Original Release Date: May 16, 2000
Record Label: Epic
Singles:
"Nothing As It Seems" (April 25, 2000)
"Light Years" (July 10, 2000)
Producers: Tchad Blake & Pearl Jam
Sales: 500,000 US

Riot Act
Original Release Date: November 12, 2002
Record Label: Epic
Singles: "I Am Mine" (October 8, 2002); "Save You" (February 11, 2003); "Love Boat Captain" (February 24, 2003)
Producers: Adam Kasper & Pearl Jam
Sales: 500,000 US

Lost Dogs
Original Release Date: November 11, 2003
Record Label: Epic
Producers: Tchad Blake, Adam Kasper, Brendan O'Brien, Rick Parashar & Pearl Jam
Sales: 500,000 US

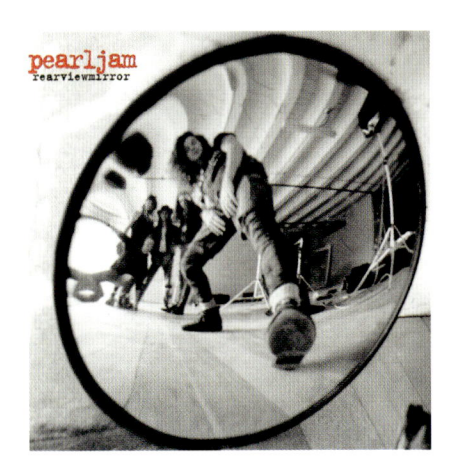

Rearviewmirror (Greatest Hits 1991–2003)
Original Release Date: November 16, 2004
Record Label: Epic
Producers: Tchad Blake, Brett Eliason, Adam Kasper, Brendan O'Brien, Rick Parashar & Pearl Jam
Sales: 1 million US

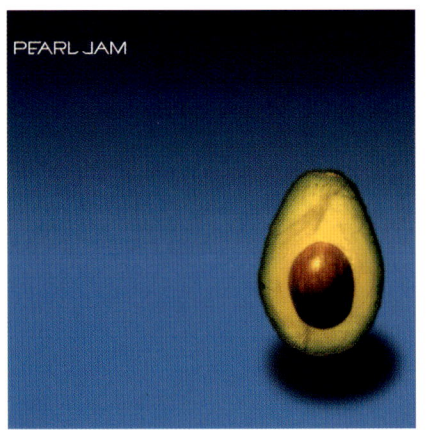

Pearl Jam
Original Release Date: May 2, 2006
Record Label: J Records
Singles: "World Wide Suicide" (March 14, 2006); "Life Wasted" (August 28, 2006); "Gone" (October 7, 2006)
Producers: Adam Kasper & Pearl Jam
Sales: 500,000 US

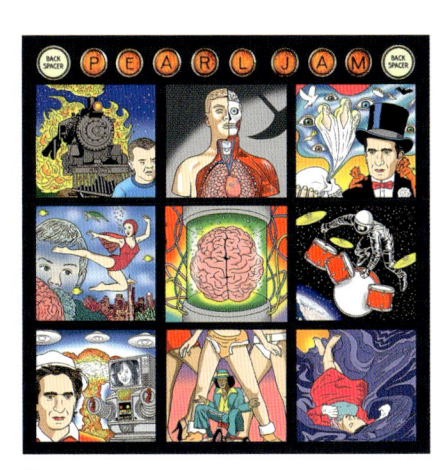

Backspacer

Original Release Date: September 20, 2009
Record Label: Monkeywrench
Singles: "The Fixer" (August 24, 2009); "Got Some"/"Just Breathe" (October 31, 2009); "Amongst The Waves" (May 17, 2010)
Producer: Brendan O'Brien
Sales: 500,000 US

Lightning Bolt

Original Release Date: October 15, 2013
Record Label: Monkeywrench/Republic
Singles: "Mind Your Manners" (July 11, 2013); "Sirens" (September 18, 2013); "Lightning Bolt" (March 4, 2014)
Producer: Brendan O'Brien
Sales: Approximately 250,000 US

Gigaton

Original Release Date: March 27, 2020
Record Label: Monkeywrench/Republic
Singles: "Dance Of The Clairvoyants" (January 22, 2020); "Superblood Wolfmoon" (February 18, 2020); "Quick Escape" (March 25, 2020); "Retrograde" (May 14, 2020)
Producers: Josh Evans & Pearl Jam
Sales: Approximately 175,000 US

Dark Matter

Original Release Date: April 19, 2024
Record Label: Monkeywrench/Republic
Singles: "Dark Matter" (February 13, 2024); "Running" (March 22, 2024); "Wreckage" (April 17, 2024); "Waiting for Stevie" (September 10, 2024)
Producers: Andrew Watt & Pearl Jam
Sales: Approximately 125,000 US

AWARDS & NOMINATIONS

American Music Awards

Favorite Pop/Rock New Artist 1993 (Won)

Favorite New Heavy Metal/Hard Rock Artist 1993 (Won)

Favorite Pop/Rock Band/Duo/Group 1994 (Nominated)

Favorite Heavy Metal/Hard Rock Artist 1994 (Nominated)

Favorite Heavy Metal/Hard Rock Artist 1995 (Nominated)

Favorite Alternative Artist 1996 (Won)

Favorite Heavy Metal/Hard Rock Artist 1996 (Won)

Favorite Alternative Artist 1999 (Won)

Favorite Alternative Artist 2006 (Nominated)

Golden Globes

Best Original Song, "Man Of The Hour," 2004 (Nominated)

Grammys

Best Rock Song, "Jeremy," 1993 (Nominated)

Best Hard Rock Performance, "Jeremy," 1993 (Nominated)

Best Rock Performance by a Duo or Group with Vocal, "Daughter," 1995 (Nominated)

Best Hard Rock Performance, "Go," 1995 (Nominated)

Best Rock Album, Vs., 1995 (Nominated)

Best Hard Rock Performance, "Spin the Black Circle," 1996 (Won)

Album of the Year, Vitalogy, 1996 (Nominated)

Best Rock Album, Vitalogy, 1996 (Nominated)

Best Hard Rock Performance, "Do The Evolution," 1999 (Nominated)

Best Music Video, Short Form, "Do The Evolution," 1999 (Nominated)

Best Recording Package, Yield, 1999 (Nominated)

Best Hard Rock Performance, "Grievance," 2001 (Nominated)

Best Rock Song, "The Fixer," 2010 (Nominated)

Best Rock Album, Backspacer, 2011 (Nominated)

Best Recording Package, Lightning Bolt, 2015 (Won)

Best Rock Performance, "Dark Matter," 2025 (Nominated)

Best Rock Song, "Dark Matter," 2025 (Nominated)

Best Rock Album, Dark Matter, 2025 (Nominated)

MTV VMAs

Best Alternative Video, "Alive," 1992 (Nominated)
Video of the Year, "Jeremy," 1993 (Won)
Best Group Video, "Jeremy," 1993 (Won)
Best Metal/Hard Rock Video, "Jeremy," 1993 (Won)
Best Direction, "Jeremy," 1993 (Won)
Viewer's Choice, "Jeremy," 1993 (Nominated)
Best Special Effects, "Life Wasted," 2006 (Nominated)

Rock & Roll Hall of Fame

Inducted in 2017

Pearl Jam appearing at the 1993 MTV Video Music Awards in Los Angeles, California on September 3, 1993.

AWARDS & NOMINATIONS

SELECTED SOURCES

Apple Music. "Pearl Jam: The 'Dark Matter' Interview." April, 2024. https://www.youtube.com/watch?v=ZpuuIpsgaPQ

Bass Player. "Godfather of the 'G' Word." April, 1994. Archived on Five Horizons. https://www.fivehorizons.com/archive/articles/bp0494.shtml

Billboard chart history. https://www.billboard.com/artist/pearl-jam/chart-history/hsi/

Billboard. "Pearl Jam: The 'Backspacer' Q&As." September, 2009. https://www.billboard.com/music/music-news/pearl-jam-the-backspacer-qas-267474/

Billboard. "Pearl Jam: Spreading The Jam." March, 2001. https://www.billboard.com/music/music-news/pearl-jam-spreading-the-jam-80213/

Billboard. "Pearl Jam's Eddie Vedder Talks Surfing, Story Behind 'Jeremy' In Rediscovered 1991 Interview." April, 2017. https://www.billboard.com/music/rock/pearl-jam-eddie-vedder-1991-interview-vintage-7751635/

Billboard. "Pearl Jam's 'Lightning Bolt': Billboard Cover Story." October, 2013. https://www.billboard.com/music/music-news/pearl-jam-lightning-bolt-billboard-cover-story-5755381/

Billboard. "Pearl Jam's 'New' World Order." April, 2006. https://www.billboard.com/music/music-news/pearl-jams-new-world-order-58752/

Billboard. "Pearl Jam's Stone Gossard Talks Brad, PJ & More." August, 2010. https://www.billboard.com/music/music-news/pearl-jams-stone-gossard-talks-brad-pj-more-956709/

Billboard. "*Riot Act* track-by-track." October, 2002. Archived at Internet Archive. https://web.archive.org/web/20021028101929/http://www.billboard.com/billboard/specialreport/pearl_jam/pearl_jam1.jsp

Broken Record Podcast. "Pearl Jam's Stone Gossard & Jeff Ament on Their Professional Relationship and How It's Evolved." April, 2024. https://www.youtube.com/watch?v=TrEn8DRajB4

CBS Sunday Morning. "Pearl Jam's Jeff Ament and Eddie Vedder on the road." September, 2024. https://www.cbsnews.com/news/pearl-jam-dark-matter-eddie-vedder-and-jeff-ament-on-the-road/

Cleveland.com. "Pearl Jam guitarist Mike McCready talks new 'MTV Unplugged' release, 'Gigaton' album & more." October, 2020. https://www.cleveland.com/entertainment/2020/10/pearl-jam-guitarist-mike-mccready-talks-new-mtv-unplugged-release-gigatron-album-more.html

CNN. "Pearl Jam - Binaural Tour 2000." 2000. Archived on YouTube. https://www.youtube.com/watch?v=-ZkMLCFGmfw&t=219s

Consequence. "Jeff Ament's Art Helped Define Pearl Jam." August, 2021. https://consequence.net/2021/08/pearl-jam-jeff-ament-art-the-opus-ten-2/

Daily Record. "Q+A session with Pearl Jam." March, 2009. Archived on Internet Archive. https://web.archive.org/web/20090312072753/http://www.dailyrecord.co.uk/entertainment/music/music-news/2009/03/09/q-a-session-with-pearl-jam-86908-21184381/

Goldmine. "Intrigue and Incest: Pearl Jam and the Secret History of Seattle." August, 1993. Archived on Five Horizons. https://www.fivehorizons.com/archive/articles/gm082093_2.shtml

Grammy Award history. https://www.grammy.com/artists/pearl-jam/8448

Grungery. "Toni Wood: Andy loved the sparkle he put in people's eyes." September, 2018. https://grungery.hu/toni-wood-andy-loved-the-sparkle-he-put-in-peoples-eyes/

Guitar Player. "Blood on the Tracks: Pearl Jam cut their deepest grooves yet on *Vs*." January, 1994. Archived on Five Horizons. https://www.fivehorizons.com/archive/articles/gp194.shtml

Guitar World. "ALIVE - Pearl Jam's Mike McCready Says Goodbye To Drugs and Alcohol And Is a Better Man For It." April, 1995. Archived on Five Horizons. https://www.fivehorizons.com/archive/articles/gw04951.shtml

Guitar World. "All For One: Pearl Jam yield to the notion that united they stand and divided they fall." March, 1998. Archived on Five Horizons. https://www.fivehorizons.com/archive/articles/gw0398.shtml

Guitar World. "Spit Fire." February, 1995. Archived on Five Horizons. https://www.fivehorizons.com/archive/articles/gw0295.shtml

Jessica Letkemann. *Music for Rhinos: The Making of Pearl Jam* (excerpt). https://www.revolutioncomeandgone.com/articles/11/momma-son-and-the-making-of-pearl-jam.php

Juice Magazine. "Interview with Jeff Ament." December, 2005. https://juicemagazine.com/home/pearl-jam/

Lightning Bolt, A Short Film by Danny Clinch. 2013. https://www.youtube.com/watch?app=desktop&v=yxHE1A_C9QQ&t=81s

Live on 4 Legs Podcast. https://liveon4legs.com/

Los Angeles Times. "COVER STORY: He Didn't Ask for All This: Eddie Vedder always wanted his band Pearl Jam to make music that mattered. He can sometimes feel, as Kurt Cobain did, the pressure of mattering too much to his fans, but he's finding a way to deal with it." May, 1994. https://www.latimes.com/archives/la-xpm-1994-05-01-ca-52475-story.html

Los Angeles Times. "Pearl Jam Does the Evolution." October, 2000. https://www.latimes.com/archives/la-xpm-2000-oct-19-ca-38639-story.html

Los Angeles Times. "Pearl Jam, Ticketmaster and Now Congress: America's biggest band sent shock waves through the music business when it filed a complaint with the Justice Department about Ticketmaster. Now, Congress is holding a hearing. How'd it all get so far?" June, 1994. https://www.latimes.com/archives/la-xpm-1994-06-30-ca-10438-story.html

The Love Bone Earth Affair. 1993: PolyGram. https://www.youtube.com/watch?v=cEOh17Spuo0

Magnet. "A Conversation with Eddie Vedder (Pearl Jam)." July, 2006. https://magnetmagazine.com/2006/07/19/qa-with-eddie-vedder/

Medium.com (Shelly Underwood). "The Off Ramp — Let Me Set the Scene." November, 2020. https://shellyunderwood.medium.com/ the-off-ramp-let-me-set-the-scene-77cd24d60293

MTV. "Lollapalooza Lookback 1992: Meet Pearl Jam." August, 2010. Archived on Internet Archive. https://web.archive.org/web/20160909120049/http://www.mtv.com/news/1644863/lollapalooza-lookback-1992-meet-pearl-jam/

The New York Times. "Grunge: A Success Story." November, 1992. https://www.nytimes.com/1992/11/15/style/grunge-a-success-story.html

Paste Magazine. "All Those Yesterdays: Brendan O'Brien Reminisces on the Evolution of Pearl Jam and the Making of *Backspacer*." September, 2009. https://www.pastemagazine.com/music/brendan-obrien/all-those-yesterdays-brendan-obrien-reminisces-on

PearlJam.com. https://pearljam.com/

Pearl Jam Concert Chronology. https://pearljamconcertchronology.com/

Pearl Jam Twenty book. Compiled by Jonathan Cohen and Mark Wilkerson. Simon & Schuster, 2011.

Pearl Jam Twenty film. Directed by Cameron Crowe. 2011.

Philadelphia Inquirer. "Eddie Vedder's evolution puts emotion out front." November, 2002. Archived on Internet Archive. https://web.archive.rg/web/20021119092501/http://www.philly.com/mld/philly/entertainment/4482381.htm

Recording Industry Association of America chart history. https://www.riaa.com/gold-platinum/?tab_active=default-award&se=pearl+jam#search_section

Rick Beato. "Brendan O'Brien Interview: The Unsung Hero Of Rock Music." May, 2024. https://www.youtube.com/watch?v=FfoOvO6Xguw

Rock & Roll Hall of Fame. https://rockhall.com/inductees/pearl-jam/

Rolling Stone. "Eddie Vedder's Combat Rock." May, 2003. https://www.rollingstone.com/music/music-news/eddie-vedders-combat-rock-233360/

Rolling Stone. "Five Against the World." October, 1993. Archived on Internet Archive. https://web.archive.org/web/20070619084803/http://www.rollingstone.com/

Rolling Stone. "Grunge City: The Seattle Scene." April, 1992. https://www.rollingstone.com/music/music-news/grunge-city-the-seattle-scene-250071/

Rolling Stone. "Lollapalooza '92: On The Road With the Chili Peppers, Pearl Jam and Soundgarden." September, 1992. https://www.rollingstone.com/music/music-news/lollapalooza-92-on-the-road-with-the-chili-peppers-pearl-jam-and-soundgarden-249442/

Rolling Stone. "Pearl Jam: The Second Coming." June, 2006. https://www.rollingstone.com/music/music-news/pearl-jam-the-second-coming-237589/

Rolling Stone. "Temple of the Dog: An Oral History." September, 2016. https://www.rollingstone.com/music/music-features/temple-of-the-dog-an-oral-history-120453/

Seattle Post-Intelligencer. "Energized Pearl Jam makes an explosive return." May, 2006. https://www.seattlepi.com/entertainment/ music/article/energized-pearl-jam-makes-an-explosive-return-1202745.php

The Seattle Times. "The story of Pearl Jam, from a Seattle basement to the Rock & Roll Hall of Fame." March, 2017. https://www.seattletimes.com/pacific-nw-magazine/pearl-jams-hall-of-fame-career-began-in-a-seattle-basement/

Seattle Weekly. "A Brief History of Pearl Jam's Drummers." March, 2017. https://www.seattleweekly.com/music/a-brief-history-of-pearl-jams-drummers/

Seattle Weekly. "Yield Not: The members of Pearl Jam break their silence to talk about the changes, challenges, and motivation behind staying together and the making of their latest, Riot Act." October, 2006. https://www.seattleweekly.com/music/yield-not/

Single Video Theory. Directed by Mark Pellington. 1998.

Singles. Directed by Cameron Crowe. 1992: Warner Bros.

SPIN. "Eddie Vedder Breaks His Silence: Our 1995 Pearl Jam Cover Story." 1995. Archived. https://www.spin.com/2019/11/pearl-jam-cover-story-1995/

SPIN. "Revisit Our August 2001 Pearl Jam Oral History: Past Ten." August, 2001. Archived. https://www.spin.com/2017/08/pearl-jam-oral-history-2001/

SPIN. "The Road Less Traveled." February, 1997. Archived on Five Horizons. https://www.fivehorizons.com/archive/articles/spin0297.shtml

Time Magazine. "Rock's Anxious Rebels." October, 1993. https://time.com/archive/6685595/rocks-anxious-rebels/

Uncut. "Artist Interview: Pearl Jam's Jeff Ament and Stone Gossard." March, 2009. https://www.uncut.co.uk/features/artist-interview-pearl-jam-s-jeff-ament-and-stone-gossard-37417/

INDEX

3rd Secret, 144
10 Minute Warning, 33

A
Abbruzzese, Dave, 12, 59, 69, 70, 88, 92, 114, 133, 134, 135, 138
Above (Mad Season), 143, 144
Academy (New York), 89
Acevez, April, 200
Adams, Paul, 71–72
Akre, Carrie, 144
Albani Music Club (Winterthur, Switzerland), 88
albums. *See also* set lists; songs; videos
   9.11.2011 Toronto Canada, 158
   Backspacer, 203, 205, 243
   Binaural, 169–170, 176, 186, 187, 241
   Dark Matter, 12, 192, 233, 236, 243
   Europe Bootlegs, 171–172
   Gigaton, 220, 226, 227–229, 231, 243
   Give Way, 158
   Let's Play Two, 158, 220
   Lightning Bolt, 51, 215, 216, 217, 219, 220, 243
   Live at Benaroya Hall, 196
   Live At Benaroya Hall, 158
   Live at Easy Street, 158, 195
   Live at Lollapalooza 2007, 158
   Live at the Gorge 05/06, 158
   Live At Third Man Records, 158
   Live In NYC, 158
   Live on Two Legs, 156, 158
   Lost Dogs, 61, 191, 195, 242
   Merkin Ball EP, 139
   Momma-Son demo tape, 35, 42, 47, 60, 61
   No Code, 70, 125, 149, 150–151, 154, 193, 203, 241
   North America Leg 1 Bootlegs, 171–172
   North America Leg 2 Bootlegs, 171–172
   Pearl Jam (avocado album), 196–200, 242
   Rearviewmirror Greatest Hits 1991–2003, 195, 242
   Riot Act, 173, 177, 188, 190, 191, 195, 215, 242
   Ten, 12, 29, 35, 42, 59, 60–61, 63, 64–65, 66, 67, 69, 71, 72–73, 83, 88, 89, 92, 104, 105, 110, 128, 240
   Vitalogy, 70, 111, 121, 133–134, 135, 149, 200, 240
   Vs., 70, 111, 112–114, 119, 128, 133, 240
   Yield, 70, 151–152, 154, 176, 201, 204, 241
Alice In Chains, 10, 19, 24, 26, 45, 49, 50, 51, 54, 91, 110, 134, 135, 143, 190
"Alive" (Pearl Jam), 12
"All Night Thing" (Temple of the Dog), 53
Allstate Arena, 176, 177
Almost Famous (movie), 24
Alpine Valley Music Theatre, 176, 186
Alpine Valley (Wisconsin) Festival, 29
Altieri, Kevin, 154
Ament, Barry, 64
Ament, Jeff, 9, 10, 11, 12, 21, 26, 29, 32, 33, 35, 37–38, 39, 40, 41, 42, 45, 46, 48, 50, 53, 56, 59, 60, 61, 64–65, 71, 92, 97, 99, 111, 122, 130, 133, 135, 141, 142–143, 151, 154, 155, 161, 173, 175, 179, 186, 187, 188, 195, 198, 205, 220, 224, 226, 228–229, 236, 237
American Music Awards, 65
Ames Bros design team, 64, 151, 154

A&M Records, 54
"Aneurysm" (Nirvana), 10
Anthrax, 67
Apache Survival Benefit Show, 113, 114–115
"Ape/Man" sets, 176, 186
Appetite for Destruction (Guns N' Roses), 65
Apple (Mother Love Bone), 33, 67
A&R, 43, 59, 65, 195
Arm, Mark, 26, 238
Arthur, Joseph, 143
AT&T Amphitheatre, 115

B
"Baba O'Riley" (the Who), 177, 204, 238
Bacchanal (San Diego), 49
Bad Animals Studio, 23–24, 196
Badmotorfinger (Soundgarden), 54
Bad Radio, 40, 46
Ball (Neil Young), 139
band name, 59, 60
Banks, Ernie, 216
Bayleaf (Stone Gossard), 142
the Beatles, 67
Beato, Rick, 111, 134
Bienstock, Richard, 97–98, 102, 105
Bierman, Tim, 163
Bikini Kill, 23
Billboard charts, 65, 114, 134, 151, 154, 164, 170, 191, 196, 198, 203, 219, 231, 236
Black Dog Forge, 45
Black Flag, 21, 161
Blake, Tchad, 169
Blaylock, Mookie, 71
Blood Sugar Sex Magik (Red Hot Chili Peppers), 72, 111
BMO Harris Bradley Center (Milwaukee), 204
"Boeing Bust," 20
Bonnaroo Festival, 202, 220
Bono, 132
bootlegs, 7, 89, 137, 150, 158, 162, 170–172, 185, 186, 187, 195
The Borderline (London), 88
Boston Marathon set, 187, 189
Brad (band), 141
Branigan, John, 71
Bratmobile, 23
Bray, Ryan, 151
Brecheisen, Barry, 103
Bridge School Benefit, 137–138, 234
Brisbane Entertainment Centre, 116–117
Broken Record Podcast, 35
Bush, George W., 170, 177, 187, 188, 191, 192, 197, 198, 201, 209
the Butts, 40

C
Cameron, Matt, 11, 27, 39, 53, 56, 69, 70, 71, 144, 147, 155, 156, 161, 169, 186, 187, 190, 195, 196, 198, 200, 205, 208–209, 226, 228, 239
Cantrell, Jerry, 45, 51
Casablancas, Julian, 209
Catastrophic Metamorphic (Deaf Charlie), 143
Cathouse (Los Angeles), 49, 51
Cavedweller (Matt Cameron), 147
CBGB, 73
Central Saloon (Seattle), 25
Chamberlain, Matt, 69, 70, 142
Chaney, Chris, 147
Chicago Recording Company, 149

"Chloe Dancer/Crown Of Thorns" (Mother Love Bone), 29, 213
Christgau, Robert, 65
the Clash, 37–38, 40
Clinch, Danny, 217, 219, 220
Clinton, Bill, 127
Club Babyhead (Providence), 71
Cobain, Kurt, 10, 13, 19, 73, 110, 114, 121, 122, 127, 129–131, 131–132, 137, 190, 207–208
Cohen, Jonathan, 209
Coleman, Jaz, 144
Come On Down EP (Green River), 27
Cook, Jan, 45
Corgan, Billy, 73
Cornell, Chris, 10, 11, 12, 19, 27, 39, 50, 53, 54, 56, 57, 67, 71, 173, 188, 209, 224–226, 229, 236
Costello, Elvis, 145
COVID-19 pandemic, 69, 93, 142, 143, 229, 231
Cow Palace (Daly City, CA), 75
Crane, David, 105
Crash Worship, 10
"Crazy Mary" (Victoria Williams), 176
Crohn's & Colitis Foundation of America, 84
Cross, Charles R., 42, 110, 239
Crover, Dale, 32
Crowe, Cameron, 10, 12, 24, 35, 36, 50, 74, 93, 105, 107, 112, 133, 154, 207
Crowley, Matt "The Tube," 103
"Crown Of Thorns" (Mother Love Bone), 174, 175
Cummings, Sue, 84
Curtis, Kelly, 24, 45, 54, 66, 110, 121, 127, 141, 154, 155, 164, 174, 195, 207, 209, 216, 228
Cyrus, Billy Ray, 65
C/Z Records, 27, 32

D
dates. *See* tour dates
Davis, Brittany, 142
Davis, Clive, 195
Dead Boys, 89
Dead Man Walking soundtrack, 149
Deaf Charlie, 143
Death Grips, 144
Deep Six compilation, 27, 32
Del Mar Pavilion (San Diego), 74
Deranged Diction, 37
Discovery Park (Seattle), 56
Dive on Medium (Shelly Underwood), 10
"Dollar Short" (Mother Love Bone), 35, 41
Drop in the Park, 119, 188
Dupree, Jon "Bubba," 144
Dylan, Bob, 207

E
Earthling (Eddie Vedder), 147, 234
Echols, Damien, 200
El Corazon, 10
Eliason, Brett, 172
Endino, Jack, 27
Epic Records, 42, 59
Erlandson, Eric, 208
The Esplanade (Southend, England), 87
Evans, Josh, 228
"Exhausted" (Foo Fighters), 141

F
Facelift (Alice In Chains), 49
Fadroski, Kelli Skye, 145
Fairweather, Bruce, 26, 33
fan letters, 61, 93
Fanzone, Carmen, 147

248 PEARL JAM LIVE!

Farias, Brian, 165, 167
Farley, Christopher John, 131–132
Farrell, Perry, 95, 97, 98
the Fastbacks, 125, 143
Fenway Park, 236
First Avenue (Minneapolis), 71–72
Fitz and the Tantrums, 143
Five Horizons website, 8
Flea, 75
Flemion, Dennis, 219
Foo Fighters, 141
Fox Theater (Atlanta), 134
Fragassi, Selena, 210
Frehley, Ace, 161
the Frogs, 219
Fugazi, 161

G
Gallen, Joel, 91–92, 93
Galleria Potatohead, 45, 47, 48, 65
Garcia, Jerry, 146
Gaspar, Boom, 71, 139, 190, 219
Geffen Records, 33
Geiger, Mark, 97
Gilmore, Greg, 33
Givony, Ronen, 93
Golden Globes, 147
Goldstone, Michael, 39, 42, 59, 65, 66, 174
Gorge Amphitheatre (George, Washington), 29
Gorra, Jeff, 125
Gory Scorch Cretins (Matt Cameron), 147
Gossard, Stone, 9, 10, 11, 12, 26, 29, 32, 33, 35, 36–37, 38, 39, 40, 41, 42, 46, 48, 53, 56, 59, 60, 61, 63, 71, 72, 92, 108, 109, 111, 112–113, 115, 119, 122, 133, 135, 141–142, 150, 152, 161, 170, 187, 196, 198, 200, 201, 204, 205, 208, 217, 226, 228, 235, 239
Grammy Awards, 12–13, 65, 114, 134–135, 147, 154, 170, 205, 223, 226, 233
Grateful Dead, 75, 122, 146, 149, 170–171
Great White Wonder (Bob Dylan), 170
Green River, 19, 26, 26–27, 32–33, 35, 37, 46
Green River Killer, 20, 42
Grohl, Dave, 74, 141
The Grunge Scene (YouTube), 21, 33
Gumble, Liz, 61
Guns N' Roses, 65, 114, 144

H
Hagar, Regan, 30, 141, 142
Hansard, Glen, 147
Harper, Ben, 125
Harpo's (Victoria, BC), 46, 50
Harrybu McCage, 144, 203
Hart, Mickey, 170
Harvey Dent and the Caped Crusaders, 156
Hater, 144
Hawkins, Taylor, 144
Headbangers Ball, 108–109
Heart, 11, 23, 24
Heisel, Scott, 172
Hiatt, Brian, 127
Hill, Zach, 144
Hole, 10
Hollywood Palladium, 84
Home Shows initiative, 63
Homestead Records, 27
Homme, Josh, 209
House of Representatives, 122–124
Hovercraft, 61, 141
Hoyt, John, 124
"Hunger Strike" (Temple of the Dog), 53–54, 67
Hunt, David, 30
"Hunted Down" (Soundgarden), 22
Hüsker Dü, 21

I
I Am Mine (Eddie Vedder), 40
"I Am The Highway" tribute concert, 226
Ian, Scott, 67
Indian Style, 40
Inflatable Soul, 10
In The Moment That You're Born (Brad), 141
Into the Wild (Eddie Vedder), 203
Irons, Jack, 39–40, 40–41, 70, 72, 134, 138, 149–150
"I've Got A Feeling" (the Beatles), 60, 67
Ives, Brian, 67
Ives, Maria, 89
"I Won't Back Down" (Tom Petty), 204

J
Jacobs, Marc, 128–129
Jane's Addiction, 97, 147, 225
Janicke, Rob, 102
Jasper, Megan, 129
Jeansson, Richard, 8
Jennings, Mason, 142
Johnson, Jennifer, 144
Jones, Kipper, 48
Jones, Rickie Lee, 63
J Records, 195–196

K
Kang, Tanya, 238
Kasper, Adam, 190, 196
Kaufman Astoria Studios, 91
Kaufman, Marta, 105
KCMU (University of Washington), 95
Keough, Bill, 71
Khan, Nusrat Fateh Ali, 149
Kiedis, Anthony, 73
Killing Joke, 144
Kill Rock Stars (record label), 23
King's X, 143
Klinghoffer, Josh, 71, 147
"Know Your Rights" (the Clash), 192
Krusen, Dave, 9, 11, 39, 69, 70, 223, 224
Kuzminski, Anthony, 193, 204

L
L7, 84
Lambert, Matt, 221
Lanegan, Mark, 10, 19, 144
Late Show (BBC2), 88
Lawson Productions, 23
Leeds Festival, 173, 201
Lennartz, Marty, 104
Letkemann, Jessica, 41, 42
Letterman, David, 137, 155–156, 200, 223
Letterman, Harry, 223
Levee Walkers, 144
Liebling, Beth, 41, 61, 141
Limelight (New York City), 67
Live Nation, 124
Live on 4 Legs podcast, 8
Lollapalooza, 70, 95–105, 127, 188, 201, 226, 236
London Bridge Studio, 53, 54, 60
Loosegroove Records, 142
Louder Than Love (Soundgarden), 60
Love Bone Earth Affair home video, 26, 30, 32
"Love Buzz" (Nirvana), 22
Love Chile, 36
Love, Courtney, 10, 23, 73, 225
Lowe, Zane, 235, 236
Luv Company, 37

M
Madison Square Garden, 29, 156
Mad Season, 19, 56, 141, 143–144
Malfunkshun, 22, 27, 30, 32, 32–33, 141
"Man In The Box" (Alice In Chains), 49, 54
March of Crimes, 37
Marquette University, 95–96
Mars, Johnny, 104
Martin, Barrett, 143, 144
Matchbox Twenty, 170
McCormick, Jill, 200
McCready, Mike, 9, 11, 12, 35–37, 38–39, 40, 46, 50, 53, 56, 59, 63, 64, 72, 74, 75, 77, 92, 108, 133, 134, 135, 137, 139, 143, 144, 151, 161, 162, 163, 169, 170, 171, 187, 195, 197, 198–199, 200, 221, 228, 237, 239
McDonald, Steven, 144
McFarlane, Todd, 154
McKagan, Duff, 33, 144
McKinsey, Marie, 159
the Melvins, 22, 27, 32, 144
Menke, Michele, 166
Mercer, Lance, 29, 65
Mercury Records, 33
the Minutemen, 21, 141
Mirror Ball (Neil Young), 139, 140
Moe's (Seattle), 156
Monkeywrench Radio, 141, 146, 150
Monkeywrench Records, 158, 195, 203, 217, 229
Mookie Blaylock, 9, 11, 29, 45, 48–49, 50, 51, 53, 54, 59, 60, 97
Moore, Chay Wilkerson, 50
Moore, Lisa, 95–96
Moore Theatre (Seattle), 25
Mosholt, Jannik Tai, 116–117
Mother Love Bone, 9, 11, 19, 26, 27, 29, 30, 33, 37, 39, 41, 49, 50, 51, 56, 59, 60, 61, 65, 67, 71, 97, 175, 205, 209, 213, 216, 223
Mother Love Bone Earth Affair, 162
MTV Unplugged, 84, 88, 91–93, 231
MTV Video Music Awards, 65–66, 91, 108, 114, 131, 137
Mudhoney, 10, 19, 22, 141, 156, 209, 220, 238
Mueller, Peter, 41
Muller, Don, 97, 98
Mural Amphitheatre, 72
Museum of Pop Culture (MoPOP), 29, 45
Music For Rhinos (Jessica Letkemann), 41

N
Nader, Ralph, 177, 187–188
name origin, 59, 60
Navarro, Dave, 225
Nelson, Lukas, 166
Nevermind (Nirvana), 65, 73, 83
New Orleans Jazz & Heritage Festival, 205
"The New World" (X), 145
Nicklen, Paul, 229
Nicks, Stevie, 145
Nielsen, Rick, 204
Nighttime Boogie Association, 144
Nirvana, 10, 19, 22, 23, 24, 26, 65, 73, 74, 75, 83, 105, 108, 110, 127, 128, 129, 130, 137, 141, 144
Noble House Hotels, 26
Northwest School, 196
"Nothing to Say" (Soundgarden), 22
Novoselic, Krist, 141, 144

O
Obama, Barack, 202
O'Brien, Brendan, 66, 111, 114, 133, 134, 139, 149, 152, 154, 169, 201, 217, 229
Off Ramp Café (Seattle), 7–8, 9, 10–12, 25, 60, 234
Ohana Festival, 143, 145, 185, 200
O.K. Hotel (Seattle), 60
"Once" (Pearl Jam), 12
Osborne, Buzz, 144

P
Painted Shield, 142

INDEX 249

Palmer, Tim, 63–64
Paramount Theatre (Seattle), 57
Parashar, Raj, 60
Parashar, Rick, 60
Pavitt, Bruce, 22
PearlJam.com, 8–9
Pearl Jam Concert Chronology, 8, 50, 71, 88, 100, 115, 150
"Pearl Jam: Home and Away" exhibit, 45
PearlJamOnline, 72
Pearl Jam Radio, 172, 188, 205
Pearl Jam Twenty documentary, 12, 24, 25, 27, 41, 45, 54, 69, 108, 152, 154, 155, 175, 187, 207, 209
Pellington, Mark, 107, 154
Pendleton, Don, 219
Perkins, Dan, 202
Perry Ellis clothing, 129
Petty, Tom, 204
Pfaff, Kristen, 19
Phillips, Chuck, 119
Pink Floyd, 169, 219
Pinkpop Festival, 96, 226–227
Pinnick, dUg, 143
PJ20 weekend, 9, 29, 56, 205, 209, 210
PJ Votes 2020 initiative, 229
Plant, Robert, 196
PolyGram, 26, 33, 39, 42, 59
Poneman, Jonathan, 22, 26

Q

Queens of the Stone Age, 142
The Quiet Table (Three Fish), 143

R

Rachman, Paul, 54, 56
Rachtman, Riki, 49, 51, 108–109, 128
Rage Against the Machine, 40
Ramone, Joey, 150
Ramone, Johnny, 25, 199–200
the Ramones, 150, 156, 161
Randall's Island (New York), 125
Raye, Jillian, 144
"Reach Down" (Temple of the Dog), 53
Reading Festival, 173, 201
"The Real Me" (the Who), 213
Red Hot Chili Peppers, 39, 67, 72–73, 75, 83, 97, 104, 111, 134, 145, 147, 149, 224, 225
Red Kross, 144
Rees, Dave, 30
R.E.M., 122
Reynolds, Simon, 128
Richards, Keith, 89, 111
Ridge Farm Studios, 63
RKCNDY (Seattle), 69, 72
RNDM, 143
Roach, Max, 149
Robbins, Tim, 198
Robb, Robbi, 143
Rock For Choice Benefit, 84, 86
the Rockfords, 144
"Rockin' In The Free World" (Neil Young), 67, 93, 137, 186, 223
Rock & Roll Hall of Fame, 12, 70, 137, 156, 223–224, 239
Rock the Vote, 188
Rodman, Dennis, 156
Roe v. Wade, 84, 86
the Rolling Stones, 89, 154, 196
Rollins, Henry, 132
Rooney, Andy, 129–130
Rosen, Fred, 121, 123
Roskilde Festival, 9, 13, 96, 172–173, 175, 177, 185, 186, 188, 190, 201, 209
Rubin, Rick, 235
Rust Never Sleeps (Neil Young and Crazy Horse), 137

Ryan, Jim, 172, 176–177

S

San Carlos Apache people, 114–115
Saturday Night Live, 69, 84, 93, 114, 127, 200, 205
Saunders, John Baker, 143
"Say Hello 2 Heaven" (Temple of the Dog), 53
Scar Tissue (Anthony Kiedis), 73
Schaffner, Lauryn, 230
Screaming Life EP (Soundgarden), 22
Screaming Trees, 19, 26, 143, 144
Sea.Hear.Now Festival, 236
Self-Pollution Radio, 141
set lists. *See also* albums; songs; videos
    Alpine Valley (East Troy, WI), 212–213
    Apache Survival Benefit Show, 113
    Boston Marathon, 189
    Cow Palace (Daly City, CA), 75
    Harpo's (Victoria, BC), 46
    Lollapalooza (2007), 100
    Mesa Amphitheatre (Mesa, AZ), 113
    MGM Grand (Las Vegas), 174
    Off Ramp Café (Seattle), 13
    Paramount Theatre (Seattle), 57
    Patriot Center (Fairfax, VA), 122
    Soldier Field (Chicago), 146
    Temple of the Dog, 57
    Tweeter Center (Boston), 189
    Twentieth Anniversary Shows, 212–213
    Wrigley Field (Chicago), 218
    Ziggo Dome (Amsterdam), 165
Severson, Edward Louis, Jr., 41, 147
Shadow, 36
Shame (Brad), 141
Shangri-La Studios, 235
Shay, Matt, 195
"She" (KISS), 64
Shepherd, Ben, 37, 144
Sheridan, Rob, 236
Shine in March EP (Mother Love Bone), 33, 60
Shoaf, Jimmy, 134
Shoreline Amphitheater, 234
the Showbox (Seattle), 25, 205
Silver, Susan, 11, 54, 95, 173
Singles (movie), 10, 24, 45, 69, 105, 208
Single Video Theory documentary, 154–155, 207
the Site studio, 112
Six Figure Retirement, 200
Skin Yard, 26–27, 39
Sleater-Kinney, 144, 187, 217, 224
Sloane, Owen, 171
Smashing Pumpkins, 67, 73, 144
"Smells Like Teen Spirit" (Nirvana), 19, 65, 128
Smith, Chad, 147
Smith, Mark "Smitty," 145, 228
Smith, Shawn, 141
Soldier Field, 141, 146, 149
Some Gave All (Billy Ray Cyrus), 65
songs. *See also* albums; set lists; videos
    "1/2 Full," 190
    "2,000 Mile Blues," 61
    "4/20/02," 190–191
    "Act of Love," 139
    "Agyptian Crave," 41
    "Alive," 12, 35, 41–42, 47, 60, 64, 65, 71, 72, 73, 83, 89, 91, 92, 93, 186, 223, 238
    "All Or None," 190, 238
    "All Roskilde's Children," 190
    "All The Way," 216
    "All Those Yesterdays," 152, 204, 213
    "Alone," 61, 89

"Alright," 228, 229
"Amongst The Waves," 201
"Animal," 111
"Arc," 190
"Army Reserve," 200
"Better Man," 111, 134, 159, 193, 223
"Black," 12, 47, 60, 61, 63, 92, 93, 109–110, 156, 230
"Blood," 112
"Brain Of J," 154, 204, 238
"Breakerfall," 169
"Breath," 47
"Breath And A Scream," 61
"Brother," 61
"Bu$hleaguer," 191
"Bugs," 134, 216
"Can't Deny Me," 192
"Can't Keep," 190
"The Color Red," 152
"Comes Then Goes," 229
"Corduroy," 134, 156, 193
"Crown Of Thorns," 238
"Dance Of The Clairvoyants," 228, 229
"Dark Matter," 236
"Daughter," 89, 111, 114, 172, 175, 193, 221, 238
"Deep," 60
"Dirty Frank," 89
"Dissident," 114, 186
"Do The Evolution," 152, 154, 156, 224
"Down," 213
"E Ballad," 41, 47
"Elderly Woman Behind The Counter In A Small Town," 111, 215
"The End," 203
"Even Flow," 11, 12, 47, 60, 63, 67, 89, 91, 92, 93, 102, 104, 105, 159, 176, 193
"Evil Little Goat," 61
"Faithfull," 204
"Falling Slowly," 210
"The Fixer," 201, 202, 205
"Footsteps," 42, 47, 61
"Future Days," 216, 219
"Garden," 60, 89
"Given To Fly," 117, 154, 156, 204
"Glorified G," 114
"Go," 112, 114
"Gonna See My Friend," 202, 205
"Got Some," 202, 205
"Green Disease," 221
"Grievance," 170
"Habit," 150
"Hail, Hail," 150, 156
"Hard To Imagine," 166
"Hey Foxymophandlemama, That's Me," 134
"Hold On," 61
"Hunger Strike," 236
"I Am Mine," 173, 190
"I Got Id," 139, 213
"I'm Open," 150
"Indifference," 213
"In Hiding," 154, 201, 204, 238
"In My Tree," 149, 186
"Inside Job," 200
"In The Moonlight," 209
"It's Ok," 238
"Jeremy," 42, 60, 65, 66, 73, 91, 92, 93, 193
"Johnny Guitar," 202–203
"Just A Girl," 13, 47, 61
"Just Breathe," 166, 201, 203
"Last Kiss," 84, 164
"Leash," 67, 75, 89, 112
"Let Me Sleep (Christmas Time)," 164

"Let The Records Play," 219
"Life Wasted," 199–200
"Lightning Bolt," 216
"Light Years," 169
"Long Road," 139
"Love Boat Captain," 173, 190
"Low Light," 152, 201, 215
"Lukin," 150, 176
"MFC," 156, 176
"Mind Your Manners," 216, 219
"My Father's Daughter," 200
"My Father's Son," 219
"Not For You," 115, 134, 137, 209
"Nothing As It Seems," 169
"Nothingman," 134, 215
"No Way," 152, 204
"Oceans," 47, 60, 63–64, 67, 89, 93, 238
"Off He Goes," 156
"Of The Girl," 169
"Once," 12, 42, 47
"Other Side," 221
"Pendulum," 219
"Pilate," 152
"Porch," 60, 72, 84, 89, 92, 93, 125
"Present Tense," 193, 213
"Pry, To," 134
"Pushin Forward Back," 53
"Push Me, Pull Me," 204
"Quick Escape," 229
"Rats," 112, 114, 201, 238
"React, Respond," 236
"Rearviewmirror," 111
"Red Mosquito," 150
"Release," 12, 47–48, 60, 61, 176, 215
"Retrograde," 228, 229
"Richard's E," 41, 47
"River Cross," 229, 231
"Running," 236
"Satan's Bed," 134
"Save You," 190
"Setting Sun," 236
"Seven O' Clock," 229
"Severed Hand," 200
"Sirens," 219
"Sleeping By Myself," 219
"Sleight Of Hand," 176
"Smile," 150
"Soldier Of Love," 176
"Sometimes," 125, 150
"Sonic Reducer," 150, 238
"Soon Forget," 169, 177
"Speed Of Sound," 202, 203
"Speed Wash," 89
"Spin The Black Circle," 134
"State Of Love And Trust," 67, 69, 92, 93, 209
"Superblood Wolfmoon," 229
"Swallowed Whole," 219
"Take The Long Way," 228, 229
"Times of Trouble," 53
"Troubled Times," 41, 42
"Unemployable," 200
"Waiting For Stevie," 236
"Wash," 60, 89
"Whipping," 134
"Who Ever Said," 229
"Who You Are," 149, 150
"Why Go," 60, 63, 89
"Wishlist," 116, 117, 154, 155, 204
"W.M.A.," 114
"World Wide Suicide," 198
"Wreckage," 192, 236
"Yellow Ledbetter," 60, 105, 150, 210, 230
"Sonic Reducer" (Dead Boys), 89, 108

the Sonics, 22
Son of Man, 9
Soundgarden, 10, 19, 22, 24, 25, 26, 27, 37, 39, 50, 53, 54, 56, 60, 71, 95, 97, 141, 144, 155, 190, 205, 238
Spectrum Center (Philadelphia), 189
Spix, Joe, 219
Springsteen, Bruce, 170, 205
Stafford, Paul Edgerton, 128
Staley, Layne, 19, 143, 190
"Stardog Champion" (Mother Love Bone), 29, 33, 209
Steinem, Gloria, 188
Stern, Howard, 138, 156
Stone Gossard Demos 91, 35, 39, 41, 53, 169
Stone Temple Pilots, 97, 128
"Stop Draggin' My Heart Around" (Stevie Knicks), 145
Strummer, Joe, 192
Studio X, 196
Stuverud, Richard, 142–143, 143
Sub Pop Records, 22, 26, 27, 71, 95, 129
Sub Pop Singles Club, 22
Summerfest, 141
Surf and Destroy, 40
Swift, Taylor, 7, 124

T
Temple of the Dog, 19, 29, 39, 50, 53, 54, 56, 57, 60, 67, 111, 209, 225
Ten Club, 7, 59, 93, 125, 150, 162–164, 166, 196, 231
Thayil, Kim, 11, 25–26, 95, 144, 238
"This Note's For You" (Neil Young), 137
Three Fish, 142–143
Ticketmaster, 7, 70, 115, 119–124, 134, 140, 151, 155, 161, 193
Ticketron, 121
Toback, Jeremy, 141
Tomorrow, Tom, 202
Tone Dogs, 144
Tone (Jeff Ament), 143
tour dates
    1990–1991, 16–17
    1992–2000, 78–81
    2001-Present, 180–183
Touring Band 2000 DVD, 185–186
Townshend, Pete, 132–133, 161, 175
Tres Mts, 143
Triad Artists, 71
Tribe After Tribe, 143
Trump, Donald J., 192, 220, 229, 233
Turner, Jerome, 219
Turner, Steve, 26, 35, 238
Twentieth Anniversary Shows, 212–213
Two Feet Thick website, 8

U
U2, 114, 169
Ukulele Songs (Eddie Vedder), 147, 219
the U-Men, 22, 27
Under The Bridge (Red Hot Chili Peppers), 73
Underwood, Shelly, 10
United Center, 193
Use Your Illusion II (Guns N' Roses), 114

V
Vedder, Eddie, 9, 11–12, 15, 25, 26, 33, 39, 40–41, 42, 45, 46, 47–48, 49, 50, 51, 53–54, 56, 59, 60, 61, 63, 66, 71, 72, 73–75, 84, 86, 88, 89, 92, 93, 98, 102, 103, 104, 105, 107, 108, 109–110, 111, 112, 115, 121, 125, 127–128, 130, 131–132, 133, 134–135, 137, 138, 140–141, 143, 145, 147, 150, 151, 154, 155, 156, 161, 163, 169, 170, 171, 173, 174, 176, 177, 185, 186–187, 187–188, 190, 191, 192, 193, 197, 198, 199–200, 201, 202, 204, 207–208, 215, 216, 217, 219, 224, 226, 227, 229, 231, 233, 234, 236–237, 239
Vedder, Olivia, 200
the Ventures, 22
Vic Theatre (Chicago), 201
videos. *See also* albums; setlists; songs
    "Alive," 65, 66, 69, 71, 91, 107
    "Dance Of The Clairvoyants," 231
    "Do The Evolution," 154
    "Even Flow," 93, 107
    "Hunger Strike," 54, 56
    "Jeremy," 93, 105, 107–108, 109, 111, 154, 170
    "Life Wasted," 199
    "Mind Your Manners," 217
    "Sirens," 217
    "Stardog Champion" (Mother Love Bone), 33
    "World Wide Suicide," 199
Virginia Beach Amphitheatre, 175
Virgin Records, 48
Vitalogy Foundation, 7, 84
Voters For Choice concert, 138

W
Wahlberg, Mark, 89
Wah Mee Club (Seattle), 20
Walking Papers, 144
War Babies, 37
Warrant, 32
Warrior, 36
Waters, John, 45
Waters, Roger, 219
Watt, Andrew, 147, 233–234, 236
Watt, Mike, 141
"We Belong Together" (Rickie Lee Jones), 63
Weiland, Scott, 128
Weiss, Janet, 144
Wells Fargo Center (Philadelphia), 88
Wellwater Conspiracy, 144, 190
"(What's So Funny 'Bout) Peace, Love and Understanding" (Elvis Costello), 145
the Who, 161, 171, 175, 177, 204, 207
Wicks, John, 143
Wilk, Brad, 40
Wilkerson, Mark Ian, 209
Williams, Victoria, 176
Wilson, Ann, 23, 24, 25
Wilson, Nancy, 11, 23, 24, 207, 225
Wonder, Stevie, 236
Wood, Andrew, 56
Wood, Andy, 9, 19, 22, 27, 29–32, 33, 35, 39, 41, 49–50, 53
"Wooden Jesus" (Temple of the Dog), 53
Wood, Kevin, 30
Wood, Toni, 30, 32
World Series, 216
Wrigley Field, 158, 215–216, 218, 233, 236

X
X, 145
X-Pensive Winos, 89

Y
Young, Matt, 164
Young, Neil, 59–60, 67, 93, 111, 114, 122, 137–141, 149, 223
YouTube, 21, 33, 72, 93

Z
Zapata, Mia, 19
Zappa, Frank, 171

INDEX 251

IMAGE CREDITS

Page 1: © Paul Bergen/Getty
Page 6: © Alison Braun/Getty
Page 8: © Paul Bergen/Getty
Page 10: © Anette Sa/Alamy
Page 11: © Alison Braun/Getty
Page 12: © Lindsay Brice/Getty
Page 14: © Steve Eichner/Getty
Page 18: © Alison Braun/Getty
Page 19 (above): © Paul Natkin/Getty
Page 19 (below): © Paul Natkin/Getty
Page 20: © Paul Bergen/Getty
Page 21: © Steve Eichner/Getty
Page 23: © Gary Gershoff/Getty
Page 24: © Warner Bros/Everett Collection
Page 25: © Abramorama/Everett Collection
Page 28: © Steve Eichner/Getty
Page 27: © Paul Briden/Alamy
Page 29: © Photoshot/Everett Collection
Page 30: © Photoshot/Everett Collection
Page 31: © Photoshot/Everett Collection
Page 34: © Paul Bergen/Getty
Page 36: © Ebet Roberts/Getty
Page 37: © Ebet Roberts /Getty
Page 38: © Koh Hasebe/Shinko Music/Getty
Page 39: © dpa picture alliance/Alamy
Page 40: © Ron Galella, Ltd/Getty
Page 43: © Photoshot/Everett Collection
Page 44: © Alison Braun/Getty
Page 47: © MediaPunch Inc/Alamy
Page 48: © Alison Braun/Getty
Page 49: © Gie Knaeps/Getty
Page 52: © Lisa Lake/Getty
Page 53: © Bill Tompkins/Getty

Page 55: © Jeffrey Mayer/Getty
Page 58: © Paul Bergen/Getty
Page 59: © Ebet Roberts/Getty
Page 62: © KMazur/Getty
Page 64: © Jim Bennett/Getty
Page 66: © Frank Micelotta Archive/Getty
Page 68: © Paul Bergen/Getty
Page 70: © Gie Knaeps/Getty
Page 72 (above): © Steve Eichner/Getty
Page 72 (below): © Paul Natkin/Getty
Page 74: © Paul Bergen/Getty
Page 76-7: © Anna Krajec/Getty
Page 82: © Mark Baker/Getty
Page 83: © Mick Hutson/Getty
Page 85: © Lindsay Brice/Getty
Page 86-7: © Paul Bergen/Getty
Page 90: © Niels Van Iperen/Getty
Page 92: © KMazur/Getty
Page 94: © Gie Knaeps/Getty
Page 96: © Goedefroit Music/Getty
Page 98: © Ebet Roberts/Getty
Page 99: © Lisa Lake/Getty
Page 101: © Henry Diltz/Getty
Page 105: © Rick Madonik/Getty
Page 106: © Gie Knaeps/Getty
Page 108: © Jeff Kravitz/Getty
Page 109: © Riki Rachtman
Page 110: © Gie Knaeps/Getty
Page 112: © Jim Bennett/Getty
Page 115: © John Shearer/Getty
Page 118: © Kevin Cummins/Getty
Page 120: © Raffaella Cavalieri/Getty
Page 123: © Congressional Quarterly/Getty

Page 124: © L. Busacca/Getty
Page 126: © Jeff Kravitz/Getty
Page 129: © Jeff Kravitz/Getty
Page 130: © MediaPunch Inc/Alamy
Page 131: © Paul Natkin/Getty
Page 132: © Paul Natkin/Getty
Page 135: © Ron Wolfson/Getty
Page 136: © Michael Brito/Alamy
Page 138: © Jeff Kravitz/Getty
Page 140: © Jeff Kravitz/Getty
Page 142: © Martin Philbey/Getty
Page 143: © Steve Jennings/Getty
Page 144: © John Atashian/Getty
Page 147: © TDC Photography/Shutterstock
Page 148: © Marc Serota/Getty
Page 149: © dpa picture alliance/Alamy
Page 152-3: © Ebet Roberts/Getty
Page 157: © Kevin Mazur/Getty
Page 158: © Scott Gries/Getty
Page 160: © WENN Rights Ltd/Alamy
Page 161: © KMazur/Getty
Page 162: © Lindsay Brice/Getty
Page 163: © Ian West - PA/Getty
Page 167: © ZUMA Press, Inc/Alamy
Page 168: © George De Sota/Getty
Page 172: © Jens Noergaard Larsen/Getty
Page 175: © Nils Meilvang/Getty
Page 178-9: © Jeff Kravitz/Getty
Page 184: © Anna Krajec/Getty
Page 185: © Jim Bennett/Getty
Page 188: © Evan Agostini/Getty
Page 191: © Kevin Mazur/Getty
Page 194: © Barry Brecheisen/Getty

Page 196: © Jason Kempin/Getty
Page 197: © Barry Brecheisen/Getty
Page 198: © Ted Soqui/Getty
Page 199: © Kevin Mazur/Getty
Page 202: © FilmMagic/Getty
Page 205: © C Flanigan/Getty
Page 206: © Gary Wolstenholme/Getty
Page 208: © Kevin Mazur/Getty
Page 211: © Kevin Mazur/Getty
Page 214: © Kevin Mazur/Getty
Page 216: © Marc Broussely/Getty
Page 220: © Kevin Mazur/Getty
Page 222: © Kevin Kane/Getty
Page 225: © Jim Bennett/Getty
Page 227: © Kevin Mazur/Getty
Page 228: © Kevin Mazur/Getty
Page 231: © Getty
Page 232: © Kieran Frost/Getty
Page 234: © Jim Bennett/Getty
Page 235: © Pedro Becerra/Getty
Page 237: © Jim Bennett/Getty
Page 239: © Jim Bennett/Getty
Page 245: © Jeff Kravitz/Getty

Acknowledgments

This book would not have been possible without the incredible, and often emotional, show memory submissions from my dear colleagues, new friends, and industry professionals. Thank you all for your heartfelt words and mementos. To the "three Richards"—Richard Bienstock, Richard Jeansson, and Riki Rachtman—thank you for your time and valuable expertise. And to Scott Lucas of Local H, a band I played just as long and loud as I did Pearl Jam, thank you for providing the foreword for this book in only the way you could do.

About the Author

SELENA FRAGASSI is a seventeen-year music journalist who grew up on a heavy diet of '90s rock and has been waiting her whole career to write a tribute to the scene, the community, and the harbingers of the Seattle sound. One of her early concert reviews covered the historic PJ20 mini-fest in 2011, a weekend that made her fall in love with Pearl Jam all over again. Living in Chicago, she's also been to every Wrigley Field show and lived to tell the tale after the epic weather event of 2013. Selena is currently a featured contributor for the *Chicago Sun-Times*. Her bylines have also appeared in *SPIN, Loudwire, The A.V. Club, Paste, Nylon, Popmatters, Blurt, Under the Radar,* and *Chicago Magazine*, where she was previously on staff as Pop/Rock Critic. Artists she's interviewed include Kim Thayil, Mike Inez, Rise Against, Gene Simmons, Jennifer Hudson, Andra Day, Chrissie Hynde, Demi Lovato, Debbie Harry, Slash, Deftones, Evanescence, Alice Cooper, Jack White, The Black Keys, Charlie Puth, Bon Jovi, and Bonnie Raitt, among many others. Selena's work has been anthologized in *That Devil Music: Best Music Writing* and she has appeared on televised panels regarding music matters for WTTW's *Chicago Tonight* program. She is the author of the books *New Kids on the Block 40th Anniversary Celebration; NSYNC 30th Anniversary Celebration; Alanis: Thirty Years of Jagged Little Pill* and *The Work, Life, and Style of Greta Gerwig*, with more to come. Selena is also a member of The Recording Academy.

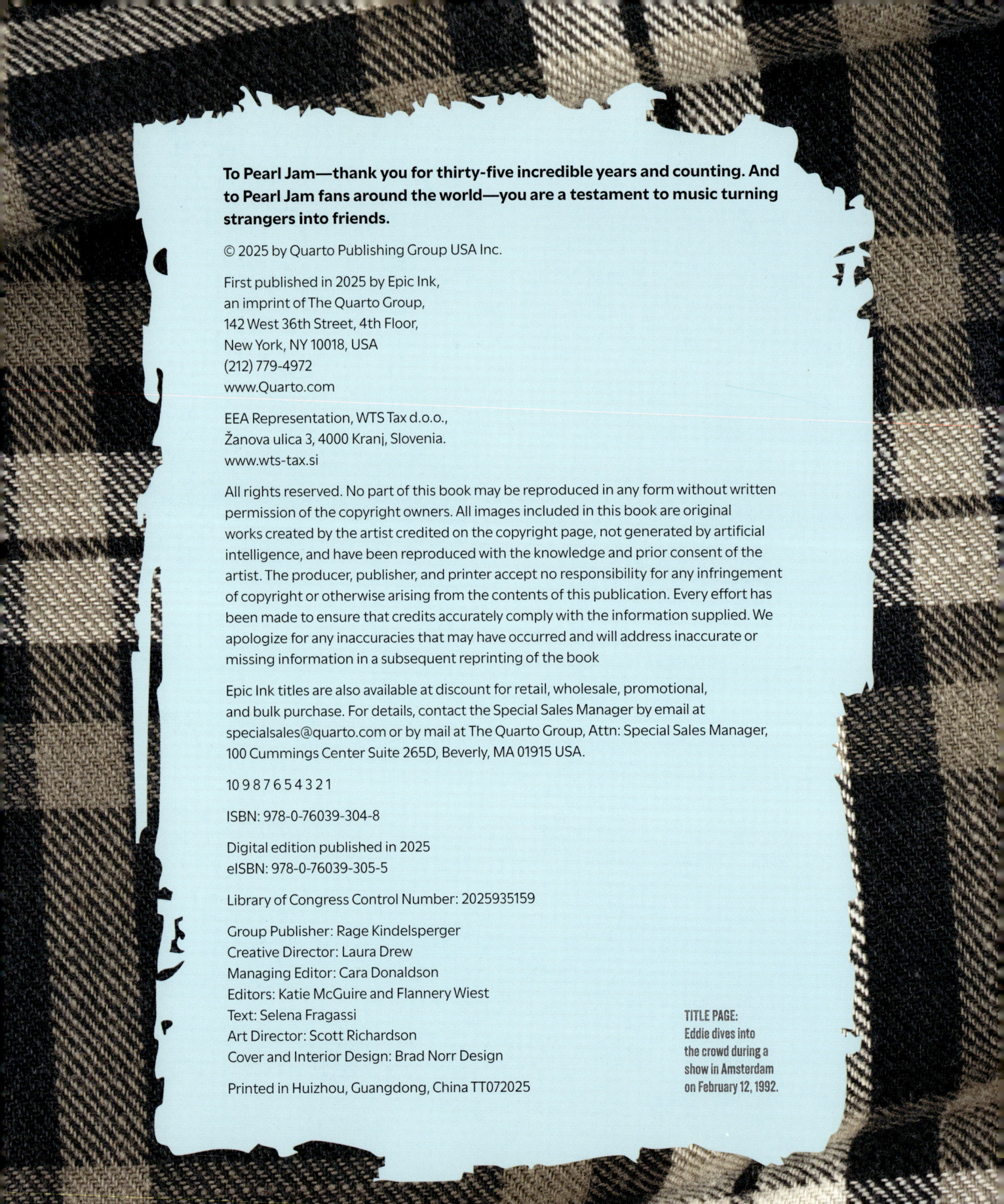

To Pearl Jam—thank you for thirty-five incredible years and counting. And to Pearl Jam fans around the world—you are a testament to music turning strangers into friends.

© 2025 by Quarto Publishing Group USA Inc.

First published in 2025 by Epic Ink,
an imprint of The Quarto Group,
142 West 36th Street, 4th Floor,
New York, NY 10018, USA
(212) 779-4972
www.Quarto.com

EEA Representation, WTS Tax d.o.o.,
Žanova ulica 3, 4000 Kranj, Slovenia.
www.wts-tax.si

All rights reserved. No part of this book may be reproduced in any form without written permission of the copyright owners. All images included in this book are original works created by the artist credited on the copyright page, not generated by artificial intelligence, and have been reproduced with the knowledge and prior consent of the artist. The producer, publisher, and printer accept no responsibility for any infringement of copyright or otherwise arising from the contents of this publication. Every effort has been made to ensure that credits accurately comply with the information supplied. We apologize for any inaccuracies that may have occurred and will address inaccurate or missing information in a subsequent reprinting of the book

Epic Ink titles are also available at discount for retail, wholesale, promotional, and bulk purchase. For details, contact the Special Sales Manager by email at specialsales@quarto.com or by mail at The Quarto Group, Attn: Special Sales Manager, 100 Cummings Center Suite 265D, Beverly, MA 01915 USA.

10 9 8 7 6 5 4 3 2 1

ISBN: 978-0-76039-304-8

Digital edition published in 2025
eISBN: 978-0-76039-305-5

Library of Congress Control Number: 2025935159

Group Publisher: Rage Kindelsperger
Creative Director: Laura Drew
Managing Editor: Cara Donaldson
Editors: Katie McGuire and Flannery Wiest
Text: Selena Fragassi
Art Director: Scott Richardson
Cover and Interior Design: Brad Norr Design

Printed in Huizhou, Guangdong, China TT072025

TITLE PAGE:
Eddie dives into the crowd during a show in Amsterdam on February 12, 1992.